AGAINST
ALL ODDS!

AGAINST ALL ODDS!

More Dramatic 'Last Stand' Actions

BRYAN PERRETT

'A mysterious fraternity born out of smoke and danger of
death.' — Stephen Crane, *The Red Badge of Courage*

'I hold it to be one of the simplest truths of war that the
thing which enables an infantry soldier to keep going
with his weapons is the near presence of a comrade.'
— Brigadier S.L.A. Marshall, *Men Against Fire*

'Refuse to be dismayed. If one must die, then inflict as
much damage on the enemy as possible. While there is life
there is hope of getting out of a seemingly impossible situation.' — Regimental Sergeant Major William Armit,
4th Royal Tank Regiment

ARMS AND
ARMOUR

Acknowledgements
I should like to express my sincere thanks to the following for their kind advice, assistance and encouragement, without which it would not have been possible for me to start, let alone finish, this book: Louise Arnold Friend of the Historical Research Branch, US Army Military History Institute, Carlisle, Pennsylvania; Mr John M. Coski, Historian, The Museum of the Confederacy, Richmond, Virginia; Lieutenant Colonel C.D. Darroch, DL, Honorary Archivist, the Royal Hampshire Regiment Museum, Winchester; Brigadier A.I.H. Fyfe, The Light Infantry Office, Taunton; Major J.H. Peters, MBE, Curator, The Regimental Museum of the Royal Gloucestershire, Berkshire and Wiltshire Regiment, Salisbury; Dr Nathan N. Prefer of Stony Brook, New York; Brigadier K.A. Timbers, Historical Secretary, The Royal Artillery Historical Trust, Woolwich; and Colonel H.B.H. Waring, OBE, The Queen's Own Royal West Kent Museum, Maidstone.

Bryan Perrett
February 1995

Arms and Armour press
An Imprint of the Cassell Group
Wellington House, 125 Strand, London
WC2R OBB

Distributed in the USA by
Sterling Publishing Co. Inc.,
387 Park Avenue South,
New York,
NY 10016–8810.

First published in 1995
This paperback edition 1997

British Library Cataloguing-in-Publication Data: a catalogue record for this book is available from the British Library

ISBN 1–85409–451–3

Cartography by Cilla Eurich.

Designed and edited by DAG Publications Ltd. Designed by David Gibbons; edited by Gerald Napier.

Printed and bound in Great Britain by MPG Books Ltd, Bodmin, Cornwall

£10.99

Contents

Introduction

In 1990, while working on the Introduction to the first volume in this series, I wrote that 'the concept of men selling their lives as dearly as possible forms an honoured part of most national histories and also the basis of much military tradition'. It seems, too, to have struck a chord in readers' imaginations to the extent that the publishers requested me to develop the theme a little further. In so doing, I have chosen another thirteen examples from the past two centuries to illustrate the factors motivating those involved. Some of these episodes are well known, others less so, and one or two were, perhaps, in some danger of sliding towards the edge of oblivion.

Those involved came from a wide variety of military backgrounds. They included elites such as the Foot Guards who defended the château of Hougoumont during Waterloo, fighting a battle within a battle that eventually absorbed the attentions of an entire French corps, and the US Marines who stormed their way across the Pacific during the Second World War; famous British county regiments such as the 13th (later Somerset) Light Infantry, who defended Jellalabad during the First Afghan War, the 66th (later Royal Berkshire) Regiment, who went down fighting in the bloody maelstrom that ended the Battle of Maiwand, the 2nd Hampshire Regiment, who fought an epic defensive action at Tebourba in Tunisia, and the 4th Queen's Own Royal West Kent Regiment, who bore the burden of the horrific Siege of Kohima in Burma; American line regiments whose soldiers defeated the German counter-attack at Mortain in Normandy and the Red Chinese hordes on Pork Chop Hill, Korea; the citizen soldiers who fought for the Union and the Confederacy during the American Civil War; the hotchpotch of soldiers and marines from many countries that defended the Peking Legations for 55 days; the colonial frontiersmen who formed the largely amateur garrison of Mafeking; and the Japanese, dedicated as always to death in the Emperor's service, whose tenacious defence of Iwo Jima was one of the factors which led to the use of nuclear weapons against their homeland.

Once again, it can be seen that the fierce motivation of the participants stems from a number of causes including anger, fear, detestation of the enemy, the desire for revenge, profound belief in a cause, esprit de corps, tradition, discipline, loyalty, willing self-sacrifice on behalf of others and, of course, the hope of ultimate survival. Some of these elements can easily be identified in most of the episodes described, but rarely all. Sometimes, too, imponderable factors were at work. At Antietam, or Sharpsburg as it is known in the South, a day of bitter fighting had resulted in General Robert E. Lee's Confederate Army of Northern Virginia being pinned back against an unfordable stretch of the Potomac river with both its flanks turned. Had events followed their most probable course, the Confederates would have made a courageous stand but in due course Lee would have asked for terms and the Civil War would have followed a different course. However, he had already ordered Major General Ambrose Hill's division to join him by forced march from Harper's Ferry. A more cautious commander might have declined to risk his command in a battle already lost, but Hill was driven by a burning hatred of General George McClellan, the Federal Army Commander, and smashed through his left wing, commanded by the lethargic Major General Ambrose Burnside, so restoring the Confederate fortunes. In passing, it is worth mentioning that the cause of Hill's personal enmity was his rivalry with McClellan for the hand of a Miss Ellen Marcy in their youth, a contest won by McClellan using somewhat dubious means.

Inevitably, leadership in its various forms played a critical part in all these actions. At Jellalabad Sir Robert Sale kept his men fully occupied and raised their spirits by making his opponents' lives a misery; the same was true of Colonel Robert Baden-Powell, the future founder of the Scout Movement, at Mafeking. During the 1918 American offensive in the Argonne Forest the senior officer present with the Lost Battalion – actually elements from several battalions – was Major Charles Whittlesey, an academic Wall Street lawyer referred to derisively by his men as Bird Legs; yet, when it came to it, it was Bird Legs who provided the leadership that enabled them to hold out against all comers. At Peking it was Sir Claude MacDonald, a diplomat with previous military experience, who somehow persuaded contingents from eight nations, each of which normally regarded the others as rivals, to combine in a coherent and effective defence. In some cases it will be seen that it was the troops' absolute confidence in their commanding officer that saw them through their ordeal; in others that the burden rested on the junior officers and NCOs. At Fort Phil Kearny on the Bozeman Trail, however, the mutinous attitude of some officers culminated in the notorious Fetterman Massacre, the most serious reverse sustained by the United States Army on the western frontier until the Custer debacle a decade later; yet, the following year, the Bozeman Trail garrisons restored the Army's prestige in two actions that might themselves have ended in disaster.

In considering all these episodes, in which men were tested far beyond the normal call of duty, it is probable that the reader, like the author, will find his thoughts turning to how he would have reacted in similar circumstances. Thankfully, for most of us the question is likely to remain unanswered.

1
The Defence of Hougoumont

In retrospect, few doubted that the Emperor Napoleon had passed the peak of his abilities, although at the time only those who knew him best had begun to suspect the fact. With them he was morose, irritable and subject to periods of lethargy in which he seemed unwilling to grapple with difficult decisions. Later, the knowledge that he was suffering from piles and cystitis provided an explanation for these symptoms, but it could not conceal the decline in his strategic and tactical abilities.

Nevertheless, he was still a formidable commander who could inspire his troops to perform prodigies for him, and no opponent dare take him for granted. On 15 June 1815 he had crossed the Netherlands frontier at the head of his 125,000-strong Army of the North, intending to deal first with the threat posed by two Allied armies in Belgium, then turn against the Austrian and Russian armies that were assembling against him on the Upper and Middle Rhine.

His enemies in Belgium consisted of an Anglo-Dutch-Belgian force of 107,000 men commanded by the Duke of Wellington and a 128,000-strong Prussian army under Field Marshal Prince Blücher. When confronted by converging hostile armies in the past, his strategy had been to separate them and defeat each in turn. This he intended repeating and on 16 June detached one-third of his troops under Marshal Michel Ney to drive back Wellington's advance guard at Quatre Bras while with the rest he simultaneously attacked Blücher at Ligny. Ney, whom Napoleon believed was overawed by Wellington's reputation, made little progress at Quatre Bras, but at Ligny the Prussians were defeated after a hard fight.

At this point Napoleon made a strategic error of critical importance. He had hoped that the Prussians would withdraw eastwards through Namur in the direction of Germany and, convinced that they were in fact doing so, sent 33,000 men under Marshal Emmanuel de Grouchy in pursuit while he concentrated on the destruction of Wellington's army. However, General Count von Gneisenau, in temporary command of the Prussians while Blücher recovered from an injury sustained in the battle, was well aware of the importance of remaining in contact with Wellington and directed the army's retreat northwards to Wavre. By the time Grouchy discovered the truth most of 17 June had been wasted.

Wellington conformed to the Prussian withdrawal. He did not like the position at Quatre Bras and indeed the Prussians' departure made it untenable. Once, Napoleon would have moved quickly to pin him down, but on 17 June the Emperor displayed no sense of urgency so that, by the time the

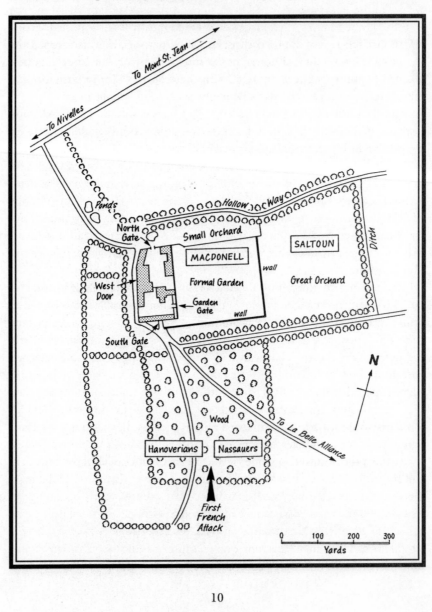

French began moving, most of Wellington's troops were well on their way back to a position previously selected by the Duke, lying along a ridge named Mont St Jean, some eight or nine miles north of Quatre Bras and two miles south of the village of Waterloo.

While Wellington had reasonable grounds for satisfaction thus far, the composition of his army caused him some concern. Most of the battle-hardened and utterly reliable British infantry units that had won him victory after victory in the Peninsula War had been shipped across the Atlantic for the war with the United States, their place being taken mostly by unseasoned second battalions. The rest of the army consisted of Dutch, Belgian, Hanoverian and North German units whose performance under pressure remained a largely unknown quantity. One veteran, Captain John Kincaid of the Rifle Brigade, was far from impressed by what he had witnessed at Quatre Bras:

'We are, take us all in all, a very bad army. Our foreign auxiliaries, who constituted more than half our numerical strength, with some exceptions, were little better than a raw militia – a body without a soul, or like an inflated pillow that gives to the touch and resumes its shape again when the pressure ceases – not to mention the many who went clear out of the field, and were only seen while plundering our baggage during the retreat.'

Kincaid's exceptions would undoubtedly have included the units of the King's German Legion, which consisted mainly of Hanoverian exiles and had fought throughout the Peninsular War, earning the sincere respect of their British comrades. As for the rest, some fought outstandingly well and others had no intention of fighting at all; one could only speak as one found.

The withdrawal commenced in a sulphurous heat that soon stained the uniforms of the trudging columns with sweat. During the morning there was the occasional heavy-dropped shower that freshened the air a little, but as the day wore on the sky was overcast with low, heavy, black clouds and it became humid again. The artillery of the rearguard paused to fire whenever the opportunity presented itself and Allied cavalry squadrons mounted local counter-attacks if the French pressed too close.

Without doubt, the most unusual unit in the rearguard was Captain E.C. Whinyates' No 2 Rocket Troop, equipped with 12-pdr explosive rockets with the then astonishing range of 3500 yards. Impressive as this was, the rockets themselves were wildly unpredictable in flight and the Duke, conservative by nature, saw no merit whatever in them. He had even given orders that they should be returned to store but relented on the urging of his senior artillery officer, Colonel Sir George Wood. Now, Whinyates had his day out and the chance to prove himself. His gunners erected their iron launching tripods, carefully aimed the first rocket at a French battery and lit the propellant fuse. The missile took off, trailing smoke, and hissed towards its target like an arrow to burst between the wheels of a gun, the crew of which were felled by the explosion. The remaining French gunners promptly abandoned their weapons and took cover until they observed that subsequent missiles were careering in every possible direction save that in which they were intended to fly. One looped the loop and chased one of Whinyates' colleagues, Captain Cavalié Mercer, whose troop of Royal Horse Artillery was to earn itself immortality the following day, until it lost interest and blew up.

Mercer's troop was taking its turn in the rearguard line when the long awaited storm broke.

'The first gun that fired seemed to burst the clouds overhead, for its report was instantly followed by an awful clap of thunder, and lightning that almost blinded us, whilst the rain came down as if a water spout had opened over us....Flash followed flash and the peals of thunder were long and tremendous; whilst, as if in mockery of the elements, the French guns sent forth their feebler glare and now scarcely audible reports – their cavalry dashing on at a headlong pace, adding their shouts to the uproar. We galloped for our lives through the storm, striving to gain the enclosures about the houses of the hamlets, Lord Uxbridge urging us on, crying, "Make haste, make haste! For God's sake gallop or you will be taken!".'

So intent was the rearguard on the business in hand that it suddenly found the final stages of its withdrawal being covered by artillery firing from Mont St Jean itself. The army had taken up position along the crest of a gently sloping ridge and was now occupying a frontage approximately four miles long. Wellington, determined to dominate No Man's Land, also established advance posts in two groups of buildings, the farm of La Haye Sainte beside the Brussels-Charleroi road, opposite his centre, and the château of Hougoumont, just east of the Brussels-Nivelles road, covering his right, with strict instructions that these were to be held at all costs. By degrees the French arrived and established themselves along a parallel ridge to the south, leaving the two armies separated by a shallow valley.

Among those rearguard units rejoining the parent formations on the Mont St Jean ridge were the light companies of Major General George Cook's 1st Division. This consisted of the 1st Guards Brigade (2nd and 3rd Battalions First (now Grenadier) Guards) under Major General Peregrine Maitland, and the 2nd Guards Brigade (2nd Battalion Coldstream Guards and 2nd Battalion Third (now Scots) Guards) under Major General Sir Julian Byng. The light company men had hardly shrugged off their packs and begun to assemble their blanket tents when, at about 1900, they were ordered to occupy the Hougoumont estate, lying some 500 yards to their immediate front. The order was well received, for, with one or two periods of respite, the rain continued to sheet down, turning the ground into a quagmire, and the buildings of the château offered shelter. In the event, only the Coldstreamers benefited, as they were told to fortify the buildings; the Scots were made responsible for the walled garden and other areas, and the Grenadiers occupied the forward edge of the adjoining orchard. Commanding the troops in the château and garden was Lieutenant Colonel James Macdonell of the Coldstream, while those in the orchard were under Lieutenant Colonel Lord Saltoun, a Grenadier, both being experienced and capable officers.

French cavalry probed the position shortly after the Guards had moved in, but retired to their own lines after a few volleys had confirmed that it was held in some strength. Thereafter, Macdonell's men spent the short midsummer night knocking loopholes in walls, building firing platforms and removing areas of tiles from some of the roofs to obtain better vantage points. As they worked, they gradually became familiar with the geography of the compact Hougoumont estate. The château itself lay in its north-eastern corner and around its small medieval core successive generations had built ranges of domestic and farm buildings, so that its form now consisted of interconnected north and south courtyards. Gates existed to the north and south, the former being left open to admit reinforcements while the latter was closed and barricaded; there was also a small door in the west wall. To the east was an extensive walled garden overlooked by a terrace and beyond that was the orchard in which Saltoun's men had spent a miserable night. To the south of the château lay a wood, and south of the orchard was an area of pasture. Along the northern edge of the property ran a sunken lane that was to play an important part in the fighting.

It was still raining at dawn when Saltoun's Grenadiers were relieved by a battalion of green-clad Nassauers, accompanied by 300 Jäger and 100 men of the Lüneburg battalion of Count Kielmansegge's 1st Hanoverian Brigade. Saltoun fell in his men and was on the point of marching them back to the ridge when he encountered Wellington, who was accompanied by his Military Secretary, Lord Fitzroy Somerset, later Lord Raglan. The Duke told Saltoun to remain where he was, in the area of the sunken lane. He then rode on into the orchard and ordered the Germans to take up positions at the forward edge of the wood, which lay only 300 yards from the French front lines. Shortly after 0800 the rain eased and finally ceased altogether. From both armies there came the sound of continuous popping as soldiers cleared their damp muskets in readiness for the day ahead.

Napoleon conferred with his senior officers at about 0900. The Army's Chief of Staff, Marshal Nicolas Soult, had, like the majority of the Emperor's commanders, been beaten by Wellington in the Peninsula at one time or another and, aware that the Duke was now holding just the sort of position from which he liked to fight, he urged caution. Napoleon, who had never faced Wellington before, was scornful in his reaction: 'Because you have been defeated by Wellington you think him a great general. I tell you that he is a bad general, that his English are bad troops, and that this will be a picnic!'.

Napoleon, as yet unaware that two Prussian corps had begun marching towards Waterloo from Wavre, would not be hurried. He decided that his main attack would not be launched until approximately 1300. This would give the sodden ground time to dry out, permitting freer movement of his artillery and also enable its balls to graze and ricochet rather than thud uselessly into the mud. This was reasonable enough, but he still clung to the delusion that he had separated Wellington from Blücher and believed that the former, if defeated, would retire in a north-westerly direction, opening the gap still further. In fact Wellington's plans, if the worst came to the worst, were to retire in the direction of Brussels, maintaining contact with the Prussians the while. Nevertheless, Napoleon remained firmly convinced that the Duke was sensitive about his right wing and would willingly commit his reserves there in order to preserve his escape route. Therefore, reasoned the Emperor, the battle would begin with an attack by Reille's corps on Hougoumont. Wellington would move troops to the threatened flank and, when the moment came, D'Erlon's corps would deliver the main attack, smashing its way through the weakened Allied centre. Having accepted this plan of battle, the generals dispersed to their respective duties.

Reille immediately called an orders group of his own at which he detailed the troops for the attack on Hougoumont. The attack itself would be made by the 6th Division which, despite its low number, was a very prestigious formation commanded by the Emperor's brother Jerome. It consisted of two brigades (Bauduin's 1st with seven battalions of the 1st and 3rd Légère, and Soye's 2nd with six battalions of the 1st and 2nd Line) and its strength amounted to almost 8000 men, nearly twice that of every other infantry division in the corps. To cover the open left flank of Jerome's advance Reille detailed Piré's 2nd Cavalry Division, consisting of two chasseur and two lancer regiments.

At about 1000 a wave of cheering spread along the French line as Napoleon, mounted on his distinctive grey, galloped along the ranks, accompanied by his glittering staff. An hour later Wellington, believing that the start of the battle could not be delayed much longer, rode down to Hougoumont again and reminded Macdonell that the position was to be held 'to the last extremity'.

Shortly after, Reille's corps began deploying for its attack. Piré's squadrons cantered off to the east of the wood and, swinging right, halted facing the Allied flank. Throwing out a screen of skirmishers, Jerome's division formed columns of assault and closed in on the wood with its drummers beating out the Advance. All the Peninsula veterans in Wellington's army were familiar with the menacing sound, which they referred to as 'Old Trousers' because of the cadence of the strokes.

Almost immediately a splutter of musketry broke out along the southern edge of the wood as the Germans opened fire. The Jägers were excellent shots and soon began to take their toll. They were, however, heavily outnumbered by a very determined enemy and were pushed slowly back, tree by tree, while balls smacked into the trunks and clipped a shower of leaves and small branches from overhead. The wood was denser than the French had imagined, forcing them to advance in a more open order in which their formation was lost, but by noon they had cleared most of the wood. At this point the Germans disengaged neatly and took up position along the forward edge of the orchard.

Emerging from the trees, the French saw their objective just a short distance ahead of them. A great cheer went up, the drummers beat the staccato 'pas de charge' and, led by their officers, the mass surged forward. Suddenly, from every loophole and window and along the garden walls, they were met by a blaze of musketry that collapsed the leading ranks. The remainder came on, attempting to return the fire. Some tried to break through the South Gate, battering it with axes and musket butts, until they were shot down and their piled bodies impeded the progress of those behind. Others tried to scale the garden walls but were bayoneted or clubbed as soon as their heads cleared the top. On the right they were doing rather better and were forcing the Germans back across the orchard towards the sunken lane, albeit galled by fire from the west wall of the garden to their left.

Wellington had been watching the progress of the attack closely. Someone had again ordered Saltoun's companies back from the sunken lane to rejoin their battalions. They had just arrived when, visibly annoyed, the Duke ordered them to counter-attack at once: 'In with you, my lads – and let me see no more of you!'. Bayonets levelled, the Grenadiers swept across the orchard, driving the French back into the wood.

The Duke also brought up a troop of six 5½in howitzers with the intention of firing into the packed ranks of the French between them and the wood, over the heads of the troops defending the château, orchard and garden. As the task demanded fine judgement, he first verified its feasibility with the senior Royal Horse Artillery officer present, Colonel Sir Augustus Frazer: 'You are going to do a delicate thing. Can you depend upon the force of your howitzers?'. Frazer answered that 'He could perfectly depend upon the troop,' which was not quite the same thing, but satisfactory enough.

In command of the troop was Major Bull, a very capable officer who had greatly distinguished himself during the fighting in Spain and Portugal. His first salvo was exactly on target and, according to one French source, killed seventeen men; in the nature of things, it would also have wounded twice that number. The sudden line of erupting shellbursts seemed to break the back of the French attack and they began edging back into the wood. Bull, located on the ridge immediately above Hougoumont, did not have a direct line of sight, but he was able to walk his barrage after them with the assistance of an old comrade-in-arms, Captain Norman Ramsay, who commanded the battery to his immediate left, and was able to observe where the shells were falling. Quite possibly, this was the first recorded instance of artillery fire being adjusted by an observer on the flank.

By 1150 the French attack had clearly been repulsed. Wellington sent the Nassauers back to their brigade but left the Hanoverians with Saltoun and moved a brigade of the King's German Legion into a position of depth behind the 1st Division on the ridge. For his part, Jerome had sustained no less than 1500 casualties, the majority incurred by his 1st Brigade, the commander of which, Major General Bauduin, had been killed. Reille was satisfied that the attack had achieved its purpose in drawing Wellington's attention to his right flank but Jerome was chagrined by the decisive manner in which he had been repulsed and insisted on attacking again. This time, Soye's 2nd Brigade would advance through the wood while the remainder of the division, covered by Piré's cavalry, would attack the château from the west.

The attack commenced at about noon and, since it was no longer necessary to clear the wood, closed in on its objective very quickly. Soye's brigade was halted by heavy fire from the southern walls but on the left flank the élan of Colonel Cubires' 1st Légère, one of the best regiments in the French service, soon brought it to a lane running down the western side of the château. The 100 or so men of the Scots Guards' light company positioned in the lane had barely time to fire a volley or two before they were pushed steadily back towards the north-west angle of the buildings in fierce hand-to-hand fighting. Cubires cut at Sergeant Ralph Fraser with his sword but the latter took the blow on his pike then wounded and unhorsed the French officer with a quick riposte. Mounting the horse, he galloped towards his comrades, who were now streaming through the still-open North Gate.

Hot on their heels came the 1st Légère, led by a huge axe-wielding lieutenant named Legros, otherwise known to his comrades as The Smasher. Hacking aside attempts to close the gates, he shouldered his way through and, followed by 30 or 40 men, charged into the northern courtyard.

Fortunately, Colonel Macdonell had anticipated the danger. Together with five other Coldstreamers (Lieutenant Colonel Henry Wyndham, Ensign James Hervey, Ensign Henry Gooch and two brothers, Corporals James and Joseph Graham), and four Scots Guards (Sergeants Ralph Fraser, Bruce McGregor, Joseph Aston and Private Joseph Lester), he fought his way through the intruders to the gates. Putting their backs and shoulders to the panels, the group strove to close them against the mass of Frenchmen struggling to force their way through.

Of The Smasher and his men, only an unarmed drummer boy survived; the rest died in hand-to-hand fighting or were shot down from the windows. Having settled this issue, more and more of the garrison converged on the North Gate until its two halves could be closed, shored with timber and their heavy crossbar dropped into place. At this very moment the head and shoulders of a Frenchman appeared above the wall. He aimed at Wyndham but took rather too long about it and was himself shot through the head by James Graham.

The crisis around the North Gate had been closely watched by Major General Byng, commanding the 2nd Guards Brigade. He ordered Colonel Alexander Woodford to counter-attack with three companies of the 2nd Coldstream Guards. These reached the scene shortly after the gates had been closed and promptly charged the now-disorganised 1st Légère, driving it along the lane and back into the wood. They then entered Hougoumont and were joined shortly after by the battalion's two remaining companies, augmenting the strength of the garrison by approximately 600 men; many of the new arrivals were posted along the east wall of the garden, where they were to play a significant part in the events of the afternoon. Although he was senior to Macdonell, Woodford was content to leave the continued defence of the position in the latter's hands.

From this point on, it is difficult to decide whether it was Reille or Jerome who commanded the French II Corps. Reille, as we know, felt that sufficient had already been done in the matter of Hougoumont. Jerome, on the other hand, had been infuriated by his rebuffs and he insisted that Reille should continue committing troops to the attack. Though Jerome was nominally his subordinate, Reille was conscious that he was also the Emperor's brother, and complied. This produced a situation that was exactly the opposite of what Napoleon had intended. More and more French troops were sucked into a battle that had been designed as a feint. Yet even in this respect it had failed, for such was the tenacity of the defence that Wellington did not have to weaken his centre to maintain his right flank; the reinforcements reaching the château were drawn from the right flank itself. In later years, when questioned as to why he had allowed himself to develop such a fixation, Jerome claimed that at about the time his second attack was thrown back he had held a conversation with the Emperor, during which the latter had said that unless Grouchy rejoined the Army or Hougoumont was captured the battle would be lost. At first glance this seems incompatible with the facts, for Napoleon was still firmly committed to his original plan of battle; on the other hand, at about 1300 the distant advance guard of two Prussian corps had become visible, converging on the battlefield from the east, and in due course it would become necessary for the Emperor to detach Lobau's VI Corps from the centre in an attempt to contain the threat; Grouchy was being held off by a third Prussian corps and by now it must have become apparent that the prospects of his decisive intervention were remote indeed. It seems, therefore, that Jerome was privy to information that Napoleon was deliberately concealing from the rest of the army, and that while the Emperor still believed that he had time in which to beat Wellington, he was in urgent need of a success that he could exploit. This alone offers a reasonable justification for Jerome's subsequent actions.

At about 1245 Lieutenant General Count Foy's 9th Division launched an attack to the east of the orchard with the clear intention of isolating the château from the ridge. It was made on a brigade frontage and not only ran into artillery fire, but was also raked by musketry from the east wall of the garden. Finally, halted by mounting losses, the French were driven back by two Scots Guards companies sent down by Byng. Saltoun and his Grenadiers now moved forward to reoccupy the forward edge of the orchard.

While this was taking place Napoleon had established his Grand Battery of over 80 guns opposite the Allied centre. This opened fire to prepare the way for what was intended to be the decisive attack of D'Erlon's I Corps, east of the highway. In the event, D'Erlon's 16,000 infantry were sharply repulsed by disciplined musketry, then routed when they were charged by the heavy cavalry of the Household and Union Brigades, who were in turn cut up by the French cavalry when they over-extended their pursuit. The attack cost D'Erlon some 7000 casualties, but he rallied his broken divisions and began to assault La Haye Sainte, the epic defence of which was conducted by the King's German Legion.

For those involved, a battle is a very local experience. There was doubtless some relief among the defenders of Hougoumont that someone else was having a turn, but almost immediately they were confronted by further problems of their own. The French had brought up a howitzer to the north-east corner of the wood and began to batter the buildings, to some effect. Perhaps unwisely, Saltoun decided to attack and capture the weapon. His two companies, accompanied by the Scots' Grenadier Company and the 50 or so remaining Jägers, charged into the wood only to find themselves confronted by the remnants of three French brigades. They were driven out of the trees and back across the orchard to the sunken lane, where Byng quickly reinforced them with the remainder of 2nd Scots Guards under Colonel Francis Hepburn. Saltoun, who had had four horses shot under him during the day but was miraculously unscathed, was ordered to take his companies back to the ridge. Sadly, he noted that of every three men who had entered the orchard the previous night, only one remained on his feet; the battle, however, was not over for them just yet.

Wellington, now in no doubt as to the importance the French attached to Hougoumont, further adjusted the position of the troops forming his right wing. Hepburn's counter-attack had recovered the orchard and two battalions of the King's German Legion were sent to support him from the sunken lane. A Brunswick battalion, somewhat sinister in its black uniforms, was also sent into the château buildings to reinforce Macdonell.

The fifth French attack, delivered by Lieutenant General Baron Bachelu's 5th Division, came in at approximately 1430 along an oblique axis directed at the south-eastern corner of the orchard. It was broken up by concentrated Allied artillery fire before it could reach its objective.

At this point Jerome and Reille did what they should have done some hours earlier and brought up a howitzer battery, ordering its commander to set Hougoumont ablaze with incendiary shells. For those within, what followed was a horrifying ordeal the memory of which would never leave them. Thatched roofs began to burn at once, but in the more substantial buildings the shells smashed their way through tiles to start fires below. With horrifying speed the flames spread throughout the entire complex, which began to consume itself in a self-generating fire storm. Panic-stricken horses broke out of their stables into the courtyards then, in their terror, ran back into the flames. There were wounded men in every building and as the fire travelled they began to shout for help. In the blistering heat, regardless of the French shells, or the masonry crashing and burning timbers falling around them, others struggled to move them to safety, sometimes in vain.

Observing the fire, Wellington remained icily cool. He took out one of the slips of ass's skin he used for messages and scribbled a note for Macdonell.

'I see that the fire has communicated itself from the hay stack to the roof of the château. You must however still keep your men in those parts to which the fire does not reach. Take care that no men are lost by the falling-in of the roof or floors. After they have both fallen in, occupy the ruined walls inside of the garden; particularly if it should be possible for the enemy to pass through the embers in the inside of the house.'

The note was delivered by an aide, who handed it to Colonel Home of the Scots Guards. Asked if he fully understood what was required, Home replied: 'You can tell the Duke from me that unless we are attacked more vigorously than we have been hitherto, we shall maintain the position without difficulty.' He then went inside and handed the order to Macdonell, who concurred with his response.

If Jerome had hoped that the inferno would drive out the garrison, he was sadly disappointed. Some had no intention of leaving and others were kept in place by their discipline. With the fire raging below, one subaltern kept his men at the window of an upper room, from which they were trading shots with the French at the edge of the wood, although the floor was in danger of collapsing as the joists burned through. Only when flames began to lick through the boards did he stand aside from the doorway and let them escape down the stairwell. Those in the garden and the orchard underwent an ordeal of a different kind. For obvious reasons they could not abandon their positions, but above the roar of the fire they could hear the piercing screams of trapped men. It was, perhaps, the hardest thing of all to remain inactive and suppress instincts demanding that they should rush to their assistance.

At about this time there took place one of the most famous yet puzzling incidents in the entire battle. Aware that ammunition stocks were running dangerously low, Ensign Drummond, the Scots Guards' adjutant, requested a visiting ADC, Captain Horace Seymour, to arrange for a fresh supply as quickly as possible. Seymour galloped to the summit of the ridge and indicated to a private of the Royal Waggon Train that he should take his ammunition waggon down to Hougoumont. Disregarding both the French shellfire and the danger posed by the burning buildings, the man whipped his team into a gallop and drove straight down to the North Gate, where his horses were killed. In Seymour's words, 'I feel convinced to that man's services the Guards owe their ammunition'; and, of course, their ability to maintain the defence of Hougoumont.

The difficulty arises in establishing the identity of this extremely brave man. He has been described as Private or Corporal Joseph or Gregory Brewer or Brewster. He is said to have transferred from the Royal Waggon Train to the Scots Guards shortly after Waterloo, but does not appear in the records of either. Sir Arthur Conan Doyle, the creator of Sherlock Holmes, based his short story *A Straggler of '15* on the incident. The story is set during the winter of 1881-82 and describes the last days of former Corporal Gregory Brewster, late of the Third or Scots Guards. Conan Doyle uses the device of a newspaper cutting to describe the action, which begins with Byng telling Brewster to chase up the reserve ammunition. Although this places him on the ridge, it is not incompatible with the facts, for while the bulk of the battalion was in the orchard, the Colours, and a suitable escort, had been left behind in its original position. The cutting continues:

'Brewster came upon two powder tumbrels of the Nassau division, and succeeded, after menacing the drivers with his musket, in inducing them to convey their powder to Hougoumont. In his absence, however, the hedges surrounding the position had been set on fire by a howitzer battery of the French, and the passage of the carts full of powder became a most hazardous matter. The first tumbrel exploded, blowing the driver to fragments. Daunted by the fate of his comrade, the second driver turned his horses, but Corporal Brewster, springing upon his seat, hurled the man down, and urging the powder cart through the flames, succeeded in forcing a way to his comrades.'

On the one hand, the story may be nothing more than an historical and literary curiosity; on the other, Conan Doyle, who was also the creator of the incorrigible Brigadier Gerard, was thoroughly versed in the history of the Napoleonic Wars, and it would not have escaped his attention that the last of Hougoumont's defenders, a Nassau officer named von Trovich, also passed away in 1882. Whatever the truth, the basic facts of the event remain uncontested.

At about 1600 a number of developments occurred simultaneously. General Cooke, commanding the 1st Division, was seriously wounded and his place was taken by Byng. Hepburn, commanding the Scots Guards, assumed command of the 2nd Guards Brigade, but as both of its battalions, save for the Colour parties, were already committed to the defence of Hougoumont, the only practical difference this made was to extend his responsibilities to maintaining communications between the château, the orchard and the ridge.

While these adjustments were being made, a further attack was launched on the southern edge of the orchard by Foy's and Bachelu's divisions. It was pressed home with such determination that the Scots Guards and the two King's German Legion battalions, outnumbered and outflanked to the east, were forced to give ground. Within a short space of time every one of the Scots' remaining officers had been hit, command of the battalion passing to a senior sergeant. However, once the French had drawn level with the garden wall the Coldstream opened such a destructive fire into them that they were forced to abandon all their gains.

Since the failure of D'Erlon's attack Napoleon's Grand Battery had been firing continuously at the Allied troops on the ridge. Wellington's response was to pull back his most vulnerable units behind the crest. Ney, whom Napoleon had left in tactical control of the battle while he rested, mistook the movement for a withdrawal and decided to turn the apparent retreat into a rout with a series of concentrated cavalry attacks. It was, in fact, the left flank of the first of these that the sixth French attack on Hougoumont had been intended to cover.

Altogether, between 1600 and 1730 the French cavalry mounted twelve separate attacks on the centre of the Allied line, each attack following the pattern of that which had gone before. Superbly uniformed and equipped regiments of cuirassiers, carabineers, lancers, hussars and dragoons breasted the slope between Hougoumont and La Haye Sainte, losing riders and horses as they were fired at by the garrisons of both. Further gaps were blown in the serried ranks by the Allied artillery until, at the last possible moment, the gunners ran back into the shelter of the waiting infantry squares, taking their rammer staves with them. Swarming round the bristling four-deep hedges of bayonets, the cavalrymen struggled in vain to hack their way in, more and more of their saddles being emptied by disciplined volleys. Finally, when the French had become thoroughly disorganised, they were counter-charged and driven off the ridge by the British cavalry, sped on their way by fire from the guns, the result of each charge being to leave the slopes encumbered with debris that would impede the next.

The Allies, too, suffered severely. With each attack, men were speared, cut down or shot dead with pistols or carbines; and, between charges, French artillery renewed its fire on the solid scarlet masses. At the end of it, however, while some regiments lay dead in their squares, Napoleon's cavalry had been fought to the edge of destruction.

Having recovered from his attack of lethargy, the Emperor resumed command. In his view, the key to victory now lay in capturing the outposts of Hougoumont and La Haye Sainte, possession of which would expose Wellington's right and centre, and both were attacked at 1830. At Hougoumont Foy again advanced into the orchard while Jerome assaulted the buildings from the west; both were repulsed. At La Haye Sainte, however, the ammunition supply failed and D'Erlon's re-formed troops were able to drive out the few gallant defenders who had survived. Ney promptly brought up a battery that opened fire just 300 yards from the Allied line, upon which a cloud of skirmishers also converged. Ignoring advice that a vengeful French cuirassier unit was now positioned immediately behind La Haye Sainte, the young Prince of Orange, serving as Wellington's Second-in-Command, ordered a King's German Legion battalion to deploy into line and drive off the skirmishers; when the cuirassiers charged, the battalion was ridden over and wiped out in less than a minute. This proved to be too much for some Allied units in the immediate vicinity. A Hanoverian brigade withdrew out of range and the Nassau brigade took to its heels, being overtaken by a fashionable Hanoverian hussar regiment that galloped all the way to Brussels with the news that the battle was lost.

By 1900 a yawning gap had appeared in the centre of Wellington's line. If Napoleon had possessed the resources, he could have driven straight through, but they were not immediately to hand. His cavalry was a spent force and of his three corps commanders Lobau was now barely holding his own against the Prussians, D'Erlon was too weak in numbers and Reille was tied down in front of Hougoumont. There was nothing for it but to bring forward the Imperial Guard, and that would take a little time. During the respite thus granted Wellington methodically closed the gap in his centre with troops moved from other sectors of the line, so that by 1930 it no longer existed.

The attack, delivered in columns by the Middle Guard, commenced at about the same time. Perversely, it was not directed up the highway past La Haye Sainte, but instead inclined to the left just short of the farm and followed an oblique route up the strewn slopes against Wellington's right centre. Weariness forgotten, the rest of the French watched the spectacle in growing excitement, believing that they were on the verge of victory. The Guard is going in! The Guard has never been beaten! The Guard always gives the coup de grâce!

Disregarding the heavy casualties inflicted by the Allied artillery, the columns overran the gunline and crossed the crest to confront Wellington's infantry, waiting in line. For approximately ten minutes there was a furious exchange of musketry. In this the firepower produced by extended lines proved far superior to that of the columns, for only those at the front of the latter could use their weapons and, in any event, the leading ranks were repeatedly shot away. The French left suddenly found itself receiving devastating volley fire from the 1st Battalion 52nd (Oxfordshire) Regiment, part of Major General Sir Frederick Adams' 3rd Brigade, which had wheeled out of line to engage the flank of the nearest enemy column; simultaneously, the French right was laced through and through at a range of only 100 yards with round after round of canister shot fired by Captain Krahmer de Binche's horse artillery battery, part of Lieutenant General Baron Chassé's newly-arrived 3rd (Netherlands) Division; in the centre, Maitland's 1st Guards Brigade, including the remnants of Saltoun's light companies, was one of several British formations whose punishing volleys halted the French advance in its tracks. It was more than flesh and blood could stand. The Middle Guard began shredding away to the rear, then suddenly bolted en masse when the British and Dutch charged with the bayonet.

Those in the valley below and on both flanks watched the rout in stunned disbelief. There arose a cry of 'La Garde recule!' born of despair, for if the hitherto invincible Guard had been put to flight, what chance did the rest of the army have?

Hard on the heels of this disaster came the news that the Prussians had broken through. Within fifteen minutes the entire Army of the North had disintegrated into a panic-stricken mob, streaming away to the south. Among the last to go were those opposite Hougoumont, who continued to fire at the defenders until the news reached them, then faded away through the wood. Only the Old Guard preserved its discipline to the end, escorting the Emperor safely off the field, although two of its battalions were totally destroyed in the process.

Hougoumont was now little more than a blazing charnel house. Thankfully, its exhausted, smoke-blackened defenders moved out and bivouacked for the night in the fields behind. Later, Wellington was remark that 'The success of the Battle of Waterloo turned upon the closing of the gates of Hougoumont', but the achievements of the garrison went far beyond this single episode. Altogether, some 3500 men (Guards, King's German Legion, Nassauers, Hanoverians and Brunswickers) had played a part in the defence, and they had tied down the entire left wing of the French army throughout the day. It can thus be seen that if Hougoumont had fallen, not only would Wellington have been forced to react to the increased threat to his right, but also that Napoleon would have had plenty of infantry available to exploit the gap which appeared in the Allied centre following the fall of La Haye Sainte. The garrison sustained approximately 1500 casualties, a ratio of 43 per cent, which can be regarded as high by any standards. Of the 15,000 French employed in the seven major attacks, as well as the continuous periods of sniping between them, some 5000 were killed or wounded.

On the morning after the battle some of garrison entered the still-smoul-
dering, shot-battered, bullet-pocked and in places roofless ruins to search for
the bodies of comrades. They had no hope of finding those within the gutted buildings, but many also lay in the open spaces between; such had been
the heat that, according to one soldier, they were 'completely dried up'. It
was also observed with some surprise that the flames had not penetrated the
chapel. They had licked through the door, charred the feet of the wooden
figure of Christ Crucified above, but penetrated no further. Local people
regarded the event as a miracle; the soldiers, more pragmatic, took it as proof
that the Almighty does not always side with the big battalions.

2
'An Old Dilapidated, Ruined Fort' – Jellalabad 1841–42*

The Nineteenth Century equivalent of the recent Cold War was known as The Great Game, the two protagonists being Great Britain and Imperial Russia. The latter was engaged in expanding her boundaries steadily into central Asia, to the point that the British believed that their interests in India were seriously threatened. As for the Russians, they may or may not have had designs on the wealth of British India, but it suited them to divert British attention away from Europe, where the Tsar's ministers were also engaged in the machinations of realpolitik with their Continental neighbours.

Separating the British in India from the Russians in central Asia was the kingdom of Afghanistan, a poor country of soaring mountains and semi-desert plains, bitterly cold in winter and unbearably hot in summer. Here a cruel land begat a cruel people, combining charm and generous hospitality with a capacity for sadistic savagery. Tribes nominally subject to the king fiercely resisted any attempt to deprive them of their independence. In the prosecution of blood feuds that passed from generation to generation, treachery and torture had become art forms that could be relished for their own sake. Fighting, too, was a sport that was universally enjoyed, provided the prospects of defeat did not exist. The Afghan was a master of the ambush, his long jezail out-performing the service muskets of the day in both range and accuracy. He knew, too, that the best results were obtained by picking off the enemy's officers; as Kipling was to put it years later, a puff of smoke high on a rocky hillside, followed by a crack, was often enough to send an expensive education rolling in the dust. With the exception of the religious fanatics known as ghazis, who believed that their place in Heaven would be guaranteed if they died fighting against the infidel, most Afghans were reluctant to close with their foes unless the latter were at their mercy, and then the long Khyber knives and tulwars would go to work with a vengeance. If, on the other hand, an unshaken enemy went for them, the Afghans saw no disgrace

(from a letter written by a member of the garrison)

in beating a hasty retreat to fight another day. Most commanders, from Alexander the Great onwards, recognised the fundamental truth that although Afghanistan was relatively easy to invade, the country contained little of value and since the military economics of remaining were prohibitive, the most sensible policy was to withdraw at the earliest opportunity. Nothing, in fact, was more likely to unite the Afghans than a foreign invasion, however much they might fight among themselves. Again, being devout followers of Islam, they particularly resented any form of rule imposed by Christian ferenghis (their general term for Westerners) or Hindus.

In 1838 Afghanistan was ruled by Dost Mohammed, who was not a member of the legitimate dynasty but had carved his own bloody path to the throne. A reformed rake, he had proved to be a strong and able monarch capable of imposing something like unity on his turbulent subjects. It was his misfortune, and that of a great many other people, that in 1836 Lord Auckland became Governor General of India.

To reduce a long and discreditable story to its simplest, Dost Mohammed was having problems with his Russian-backed Persian neighbours to the west and with the Sikhs to the south. Auckland not only declined assistance but took the greatest exception to the appearance of a Russian emissary at the court in Kabul. He wrote to the king in dictatorial tones that no self-respecting monarch would find acceptable. Not surprisingly, Dost Mohammed turned to the Russians, who quickly resolved his problems with Persia. Auckland, now seriously alarmed, believed that this was merely a prelude to the extension of Russian influence to the very borders of British India. Without hesitation, he took the decision, high handed and ill-considered to the point of imbecility, to invade Afghanistan and replace Dost Mohammed with a king of his own choice. That choice fell on Shah Shuja, whose claim was that he belonged to the legitimate dynasty and had ruled for six years before being deposed as long ago as 1809. Since 1816 he had lived in India as a pensioner of the East India Company. In 1833 he had made an attempt to recover his throne, the decisive failure of which provided a clear indication that the Afghans wanted nothing to do with him.[1] At home the opinion of the now ageing Duke of Wellington coincided with that of anyone who knew anything about the subject, namely that Auckland was getting himself and the Army into a situation from which withdrawal was going to be difficult, if not impossible.

In the spring of 1839 the 21,000-strong Army of the Indus, commanded by General Sir John Keane, began its march on Kabul by way of Kandahar and Ghazni. The bulk of the troops belonged to the East India Company, which had begun life as a trading organisation but was now responsible for administering British possessions in India on behalf of the Crown. They included Native regiments with British officers, European regiments consisting of men who accepted virtual exile in India in return for better pay and conditions than could be obtained in the Regular Army, and a small number of 'Queen's' i.e. regular regiments of the British Army, hired by the Company to provide a stiffening. Accompanying the army were no less than 38,000 camp followers, without whom any campaign in India would not have been complete, providing every possible service that might be needed, including laundry and water carrying.

The only serious opposition encountered was at Ghazni, a strong fortress surrounded by a moat and a wall 70 feet high. Keane decided to storm the place without delay, blowing in the one gate that had not been bricked up, after which an assault column fought its way through the interior. In command of the assault was Brigadier General Robert Sale, more commonly known to the troops as 'Fighting Bob'. Sale had received his ensign's commission when he was thirteen and had served under the then Sir Arthur Wellesley at the siege of Seringapatam in 1789. During the First Burma War he had personally killed the enemy's commander-in-chief in single combat. Now, though aged 57 and become a little portly, his love of a good fight remained undiminished, as is evident from Archibald Forbes' vivid description of the action.

'A pillar of black smoke shot up from where had been the Afghan gate, now shattered by the 300 pounds of gunpowder which Durand had exploded against it. The Advance was sounded and Colonel William Dennie (commanding officer of the 13th Light Infantry) and his stormers sped forward, and Sale followed at the head of the main column.

'Dennie and his gallant followers rushed into the smoking and gloomy archway to find themselves met hand to hand by the Afghan defenders. Nothing could be distinctly seen in the narrow gorge, but the clash of sword blade on bayonet was heard on every side. But some elbow room was gradually gained, and then, since there was neither time nor space for methodic street fighting, each loaded section gave its volley and then made way for the next, which, crowding to the front, poured a deadly discharge at half pistol-shot into the densely crowded defenders. Thus, the storming party won its way, till at length Dennie and his leading files discerned over the heads of their opponents a patch of blue sky and a twinkling star or two, and with a final charge found themselves within the place.

'A body of fierce Afghan swordsmen projected themselves into the interval between the storming party and the main column. Sale, at the head of the latter, was cut down by a tulwar stroke in the face; in the effort of his

28

blow the assailant fell with the assailed, and they rolled together among the shattered timbers of the gate. Sale, wounded again on the ground, and faint with loss of blood, called to one of his officers for assistance. Kershaw ran the Afghan through the body with his sword, but he still struggled with the Brigadier. At length in the grapple Sale got the uppermost, and then dealt his adversary a sabre cut which cleft him from crown to eyebrows.'

Keane resumed his march on Kabul, which he entered on 1 August. Shah Shuja's installation as king provoked no enthusiasm whatever among his subjects and it was clear that without British support his days would be numbered. The real power, as the Afghans knew well and bitterly resented, lay with Sir William Macnaghten, Lord Auckland's personal representative. As a precaution, therefore, Keane left garrisons at Kabul, Kandahar, Charikar and Ghazni before returning to India with the rest of the army. Sporadic fighting continued for a year but in the autumn of 1840 Dost Mohammed came in to surrender and was transported to India.

By the middle of 1841 the country seemed sufficiently pacified to start relieving some of the troops who had now been in Afghanistan for over two years. The calm, however, was deceptive, for Akbar Khan, Dost Mohammed's son, was plotting a carefully orchestrated general rising with the support of the tribal chiefs, who resented Macnaghten's recent withdrawal of their good conduct subsidies. In October Sale's brigade, returning to India by the Khyber route, suddenly found itself having to fight every step of the way to get as far as Gandamak. One particularly successful engagement is described by an eyewitness:

'Clever were the manoeuvres by which on that day Dennie drew the enemy into his toils and heavy the retribution which descended upon them. Placing his cavalry in ambush he brought up his infantry, ordered them to advance firing and then wheeled them about as if in panic flight. The enemy, after a brief pause of wonderment, believed they had accomplished a great victory, sent up wild shout and then rushed in pursuit of the flying ferenghis. They were soon on the clear open space to which Dennie had designed to lure them. The cavalry whom they had laughed at from the hills, able now to operate freely, dashed at them with sudden fury. The slaughter was tremendous, the rout was complete.'

Despite this, the brigade was in real danger. Sale had about 300 wounded with him, sufficient musket ammunition for immediate needs, but only a few days' rations in hand. Once it became clear that he was faced with something far more formidable than a Ghilzai tribal revolt, he had to make a decision. He could not remain where he was, and the cost of fighting his way back to Kabul would be prohibitive; therefore, he must continue along his route as

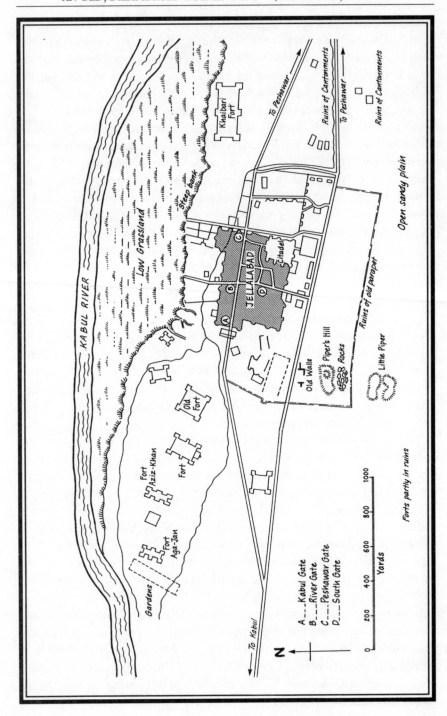

far as Jellalabad, which he could hold until a relief column arrived from India by way of Peshawar. Jellalabad lay four days' march from Gandamak, but the brigade reached it in two, arriving on 13 November.

Jellalabad contained a citadel and was surrounded by a rectangular wall some 2300 yards in length, incorporating 33 bastions and four gates. Unfortunately, all the defences had crumbled and the walls stood no more than ten or twelve feet high; only a few hundred yards of parapet remained and, being no more than two feet high, provided no protection at all. In the distant past the town had been of greater importance and covered a much wider area for, some 500 yards outside the existing walls, to the north, east and west, there were traces of an outer wall, long since crumbled into a series of sandy mounds. Within this enclosure, 450 yards south-west of the town, was a rocky knoll that later became known as Piper's Hill. To the west of the town were a number of fortified dwellings, most of them derelict. To the north was an area of grassland, 500 yards wide, separating the walls from the Kabul river, which was fordable. To the east were the quarters of the Political Mission, known as the Khaibari Fort.

Sale's command consisted of Dennie's 13th Light Infantry, 700 strong, armed with muskets that had been condemned at Kabul but would still fire; 750 men of the 35th Native Infantry, commanded by Lieutenant Colonel Monteith; a 130-strong squadron of the 5th Bengal Cavalry under Captain Oldfield; one company of Sappers and Miners under Captain George Broadfoot; the 6th Light Field Battery with five 9pdrs, commanded by Captain Abbott; a mixed battery containing one 24pdr, three 3pdrs, two 8in and three 5in howitzers, commanded by Captain Backhouse; and about 130 Afghan irregulars, 90 of whom were mounted, who were nominally loyal to Shah Shuja. In addition, up to 3000 camp followers trailed through the gates, together with 750 camels and a large number of mules and pack ponies.

Hard on their heels came an estimated 6000 tribesmen under Gul Mohammed, the local leader of the rising, who quickly invested the town. The focal point of their activities was Piper's Hill, upon which they could be seen dancing to the sound of a reed pipe. As possession of the hill, some 30 or 40 feet high, gave them the ability to fire over the ramshackle walls, Sale decided to drive them off before they could establish themselves, ordering a sortie to be mounted the following day, 14 November. This was commanded by Monteith and included 300 men each from the 13th Light Infantry and 35th Native Infantry, 100 Sappers, and two guns. Private Thomas Rowbotham of the Thirteenth subsequently described the action in a letter to his father:

'The enemy were in the ravines and gardens all round and at a precon-
certed signal out we sallied with a deafening cheer. They never dreamed we
would have attempted such a thing – they were powerless from surprise. We
instantly dispersed them with little opposition. The slaughter was immense
with only small loss on our side – a few killed and some 25 wounded. Not a
vestige of the enemy was to be seen.'

As a result of the sortie, in which about 200 of the enemy were killed, the
immediate pressure on the garrison was relieved. Neighbouring villages, anxious to do business, brought in sufficient food to satisfy immediate needs.
Sale's next priority was to put Jellalabad into some sort of defensive order.
The entire garrison, including officers, was put to work with pick and shovel
to perform this Herculean task, and if the camp followers wanted to eat they
joined in as well. Broadfoot, the chief engineer, was tireless and thorough in
his efforts. The derelict forts to the west were demolished; walls and ravines
that might provide cover for the enemy were knocked down and filled in;
trees and bushes within range of the walls were cut down; the ramparts were
widened, strengthened and given a parapet over six feet high; ramps were
constructed up which guns could be run into the bastions; and the defences
of the gateways were improved.

Towards the end of the month the villagers stopped bringing in supplies.
This was ominous and, sure enough, on the 27th the enemy again closed in
around the town, occupying one of the remaining forts to the west as well
as Piper's Hill. Sale responded with a sortie on 1 December, the composition of the force being the same as before but this time it was accompanied
by the cavalry and led by Dennie. Going in with the bayonet, the infantry
chased the tribesmen out of their positions and the cavalry cut them up as
they fled, the total number killed being in the region of 150.

Jellalabad was left severely alone for several weeks. Local supplies were
resumed and Broadfoot kept the men hard at work. It might be thought
that, trapped as they were in a savage and treacherous land, with no immediate prospect of relief, their morale might be low, but it was not. They had
confidence in Sale and, having worsted the enemy in every encounter, in
themselves. Furthermore, the constant physical labour not only kept their
thoughts occupied, but also rendered most of them fitter than they had ever
been in their lives. The real pressures were psychological and were born by
Sale alone. Contact with Kabul and India was infrequent and generally
restricted to what the tribal leaders thought should be allowed through.
Through divers sources he learned that the small Gurkha garrison at
Charikar had been overrun and that only a handful of wounded survivors
had succeeded in reaching Kabul; that Kandahar and Ghazni were under

siege; and that the Kabul garrison itself was in serious trouble. The last might not have surprised him too much, as its commander, Major General William Elphinstone, though a good soldier in his youth, was now elderly, ill, indecisive and dominated by Macnaghten, who was apparently unable to come to terms with the reality of the situation. On 17 December word was received that Akbar Khan would permit the Kabul garrison to evacuate Afghanistan. It was obvious to Sale that something akin to a capitulation had taken place and it seemed probable that when Elphinstone's troops reached Jellalabad his own brigade would be ordered to conform to the withdrawal.

Meanwhile, work continued on the fortifications without rest save on Christmas Day, when there was a church parade for the garrison's Christians and the cooks did what they could to produce a suitable dinner. Next day came the first indication that Jellalabad had not been entirely forgotten when a troop of irregular cavalry belonging to a friendly chieftain arrived with 25,000 rupees, so prolonging Sale's ability to buy in supplies.

On 2 January Sale was informed that Macnaghten had been treacherously murdered while negotiating the details of the withdrawal. A week later Major Macgregor, Sale's political officer, received the following letter from Kabul, jointly signed by Macnaghten's successor, Major Pottinger, and Elphinstone.

'It having been found necessary to conclude an agreement, founded on that of the late Sir W.H. Macnaghten, for the evacuation of Afghanistan by our troops we have the honour to request that you will intimate to the officer commanding at Jellalabad, our wish that the troops now at that place should return to India, commencing their march immediately after receipt of this letter.'

Despite Elphinstone's signature, Sale correctly chose to disregard what was an internal communication between members of the political service. In their reply Sale and Macgregor quoted their own local intelligence sources, which indicated that Akbar Khan had given instructions that the troublesome Jellalabad garrison was to be wiped out; in these circumstances, they continued, they intended remaining where they were until a safe march to Peshawar could be guaranteed. It seems unlikely that their letter was ever delivered. On 11 January Sale wrote to the Commander-in-Chief India, stating that he intended to hold out for as long as his ammunition and food supplies lasted.

At about noon on 13 January some officers on the roof of the town's tallest house spotted a single horseman slowly approaching the walls from the direction of Kabul, his mount staggering, head down, and clearly having trouble with its hind legs. The rider, also evidently in the last throes of exhaustion, waved his cap feebly. A party sent out to help recognised him as Dr William Brydon, who told them that he was the last survivor of the entire Kabul garrison.[2]

Brydon, cut about the head, left hand and knee, battered and bruised from being stoned, had a terrible story to tell. The garrison, 4500 strong with 12,000 camp followers, had left Kabul in deep snow and bitter cold on 6 January. Attacks on the column had begun almost at once. The freezing weather seemed to numb the sepoys to the point at which they became useless and many left the ranks to join their wives and families among the followers. By the end of the first day's march all order and discipline had collapsed save in the rearguard, maintained by the 44th (later the Essex) Regiment and a troop of Bengal horse artillery. By the end of the second day it was estimated that 500 soldiers and 2500 followers had been killed, while of the rest half staggered along suffering from wounds or frostbite. Day and night, the tribesmen had sniped or rushed down from the hillside on isolated parties, killing, raping and looting. The only prisoners taken were those who might prove valuable as hostages, including Elphinstone, Pottinger and Sale's wife and daughter. Elphinstone had repeatedly asked Akbar Khan to control the excesses of his men, without visible result. By 11 January the only Indian soldiers left alive were 50 troopers of the 5th Cavalry and sixteen gunners, and the 44th had been reduced to 150 men. The end came on the morning of the 13th at Gandamak, where twenty officers and 45 British soldiers, the majority from the 44th, turned off the road to make a stand on a snow-covered hillock. Pretending to be friendly, the tribesmen closed in but were driven off when they tried to snatch some of the men's weapons. The Afghans then began reducing the size of the group by sniping and, once the British had expended their last few rounds of ammunition, they swarmed forward, sword in hand, to make the first of the several charges that were required to finish the business. Captain Souter of the 44th, who had tied the regiment's colours around his waist, was wounded but spared when the Afghans took it that the richly embroidered 'sash' indicated a man of great importance who would make a valuable hostage. Uncharacteristically, and perhaps with a degree of admiration, the tribesmen also spared the lives of three or four wounded privates. Brydon was the only survivor of a small group of mounted officers who had managed to fight their way past Gandamak but been killed one by one, the last within a few miles of Jellalabad; that he had come through at all was something of a miracle, as his horse had been shot through the spine near the tail.

Sale sent out his cavalry, who confirmed that the long trail of slaughter ended just four miles from the town. Feeling unable to place any trust whatever in the Afghans, Sale turned out the entire civil population, followed by Shah Shuja's troops; the latter had given no cause for complaint, but he had no confidence that they would remain loyal and was not prepared to take risks. He then set about arming 1300 of the camp followers with jezails, muskets, swords and home-made pikes. Lieutenant Chetwynd Stapylton of the 13th recorded in his diary that on the night of Dr Brydon's arrival, 'A large lanthorn was suspended over the Kabul Gate, and the Colours of the regiment by day, our bugles sounded the Advance every half-hour during the night for the ensuing week to attract the attention of any who might have escaped and feared to approach the fort not knowing if it was occupied by friends or foes, all however without success'.

At this point it seems that a clash arose between the personalities of Broadfoot and Sale. As chief engineer, Broadfoot was largely master in his own house, and this may have given him an exaggerated idea of his own importance. Outstandingly good at his job, he was not an easy man to get along with professionally, making no secret of the fact that in his opinion the Army contained only two categories of people – engineers and lesser mortals. No doubt acting from the sincerest motives, he informed Sale that he did not consider Jellalabad was tenable against an enemy who now undoubtedly had cannon at his disposal; furthermore, small arms ammunition was in short supply, and although the men could be fed for six weeks there was only three weeks' fodder in hand for the animals. In these circumstances, therefore, he urged the brigadier to abandon the town and fight his way through to Peshawar. Sale declined, for two reasons. First, he believed that any attempt to reach Peshawar would simply result in another massacre; and secondly, he had established contact with the one hundred or so prisoners taken by Akbar Khan, who were being held at Buddiabad, only 35 miles distant. It seems that during what became a heated discussion Sale brusquely ordered his chief engineer to concentrate on strengthening the defences still further. The upshot was that the entire garrison turned out to dig a ditch twelve feet deep and between twelve and 30 feet wide around the walls.

Some days later Sale received the depressing news that a brigade from Peshawar had been repulsed in the Khyber and forced to retire. He called his senior officers to a council of war on 27 January, the minutes being taken by his principal staff officer, Captain Henry Havelock of the 13th, ahead of whom lay a brilliant career.[3] The matters for discussion included correspondence from the Government of India, confirming its intention to evacuate Afghanistan; a letter from Peshawar, indicating that the relief attempt had been suspended; a letter from Pottinger at Buddiabad, suggesting that Akbar Khan was inclined to befriend the garrison provided Dost Mohammed was released; and letters from Shah Shuja, requesting money, denying personal responsibility for the massacre of the Kabul garrison and asking Sale, in the light of the treaty that had been concluded, what his intentions were.

Obviously, the decisions taken were of critical importance, not only to those besieged in Jellalabad, but to the whole question of badly damaged British prestige throughout the Indian sub-continent. Unfortunately, the issue has been clouded by Broadfoot's dislike of Sale, which resulted in a quarrel that was still being pursued two generations later. When the siege was ended, Broadfoot resented the fact that Sale had become a national hero and believed that he had been deprived of his share of the credit for the successful defence. To some extent, Sale played into his hands by retaining the minutes himself, and after his death they remained among the family papers for the better part of 50 years. In 1843 Broadfoot put together his own version, sending it to Havelock for verification. The latter, by then having more important matters on his mind, made a few notes and returned it as 'a fair and correct statement of that which occurred'. In 1888 Broadfoot's biography was published by his grandson, suggesting that Sale and Macgregor were inclined to abandon Jellalabad and negotiate their way out, proposing that a letter should be written to Shah Shuja indicating a number of conditions which included the mutual exchange of hostages and prisoners once the brigade had reached Peshawar, the honours of war, safe escort, supplies and transport. According the Broadfoot biography the proposal was greeted with outrage but was passed by a majority with himself and Oldfield as the only dissenters.[4]

However, when this version was quoted by Archibald Forbes in his *Life of Havelock*, published in 1890, it attracted an apoplectic letter to *The Times* from Sale's grandson, Lieutenant General R.S. Sale-Hill, who informed the editor that he had recently inherited the original minutes and would shortly be publishing the truth in the columns of the *Illustrated Naval and Military Magazine*. This version reveals that the contents of the letter were somewhat different. It informed Shah Shuja that since Jellalabad was being held on his behalf, the garrison could not retire to India without his permission; that in view of the treacherous end suffered by the Kabul garrison no reliance could be placed on Afghan professions of goodwill; and that before withdrawal could even be considered Akbar Khan's following must retire to Kabul, certain royal princes would be required as hostages, and that the garrison should be provided with transport. Once again, Oldfield and Broadfoot are listed as dissenters, as is Havelock, although he was not a voting member.

Obviously, the message contained in the second version of the letter is very different from that in the first. Sale and Macgregor were well aware that

Shah Shuja, now reduced to a mere cypher in daily fear for his life, could neither grant nor enforce the conditions that were demanded, and they were simply playing for time until a fresh relief force could be assembled at Peshawar.

Sadly, the picture has been further distorted by Forbes, who was clearly nettled by criticism. In his book *The Afghan Wars*, published in 1892, he again accepts Broadfoot's version, simultaneously taking a vindictive sideswipe at Sale-Hill: 'Records and papers long lost to sight have recently been deposited among the records of the India Office, but not before their latest non-official possessor had published some extracts from them. It is to be hoped that the more important documents may be given to the public in full, since passages from documents, whether intentionally or not, may be so extracted as to be misleading.' Such was Forbes' reputation that, with very few exceptions, the Broadfoot version has been accepted without question ever since. Yet, even without Sale-Hill's evidence, it is difficult to accept that Broadfoot could counsel retreat but then decide that standing fast was the best policy just a day or so later; or that, by coincidence and within the same space of time, 'Fighting Bob' Sale would advocate standing fast then decide to negotiate a withdrawal. True, Sale had become so worried by the shortage of musket ammunition that the enemy's spent balls and the garrison's pewter tableware were alike melted down and recast; likewise, he remained perpetually anxious regarding the safety of Lady Sale and their recently widowed daughter; but the despatch of foraging parties into the surrounding country on 30 January, yielding 175 bullocks and 734 sheep, was hardly the act of a man contemplating surrender.

Shah Shuja's reply reached Sale on 8 February. Delphic in its obscurity, it was the response of a man who dared not solve the deadly conundrum he had been set: 'If you are sincere in your offers, let all the chief gentlemen affix their seals.' After this, it was decided unanimously that further negotiation with the enemy would be pointless.

In the meantime, Lord Auckland, shaken by the destruction of the Kabul garrison, had taken steps to retrieve the situation. He appointed the capable General Sir George Pollock commander of an Army of Retribution, investing him with full military and political powers. Pollock immediately began assembling his troops at Peshawar and by the middle of February he was in correspondence with Sale, who informed him that the garrison had 2263 men fit for duty and 195 sick; and that there were sufficient foodstuffs in hand to keep the British troops on full rations for 70 days and the Indians for half that period. Akbar Khan, obviously aware of Pollock's preparations, began closing in around Jellalabad on 15 February.

At about 1100 four days later a tremendous earthquake convulsed a wide area of eastern Afghanistan. About a third of Jellalabad's buildings were destroyed, the Kabul gate and several bastions collapsed in ruins, a breach opened in the eastern face of the curtain walls, and the laboriously constructed parapets were shaken apart. Sale and Havelock escaped from their quarters in the nick of time, although Monteith was buried by collapsing masonry and had to be dug out, bruised but alive. Incredibly, only five or six lives were lost, largely because almost all the troops were working on the ditch at the time.

'I never witnessed a more awful thing,' recalled Private Rowbotham. 'I could stand in the battlefield unmoved or on the ocean with its raging terrors, but this showed me the Littleness of Man and made the stoutest heart tremble. We have had more than 100 shocks since, but none of them near so terrible.'

It was heartbreaking to see the work of months destroyed in minutes, but Broadfoot reacted with characteristic energy. 'The earthquake took place at eleven o'clock in the morning,' wrote Stapylton, 'And at twelve o'clock we were all hard at work repairing damages. By dint of working day and night at the end of the week all our breaches were repaired and the works defensible.' To everyone's surprise, Akbar Khan failed to take advantage of the situation, almost certainly because many of his tribesmen had temporarily returned to their villages, which had also been badly damaged by the earthquake. Even so, parties cutting grass for fodder were attacked by Afghan horsemen on 22 February and again the following day. The attackers, estimated to number about 500, were driven off by the disciplined counter-charges of 80 of Oldfield's troopers.

Akbar Khan established a camp two miles west of the town on 26 February, and a few days later set up a second camp the same distance on the opposite side. Sale was worried that the enemy would use the guns they had captured from the Kabul garrison, but instead the tribesmen, who apparently had little enthusiasm for tackling a fortified position, resorted to psychological warfare and sniping. According to Rowbotham, 'They posted strong guards all around and sent us in word that our hour of redemption was past and they would assuredly put us all to death. They daily came up firing at the walls and occasionally hit someone on the ramparts, but did not show any inclination of scaling the walls. However, we could not endure this – we had to get grass for such of our cattle as we had not shot, and this brought on a partial engagement daily with various success. They tried many manoeuvres to seduce us out, among others sending their cattle to graze near their fort.'

Messengers from Kabul approached the garrison on 7 March, demanding that it should evacuate Jellalabad. Sale told them to go to Peshawar and talk to General Pollock, as he now commanded the British forces in Afghanistan. No doubt with an element of spiteful glee, Sale was then informed that Ghazni had fallen and that none of its garrison had survived.[5]

In a leisurely sort of way, the Afghans had begun driving entrenchments towards the north-west bastion of the town. On 11 March a strong sortie led by Dennie drove the enemy out of these, killing about 100, and filled them in, incurring little loss. The Afghans persisted and on 24 March the sortie, this time commanded by Broadfoot, was repeated, with similar results. Casualties included three killed and Broadfoot wounded. Meanwhile, Pollock had informed Sale that he had been delayed and asked whether the garrison could hold out until the end of the month. Sale replied in the affirmative, but gave orders for the camels to be destroyed so as to preserve the dwindling supply of fodder for the cavalry and artillery horses.

Hunger was now beginning to make itself felt. Stapylton records that some of the camp followers were starving and that the daily issue to his own mess of 28 members was one piece of salt meat and half a sheep, although 'the sheep here are not half the size of the English sheep and were starved like ourselves'.

On 1 April it was noticed that one of the enemy's flocks had strayed towards the walls and was about a mile from Akbar's camp. A sortie in strength was mounted immediately, during which Rowbotham seems to have enjoyed himself:

'Out we burst like a clap of thunder, slaughtered the drovers and captured 580 sheep. Out came Akbar's army, but he was too late, for we sent in the sheep by the native servants and turned about and attacked them. We made good our retreat into the fort with little loss while they, enraged at their loss, rode up to our ranks and idly sacrificed their lives. This little affair made us think that, small as was our numbers, with our discipline and courage we might eventually beat them.'

By now, whatever the bickerings that might have taken place between their senior officers, the various units of the garrison had developed a strong mutual respect for each other. On this occasion, the 35th Native Infantry, who as usual had played a full part in the sortie, gave their share of the captured animals to the 13th Light Infantry, saying that meat was less necessary for them than it was for the Europeans.

On 5 April Sale's spies produced two items of critically important intelligence. The first was that Pollock had suffered a serious check in the Khyber. In fact, the reverse was true, but as a piece of black propaganda it was to prove extremely effective. The second was that a revolution had broken out in Kabul, that the wretched Shah Shuja had been assassinated while return-ing from prayers, and that Akbar Khan was on the point of leaving for the capital to safeguard his father's interests. The sound of guns firing a royal salute in the enemy camp was taken by the garrison to be in celebration of Pollock's alleged reverse, but was more probably inspired by the coup.

Once again, Sale called his senior officers to a council of war. There was just sufficient musket ammunition left for one day's serious fighting, and Sale decided that this would be expended during a major sortie that would make or break the garrison's fortunes. His intention, now that Akbar Khan's mind was on other matters, was to strike hard and without warning. A crush-ing defeat inflicted on the tribesmen, now said to number about 6000, would not only relieve the immediate pressure on Jellalabad but also provide encouragement for Pollock.

The sortie commenced at first light on 7 April. Screened by skirmishers, the garrison advanced in three parallel columns, the 35th Native Infantry, less one company, under Monteith, on the left, the 13th Light Infantry, less one company, under Dennie in the centre, and one company each of the 13th and 35th, plus the Sappers, under Havelock, on the right. Abbott's 6th Light Battery moved forward in support, together with Oldfield's squadron of 5th Bengal Cavalry. Detachments were left behind to guard the gates and the armed camp followers had been detailed to man the walls, but otherwise every fit man in the garrison was now marching towards Akbar Khan's camp through the grey half-light.

Monteith's column made steady progress but Dennie's veered towards a ruined fort from which the Afghans had opened fire. Sale, close behind, ordered one company of the 13th to clear it. The men experienced no diffi-culty in scrambling through a gap in the outer wall but found further progress barred by a loopholed inner wall. Both sides fired at each other through the loopholes and grabbed at each other's muskets. The 13th lost one of theirs but evened the score by pulling out one of the enemy's, the markings on which indicated that it had once belonged to the massacred 44th. At about this time Dennie was shot through the side while encourag-ing his men, and the wound proved mortal. Sale instructed Abbott's guns to engage the fort, but when it became clear that they lacked the weight to make any impression he ordered the advance to continue.

The enemy, now thoroughly aroused, began pouring out of their camp. Havelock's column, somewhat ahead of the other two, was twice charged by cavalry but formed square and beat them off. The rest of the battle is described by Sale himself:

'The artillery advanced at a gallop and directed a heavy fire upon the Afghan centre, whilst two of the columns of infantry penetrated the line near the same point and the third (Havelock's) forced back the (enemy) left from its support on the river, into the stream of which some of his horse and foot were driven. The Afghans made repeated attempts to check our advance by a smart fire of musketry and by opening upon us three guns from a battery screened by a garden wall. But in a short time they were dislodged from every point of their position, their cannon taken, and their camp involved in a general conflagration. The battle was over and the enemy in full retreat by about 7 a.m. We have made ourselves masters of two cavalry standards, recaptured four guns lost by the Kabul force, seized and destroyed a great quantity of material and ordnance stores, and burnt the whole of the enemy's tents. The field of battle was strewed with the bodies of men and horses, and the richness of the trappings of some of the latter seemed to attest that persons of distinction had been among the casualties.'

During the hand-to-hand fighting Armourer-Sergeant Henry Ulyett of the 13th captured Akbar Khan's personal standard, taking it from an Afghan cavalryman whom he killed.[6] He was subsequently rewarded with a medal and an annuity of £20. Rowbotham, as usual, gives the impression of having enjoyed himself, although since he is writing to his family he deliberately spares them the more horrific aspects of the fighting:

'We first encountered the enemy's piquets and they opened a fire upon us, which alarmed the camp. They would not believe we were coming to attack the camp – they thought we were on another mutton bout. But when they saw us steadily advance, driving all the piquets before us, they thought it time to prepare. They drew up in line as if to charge, but our guns opened with terrible effect. They made several demonstrations to charge, but we kept up a sharp and well directed fire and their efforts were rendered futile. As a last resource, they formed in front of their camp and brought their guns into play. Still we steadily advanced and when near the glorious word Charge! was given. Away we went with the usual British cheer and we'll draw a veil. I cannot describe the remainder – suffice it to say in one hour we were masters of the camp.'

During the final stages of the engagement the Afghans also abandoned their outlying fort. Observing this, Lieutenant George Wade of the 13th led out a party from the Kabul Gate, bayoneted several of them and set the fire to the building.

At a total cost of fourteen killed and 66 wounded Sale's garrison had wrought its own salvation. The local chiefs hurried in to make their peace and supplies began to flow into Jellalabad. On 16 April Pollock's troops arrived, being played in by the band of the 13th with an old Jacobite air, 'Oh, but ye've been lang a'coming!' Pollock reported to Lord Ellenborough, who had replaced Auckland as Governor General, that he found the garrison 'in excellent health and spirits and in an admirable state of discipline'. Ellenborough decreed that the relief should be celebrated by the firing of a 21 gun salute at every major military post throughout India. He further announced that every man of the Jellalabad garrison present on 7 April would receive six months' additional batta, that is, field subsistence allowance.

Together, the sieges of Jellalabad and Kandahar maintained the reputation of British arms in Afghanistan, although it was the former that caught the public imagination. Acting Major General Sir Robert Sale became a Knight Grand Cross of the Order of the Bath in June. The entire garrison received a medal, two versions of which exist, the first with a mural crown and the word Jellalabad, and the second with a figure of Winged Victory and Jellalabad VII April MDCCCXLII; today their value is between £300 and £600. Those who had been present at the capture of Ghazni were also eligible for the Ghuznee (sic) Medal, the first campaign medal issued to British troops since Waterloo. The 13th (later Somerset) Light Infantry, by coincidence Sale's own regiment and that of Havelock, was granted the honorific title Prince Albert's and the right 'to bear on its colours and appointments a Mural Crown, superscribed Jellalabad, as a memorial of the fortitude, perseverance and enterprise evinced by that regiment and the several corps which served during the blockade of Jellalabad'. Well over a century of loyal service lay ahead of the regiment; sadly, the same was not true for the 35th Native Infantry, which was disbanded during the Great Mutiny of 1857 and vanished into history.

The rest of the story is soon told. Futteh Jung, Shah Shuja's second son and successor, foreseeing a very limited future for himself on the throne of Afghanistan, fled from his capital in disguise and sought sanctuary with the British. Pollock's army fought its way through to Kabul, where it was joined by the Kandahar garrison. Elphinstone had died in captivity, but the remaining British captives, including Lady Sale and her daughter, were released. It was now apparent to the government of India that the continued occupation of Afghanistan was not an economic proposition and, having destroyed the Kabul bazaar and levelled Charikar to the ground, the Army of Retribution marched back to India. Ellenborough, deciding that dealing with the devil he knew was preferable to the alternative, allowed Dost Mohammed to resume the throne. Understandably, many people felt that thousands of lives had been squandered to no purpose. Dost Mohammed was to send a con-

42

tingent to fight against the British during the Second Sikh War, but in British eyes this was a lesser sin than intriguing with the Russians, whom he succeeded in keeping at arm's length throughout the rest of his reign.

Notes

1. Shah Shuja's only other claim to fame was that he had once owned the fabulous Koh-i-noor diamond, which now forms part of the British Crown Jewels. While a fugitive from his own country he was defrauded of the stone by Ranjit Singh, ruler of the Punjab.

2. This was not quite true. Sergeant Major Lisant of the 37th Native Infantry, a merchant named Banes and a handful of camp followers also reached Jellalabad.

3. Havelock, a devout Christian, played a leading role in many subsequent campaigns in India but is best remembered for his actions during the Great Mutiny, which made him one of the great heroes of the mid-Victorian era. Worn out, he died only days after the final relief of Lucknow. For many years the neck cloths worn by some armies in tropical climates were known as Havelocks.

4. Broadfoot's unfortunate manner put him at cross purposes with many people. Monteith was criticised for not adopting his suggestions, and Dennie was described as being 'wholly unqualified to command'. At one point Sale had to intervene personally to end an ongoing row between the engineer officers and those of the 13th. Although the precise nature of his offence is unknown, Broadfoot overstepped the mark in February, receiving a formal written reprimand via the Brigade Major 'for direct and wilful disobedience of orders, and warning him if he again contravenes orders prompt and decisive measures will have to be taken by the Major General, with a view to the proper maintenance of his authority'.

5. After some of the inhabitants had led the besiegers into the town, the Native Infantry regiment holding Ghazni retired into the citadel. Starved into surrender and promised the Honours of War, it was massacred after it marched out. A few British officers were spared and joined the prisoners already held by Akbar Khan.

6. The standard, together with two more taken during the capture of Ghazni in 1839, is preserved at the Somerset Military Museum in Taunton.

3
The Bloodiest Day: Antietam (Sharpsburg), 17 September 1862

In the late summer of 1862 Confederate hopes were at their highest. In May the Federal Army of the Potomac, commanded by Major General George B. McClellan, had advanced to within sight of Richmond but after the series of engagements known as The Seven Days' Battles had been forced to retreat to Harrison's Landing on the James River, where it enjoyed the protection of the Navy's gunboats until it was shipped back to the Washington area in August. In the meantime, the newly formed Federal Army of Virginia, under Major General John Pope, had invaded Confederate territory. On learning that McClellan's army would march to join Pope as soon as it reached Washington, General Robert E. Lee, commanding the Confederate Army of Northern Virginia, recognised that the combined Union armies would have a total strength of 150,000 men, outnumbering him by three to one. He therefore decided to deal with Pope before the latter could be reinforced and inflicted a decisive defeat on him at the Second Battle of Bull Run (Manassas). The Confederate pursuit towards Washington was checked at the Battle of Chantilly by the stubborn fighting of the Federal rearguard. During this action, Brigadier General Phil Kearny, whose name would be given to the frontier fort that forms the subject of the next chapter, lost his life while courageously rallying his troops.

The stage was now set for the Confederacy to take the offensive. In the West General Braxton Bragg was to mount an invasion of Kentucky, while in the East Lee would march north into Maryland. Both states, it was believed, contained large numbers of Confederate sympathisers who would prove a valuable addition to the South's limited manpower. Furthermore, in Lee's case, once he was deep within the Federal hinterland he could not only disrupt Union communications with the Western theatre of war, but also strike at Philadelphia, Baltimore or Washington as the occasion offered. The possibilities, however, extended far beyond the purely military considerations. Lee was aware that the North possessed infinitely greater resources than the Confederacy, and that in the long term these would prove decisive in a protracted war. On the other hand, it was apparent that large sections of Northern public opinion were becoming weary of the conflict. A major victory on northern territory would make President Lincoln's Federal administration more receptive to the offers of mediation put forward by Great Britain and France. As the Confederacy had not, as yet, been recognised by a single foreign power, such mediation would be tantamount to recognition and the Confederacy would remain in being after the conclusion of a negotiated peace.

In Washington, Lincoln knew exactly what was at stake. Although the slavery issue lay simmering just below the surface, the Federal government was fighting the war on the principle that individual states could not secede from the Union. Now that the novelty of war had been replaced by a sense of its grim realities, many in the North had begun to feel that the secession question was simply not worth the huge outpouring of grief, blood and treasure, a view that might well be shared by British and French mediators, should it prove necessary to involve them. For the moment, however, he could only hope and reorganise, disbanding Pope's army and merging it with that of McClellan, who was made responsible for the defence of Washington.

Lee began crossing the Potomac on 4 September and three days later had reached Frederick, Maryland. To his disappointment, the Marylanders did not welcome his troops, nor did they provide anything like the support he had anticipated. He was also alarmed at the extent to which straggling was seriously reducing the numbers under his immediate command. There were several reasons for this. First, the weather was hot and dry, with the temperature in the middle 80s and dust rising in choking clouds from the dirt roads. Secondly, most of the troops were dressed in ragged, worn-out uniforms and many marched barefoot until they could march no more. Thirdly, until their supply wagons caught up with them, the men fed themselves on green corn taken straight from the fields and began to suffer from diarrhoea. Fourthly, notwithstanding the victories of the past few months, there was a crisis of morale. For this, the Confederacy's Conscription Act was partly responsible. Under this, those with the necessary funds could purchase a substitute to serve in their place, giving rise to the saying that a rich man's war had become a poor man's fight. Again, regiments that had been conscripted for what they believed to be a one-year term suddenly discovered that they were in a Catch 22 situation; the small print making it clear that they had enlisted for the war's duration. Finally, many of the officers and NCOs best able to maintain march discipline had become casualties in the recent battles and their inexperienced replacements, though willing enough, were not up to the job.

Despite this, Lee persevered with his plan of campaign. On 9 September he issued his Special Order No 191. The gist of this was that Major General Thomas 'Stonewall' Jackson, with six divisions, was to cut the Baltimore and Ohio Railroad and capture the Federal arsenal of Harper's Ferry, while Major General James Longstreet, with two divisions, was to maintain the general direction of the advance as far as Boonsboro. Once Jackson had taken Harper's Ferry he too would converge on Boonsboro, after which Lee's intention was that the entire army would advance on Harrisburg, Pennsylvania. Copies of the order were distributed to every divisional commander and as a precaution Jackson sent a duplicate to Major General D.H. Hill, whose division was to form the rearguard. The effect of the order would be to disperse the army across 25 miles of country divided by a major river. This was hardly a wise course to take so deep in enemy territory, but Lee knew McClellan well and, certain that he would react slowly, believed that the risk was justified. On 10 September the Army of Northern Virginia marched out of Frederick, its various elements dispersing to the north-west, west and south-west as their missions demanded.

Yet, contrary to Lee's expectations, and indeed those of Lincoln and General Henry Halleck, the Army's General in Chief, McClellan had responded quickly to the invasion of Maryland. Leaving some 26,000 men for the defence of Washington, he was already marching north with the enlarged Army of the Potomac. On 12 September he entered Frederick and there, on a former Confederate camp site, some of his soldiers discovered a bundle of cigars wrapped in what was apparently a letter of some sort. The 'letter' was, in fact, one of the few copies of Special Order No 191. Whether it had been left behind because of negligence or, as some hinted, treachery, will never be known. Be that as it may, the men recognised the importance of their find and passed it on to higher authority. McClellan was now aware of Lee's precise dispositions. All he had to do was thrust through the South Mountain passes of the Blue Ridge Mountains, insert himself between the corps of Longstreet and Jackson, who could then be overwhelmed in detail, and the Confederate Army of Northern Virginia would cease to exist. But now his customary caution returned and his advance guard did not begin probing the South Mountain passes until 14 September.

One story has it that a civilian sympathiser informed Lee that Special Order No 191 had fallen into McClellan's hands during the evening, although it not universally accepted. More probably his reaction was based on the observation's of McClellan's general dispositions by his own cavalry scouts. Deeply shocked, he realised that the strategic initiative had passed to McClellan and that his first task must be to defend the three passes if his own army was to survive. Longstreet was instructed to reinforce D.H. Hill, who was already covering Turner's and Fox's Gaps with his own division, and Major General Lafayette McLaws, part of Jackson's forces investing Harper's Ferry, was ordered to send back two brigades to cover Crampton's Gap.

During the ensuing series of engagements, known as the Battles of Crampton's Gap and South Mountain, the outnumbered Confederates fought for time throughout 14 September but were eventually driven from their positions. Deeply depressed, Lee issued an order to Jackson, telling him to abandon the attack on Harper's Ferry and cover the army's withdrawal across the Potomac into Virginia. This was countermanded shortly after when a despatch arrived from Jackson saying that Harper's Ferry was about to fall.

The position of the 12,000-strong Federal garrison of Harper's Ferry, commanded by Colonel D.S. Miles, was indeed untenable. Lying in a deep valley at the confluence of the Potomac and Shenandoah rivers, the town was vulnerable to artillery fire from the surrounding heights, which were quickly secured by Jackson's divisions. Enclosed within a ring of fire, the Federals held out until the morning of the 15th, Miles being mortally wounded at the moment of surrender. Jackson's haul amounted to 11,000 prisoners, 73 guns, 13,000 small arms, plenty of ammunition, 73 wagons, and large stocks of food, clothing and shoes. That night, leaving A.P. Hill's division to deal with the prisoners and captured stores, Jackson began the twelve-mile march north to Sharpsburg, where Lee had ordered the army to concentrate.

With his customary caution, McClellan had not exploited his success at the South Mountain passes while there was time to do so. This may have been a result of faulty information supplied by Allan Pinkerton, founder of the famous detective agency and head of the Army of the Potomac's network of intelligence gathering network. Pinkerton persistently overestimated Lee's strength, suggesting that he had invaded Maryland with 120,000 men, although the real figure was in the region of 55,000, which straggling and casualties had now reduced to 38,000. McClellan had begun the campaign with about 85,000 men and had lost about 10,000 of them through straggling and other causes. Believing that following the fall of Harper's Ferry he would be opposed by superior numbers as Lee concentrated his army again, he understandably waited until all his troops were over the passes before offering battle.

As a result of this, Lee was given time to return his house to some sort of order. After the success at Harper's Ferry a less aggressive commander might have retired into Virginia, but with the political dimension in mind Lee was seeking a major victory that would attract international attention. He decided to fight a defensive battle on Sharpsburg Ridge, lying between Antietam Creek and the Potomac, confident in his army's ability to inflict serious loss on McClellan's troops.

The terrain over which the battle would be fought consisted of rolling, well cultivated farmland with woods dotted here and there. To the east, three arched stone bridges crossed the fast-flowing Antietam Creek, and a number of fords were also available. The village of Sharpsburg, founded 99 years earlier, lay in a hollow below the western slopes of Sharpsburg Ridge. One road, the Boonsboro Pike, headed east over the ridge and crossed Antietam Creek by the Middle Bridge. A second, less important, road led southeast to cross the creek at the Lower or Rohrbach Bridge. Other roads led west to Shepherdstown and the Potomac, some two or three miles distant. Heading north from the village was another major road, the Hagerstown

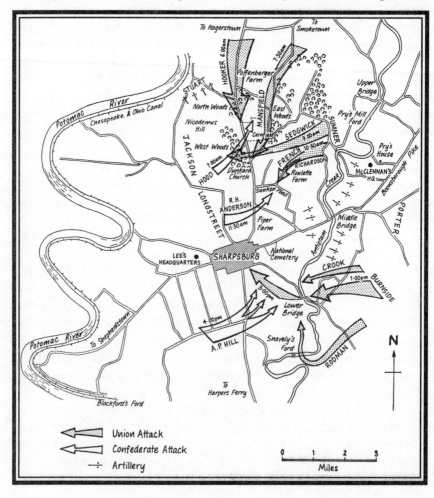

Pike. Approximately one mile to the north this road passed by the West Woods, with a small whitewashed Dunker or Dunkard Church, used by a German pacifist sect, on the left. Over some fields on the right were the East Woods; one field, belonging to a farmer named Miller, was full of corn almost ready for harvesting, extended from the northern edge of the East Woods back to the road. Some way beyond this point the Hagerstown Pike passed through the North Woods, west of which was a prominent feature known as Nicodemus Hill, sloping down to the Potomac. Anyone travelling south along the Hagerstown Pike could avoid Sharpsburg by turning left into a winding lane just beyond the West Woods, and in due course he would emerge onto the Boonsboro Pike; over the years the combined action of wagon wheels and water erosion had worn away the surface of the lane until it had become known as the Sunken Road.

On 16 September Lee completed the deployment of his re-assembled army. Fully aware that he was heavily outnumbered, he refused his left flank, positioning Stuart with fourteen guns on Nicodemus Hill. In other respects his line ran along Sharpsburg Ridge from north-west to south-east with Jackson commanding the front north of Sharpsburg and Longstreet the village itself and the line to the south, extending as far as the Lower Bridge, beyond which cavalry covered the fords downstream.

Slowly, the Army of the Potomac closed up to the position during the day, but nothing more serious than skirmishing and artillery exchanges took place. Altogether, McClellan had six corps and a strong cavalry division available, the operations of which would be supported by concentrated artillery fire from the bluffs east of Antietam Creek. He had already noted that Lee had chosen the dangerous course of fighting with the Potomac at his back and decided to exploit this the following morning by attacking in echelon of corps from the right. As each attack went in he envisaged, correctly, that Lee would transfer his reserves from his as-yet disengaged right flank to meet it. Finally, the weakened Confederate right would itself be overwhelmed and Lee, penned with the remnants of his army against an unfordable river, would be forced to surrender. Following as it did the Cannae principle, the plan was sound enough, although precise timing was essential if it was to succeed. Some of McClellan's critics have suggested that a simultaneous concentric attack would have produced a similar result for less trouble, but again timing would have been a critical factor; and, of course, since McClellan believed that he had the smaller army, he would have been less willing to risk being checked anywhere along the line.

The morale of the troops on both sides was high. Although the Federals had been repeatedly worsted by the Army of Northern Virginia, they were encouraged by their success at South Mountain. Their failures in the past they put down to poor leadership by middle-ranking commanders who were often political appointees, but they liked and trusted McClellan, whom they called Little Mac, and they had no quarrel with their regimental officers. Across the lines, there was not the slightest doubt in Johnny Reb's mind that he was a better man than the average Yankee and he could quote a string of victories to prove his point. Furthermore, he had absolute trust in Robert E. Lee, the epitome of the Southern gentleman, and he would do anything for him.

After a night of drizzle the 17 September dawned grey and misty, although it would clear as the day progressed. On the extreme right of the Federal line Major General Joseph Hooker's[1] I Corps began advancing south along the axis of the Hagerstown Pike at about 0615, harassed by Stuart's guns firing from Nicodemus Hill. Supported by five batteries, the Federals pushed steadily forward, pushing the Confederate skirmishers back through the East and West Woods and the Miller cornfield until they were in contact with Jackson's main line. An intense firefight followed until the Confederate ranks began to give way under pressure. In attempting to escape from the cornfield into the West Woods many were shot down while clambering over the post and rail fences bordering the Hagerstown Pike. Yet, as Hooker noted, the loss of life on both sides had been heavy:

'Every stalk in the Northern quarter and the greater part of the field was cut as closely as could have been done with a knife, and the slain lay in rows precisely as they had done in their ranks a few moments before. It was never my fortune to witness a more bloody, dismal battlefield.'

Worse was to follow. Jackson's line was apparently on the point of collapse when he committed Hood's Division to a counter-attack at 0700. Consisting of two brigades, Colonel William Wofford's (1st, 4th and 5th Texas, 18th Georgia, and Hampton's South Carolina Legion) and Colonel Evander Law's (4th Alabama, 2nd and 11th Mississippi and 6th North Carolina) with about 2300 men between them, this was one of the Confederacy's crack formations. The men had been cooking dough twists on their ramrods when they were called forward and were obviously not in the best of moods. Giving vent to their feelings with the fearsome Rebel Yell, they suddenly emerged from the West Woods to fire a devastating volley that felled the leading ranks of the surprised Northerners. Wheeling half-left, they began to press their shaken opponents back across the cornfield. To their left-rear, brigades from D.H. Hill's division had come forward from their position in the Sunken Road to help clear the southern end of the East Woods, and had set fire to the buildings of the Mumma farm to prevent their being used by Federal sharpshooters.

The progress made by Hood's counter-attack, however, was too good to last long. The further his men advanced, the more exposed they became to the Federal artillery, which blew great gaps in their ranks with case shot and canister. Decimated, they were finally checked by unshaken troops, but had succeeded in stabilising the situation. Of the 226 men of the 1st Texas who had gone into action just twenty minutes earlier, only 40 came out; thirteen of their comrades lay dead in one small group, around the fallen regimental colours.

Hooker's Corps pulled back towards the North Woods to regroup, having sustained one-third casualties. Jackson had sustained a similar proportion of losses but his men were permitted just ten minutes before the second of McClellan's hammer blows struck them. This was delivered by Major General Joseph Mansfield's XII Corps which took as its axis the Smoketown Road, a track leading south-west through the East Woods to join the Hagerstown Pike close to the Dunker Church. Mansfield himself was mortally wounded as soon as his troops came within range, his place being taken by Brigadier General Alpheus Williams. While Williams was discussing the overall situation with Hooker a shell splinter struck the latter in the foot and he, too, had to be carried from the field.

Luckily for Jackson, XII Corps' attack was not coordinated. On the right the units of its 1st Division went into action piecemeal as they arrived and were stopped at the cornfield. On the left, however, Brigadier General George Greene's[2] 2nd Division, emerging from the East Woods, drove off the remnants of Hood's command and advanced on the Dunker Church, causing several Confederate batteries to limber up and head for the rear. Somehow, using every formed body of troops he could lay hands on, Jackson managed to plug the gap, requesting Lee to send reinforcements as a matter of desperate urgency. Lee was forced to strip his centre and right of troops, and he promised to send up McLaws' division, which had just reached the battlefield. The effect of this was to place three-quarters of the Confederate army north of Sharpsburg, exactly as McClellan had intended.

By 0900 Greene's division had expended its ammunition and it began to seem that XII Corps had shot its bolt. Fighting died down, although away to the east the blue columns of McClellan's next attack could be seen marching towards the East Woods. This would be delivered by Major General Edwin Sumner's II Corps, containing the divisions of Major General John Sedgwick and Brigadier Generals William French and Israel Richardson. The corps advanced with Sedgwick on the right and French on the left. Richardson trailed far behind, having been forbidden to move off by McClellan until he had been relieved by a division from the reserve. The whole of the cornfield and the area between the East and West Woods was now covered with thousands of killed and wounded, blue and butternut-grey intermingled, smashed weapons and abandoned limbers. The many young recruits in Sedgwick's ranks, already taking casualties from the fire of Stuart's artillery, were severely shaken by the screams of the wounded and sickened by the sights they came across every few steps – torn bodies, severed limbs, here a kepi containing part of the owner's head, there a hand still clutching a weapon, and everywhere blood that soon splattered their boots. Nevertheless, they pressed on towards the West Woods, leaving the Dunker Church and Greene's division, now resting and replenishing its cartridge boxes, on their left. Hopes began to rise as they crossed the Hagerstown Pike and entered the trees, for there was not a live or unwounded Confederate in sight.

Jackson had decided against meeting this attack head on. Instead, he pulled back his troops deep into the West Woods, where rocky outcrops and broken ground provided excellent cover. McLaws' brigades and other reinforcements were pushed into the line as they came up until eventually Jackson had about 10,000 men deployed in a great semicircle around Sedgwick's axis of advance.

Sedgwick had entered the West Woods at about 0930. Their confidence growing, his regiments pushed on through the trees without meeting any opposition. Then, just as a warning was shouted, the woodland erupted in smoke and flame, blasting away entire ranks at close quarters. Whooping, the Confederates on their left closed in behind them. Incredibly, Sedgwick's men stuck it for about fifteen minutes before breaking, fleeing out of the woods to the north-east, their one remaining avenue of escape. They had gone into action 4500 strong and now almost half that number were down. Somewhat rashly, Jackson ordered a counter-attack against the East Woods, but this quickly foundered under the fire of 50 guns lining its edge. After this, neither side made any major moves on this sector of the battlefield and firing finally died away at about 1300.

Sedgwick, his division destroyed, was entitled to ask what had become of French's division, which should have come up on his left. The answer was that in the smoke of battle French had been drawn on by skirmishers and veered off the corps axis of advance to the left; a further, and quite unexpected, diversion was provided by a Confederate roundshot that demolished a beehive, the angry occupants of which set about and temporarily dispersed the 132nd Pennsylvania. At 0930 French's leading brigade crossed a rolling crestline and arrived in front of the Sunken Road, to which D.H. Hill's division had returned. A murderous fire-fight ensued, lasting over three hours. At about 1100 Richardson came up on French's left and some 30 minutes later Longstreet, on whose sector the battle was now raging, directed Major

General Richard Anderson's division, the Army of Northern Virginia's last reserve, to move forward and support Hill. Enjoying the limited protection provided by the banks of the Sunken Road and its post-and-rail fence, the Confederates shot down the exposed Federals in large numbers. Typical was the experience of Brigadier General Francis Meagher's mainly New York Irish Brigade belonging to Richardson's division. Meagher's intention had been to fire two volleys then charge home with the bayonet, but no sooner had his regiments appeared above the crest than they were staggered by a tremendous discharge. Bravely they followed their colours forward into a leaden sleet in which none could hope to remain upright for long and finally the attack collapsed. Two regiments, the 63rd and 69th New York, sustained 60 per cent casualties; Meagher, stunned by the fall when his horse was shot under him, was carried off the field.

Yet, for all their partial protection, the Confederates were forced to endure the heavier volume of fire and whenever they tried to counter-attack they were driven back with severe loss. The end came shortly before 1300 when the Federals finally managed to secure the eastern end of the position. The 61st and 64th New York were first into the lane, opening an enfilade fire into the flank of the remaining defenders. Thanks to a misunderstood order, many of the latter withdrew in some haste, leaving 300 of their comrades to be taken prisoner. 'In this road,' recalled an officer of the 5th New Hampshire, 'lay so many dead rebels that they formed a line which one might have walked upon as far as I could see, many of whom had been killed by the most horrible wounds of shot and shell'. From that moment onwards the Sunken Road would be known to history by another name – Bloody Lane.

One of Lee's senior artillery officers, Lieutenant Colonel E.P. Alexander, felt his heart clutched by the leaden hand of despair as he watched the Confederate line collapse in disorder. At that moment, he recalled, he sincerely believed that 'Lee's army was ruined, and the end of the Confederacy was in sight'.

Never before, and never again, during the course of the war did the Army of Northern Virginia stand in such mortal danger. Even when rallied, Hill's and Anderson's divisions were but a shadow of their former selves, and while Longstreet had brought up his reserve artillery, he was reduced to holding the horses of his staff who manned a gun, the crew of which had been shot down. It looked as though one determined Federal advance could roll over the threadbare grey line and drive on to the Potomac, completely surrounding most of Lee's troops.

At that moment such a move would certainly have succeeded. True, the divisions of French and Richardson, mauled and exhausted, had halted their advance a few hundred yards beyond Bloody Lane, but McClellan had reinforced Sumner's II Corps with two fresh divisions from Major General William Franklin's VI Corps, one of his reserve formations. Franklin had brought them forward himself and was in favour of an immediate attack. Sumner, deeply depressed by his losses, did not agree; although aged 65, he was normally a vigorous commander, but on this occasion all the fight seemed to have been knocked out of him. Minutes ticked away as the generals argued, both sending messengers back to McClellan with their respective arguments. Shortly after 1400 this brought the army commander to the front for the only time in the battle.

Sumner convinced him that I, XII and II Corps were completely exhausted and McClellan informed Franklin that in the circumstances 'it would not be prudent to make the attack'. A little later he was approached by Brigadier General George Sykes, a divisional commander in Major General Fitz-John Porter's V Corps, the Army of the Potomac's second reserve formation, who also requested permission to attack the attenuated Confederate centre. Porter is alleged to have dissuaded McClellan with the words, 'Remember, General, I command the last reserve of the last army of the Republic'. This, coupled with an earlier reluctance to engage during the Seven Days' Battle, cost Porter his career.

Few would wish to argue that McClellan's caution was not being carried to absurd lengths, although there were a number of considerations running through his mind that should be mentioned. He still thought that Lee outnumbered him and believed, correctly, that he was considering a major counter-attack; this was to have been directed at the North Woods and was only abandoned when Jackson and Stuart pointed out that it would be made in teeth of a major concentration of Federal artillery. Above all, however, McClellan still had faith in his original battle plan. The thunder of battle to the south indicated that Major General Ambrose Burnside's IX Corps was bringing pressure to bear on the Confederate right, now stripped bare to support Lee's battered left and centre. Burnside was McClellan's trump card – once he had broken through, the encirclement of Lee's army would be a fact.

One complication was that Burnside had begun the day in a sulk. He had been designated as the commander of a wing of the Army of the Potomac containing I and IX Corps. Now, I Corps had been taken away to lead the Federal attack on the right and he took the attitude that IX Corps was actually under the acting command of one of its divisional commanders, Brigadier General Jacob Cox. Thus, orders received by Burnside were passed on to Cox, which cost valuable time, although as 'wing' commander Burnside retained the right to interfere, which cost more.

Burnside's first task was to capture the Lower or Rohrbach Bridge over Antietam Creek, for which he had 12,000 men available. On the opposite bank the Confederate right consisted solely of Brigadier General D.R. Jones' division, reduced to 3000 men by demands elsewhere, and a small force of cavalry; covering the bridge itself was Brigadier General Robert Toombs' all-Georgia brigade, dug in among trees and rocks on a hillside that dominated the crossing.

At 0910 McClellan despatched an order for Burnside to commence his attack. Burnside received the order at 1000 and mounted a succession of attacks on the bridge. Each was swept away in a blast of musketry and canister that turned the structure, 125 feet long but only twelve feet wide, into a death trap. In the meantime, Burnside sent Brigadier Isaac Rodman's division downstream to find a crossing. At about noon it came upon the shallow water of Snavely's Ford and forded the river, bringing pressure to bear on the Georgians' right. Simultaneously, a brigade under Colonel George Crook located another ford just a few hundred yards upstream of the bridge and closed in on the defenders' left.

McClellan was rapidly losing patience with Burnside, to whom he sent one courier after another, stressing the need for speed. At about 1215 Burnside, rattled and ill-tempered, ordered Cox to mount another attack, the choice of troops falling on Brigadier General Edward Ferrero's brigade. Ferrero decided to use only two of his regiments, the 51st Pennsylvania and the 51st New York, and instead of assaulting along the road, which ran parallel to the river, he formed them up behind a hill only 300 yards above the bridge. Yet, when the regiments came swarming down the slope they ran into such heavy fire that they were forced to take cover behind a fence and stone wall that lay respectively to the left and right of the bridge. Then, quite suddenly, the Confederate fire seemed to slacken. The Georgians had themselves sustained serious losses, they were running out of ammunition and they were unsettled by the pressure on their flanks. From across the river they could be seen abandoning their positions and disappearing behind the opposite crest. At 1300, spurred on by their commanding officers, the two 51sts stormed across the bridge together and spread out to create a bridgehead.[3]

It was an heroic moment that would result in the bridge being known ever after as Burnside's Bridge. Unfortunately, it was largely wasted. Burnside pushed his troops across, most of his infantry brigades, artillery batteries and supply wagons all using the same narrow path. Instead of pushing forward immediately in the direction of Sharpsburg, he began methodically redeploying IX Corps. McClellan, sensing that victory lay now just within his grasp, was incensed by the delay and despatched a senior member of his own staff with orders to relieve Burnside unless the advance was resumed at once.

At 1500 Burnside authorised Cox to move off. The towers of Sharpsburg's Episcopal and Lutheran churches were clearly visible now. Between them and the advancing blue ranks were all that remained of Jones' four brigades, their ammunition replenished but few in numbers, punctuated here and there by undermanned guns. Bitterly, the Confederates contested every foot of ground but were pressed steadily back. A wild bayonet charge by the 9th New York, a Zouave regiment with baggy red trousers and floppy fezzes, effectively broke Jones' line. Only a few hundred yards separated the Federals from Sharpsburg, the streets of which were crowded with wounded and stragglers. Lee, with not a man nor a gun in reserve, was convinced that he had lost the battle when, at 1545, he observed more blue-clad columns entering the southern edge of the battlefield. Being close to a battery position, he asked an artillery officer to identify their regimental colours and was told that they were Confederate. Minutes later, the newcomers opened fire into the left flank of Burnside's corps.

Ambrose Hill's division entered the battle in the nick of time and just at the right place. Hill had set a cracking pace all the way from Harper's Ferry, alternately double-timing and quick-marching, and he had used the flat of his sword to drive the stragglers on towards the sound of the guns. While in Harper's Ferry his men had replaced their rags with fresh uniforms from the captured Federal stores and, of course, there had been no time to dye these. The result was to cause Lee a moment's despair, and a degree of bewildered hesitation among their opponents as they reached the field.

While Hill rode ahead to confer with Lee and Jones, his five brigades came into action one after another, rolling up Rodman's division and forcing it into a disorderly retreat towards the bridge. The rest of Burnside's troops, their flank stove in, had no alternative other than to abandon their advance on Sharpsburg and conform until the position was stabilised at about 1630. To all intents and purposes the Battle of Antietam was over.

It was the bloodiest single day of the entire Civil War. Confederate losses amounted to 2700 killed, 9024 wounded and about 2000 missing, a total approaching 14,000 casualties. Federal losses included 2108 killed, 9549 wounded and 753 missing, a total of 12,410. The surgeons of both armies worked together during the night and into the next day, many a man owing his life to Miss Clara Barton, one of the future founders of the American Red Cross, who reached the battlefield with a wagonload of dressings, anaesthetics and oil lamps donated by the people of Washington.

Tactically, the battle had ended in a draw. Lee had preserved his army, handling his reserves in a masterly fashion, but he had been forced to dance to McClellan's tune all day and had come within an ace of defeat. McClellan had more than once been close to winning a major victory, but his own sense of caution had proved his undoing; whereas Lee had no more troops to commit to the fighting, much of McClellan's V and VI Corps, plus a large cavalry division, had barely fired a shot by the day's end. Only Ambrose Hill, whose division had turned the scales at the critical moment, had any real cause for satisfaction; he bore McClellan a long-standing personal grudge and the fact that he had himself been responsible for wrecking the latter's grand design was a sweet revenge that he savoured until his dying day.[4]

Strategically, however, the battle put an end to Lee's invasion of Maryland and Pennsylvania. With difficulty, his senior officers persuaded him that the army was now too weak to continue the offensive. There was no fighting on the 18th and that night the Army of Northern Virginia withdrew across the Potomac.

McClellan made only a token attempt at pursuit, despite the personal urgings of President Lincoln to take more vigorous action. When Stuart's cavalry made a three-day raid through Maryland and Pennsylvania in October, riding round the still-stationary Army of the Potomac, causing $250,000 worth of damage, capturing large quantities of military stores and driving off 1200 horses, this proved to be the last straw. McClellan was dismissed on 7 November. Burnside was appointed to succeed him but was heavily defeated by Lee at Fredericksburg on 13 December.

It was at the political level that the Federals gained most from Antietam. In London, Lord Palmerston's administration had been seriously considering recognition of the Confederacy, but the inconclusive result of the battle led it to await further events. On 22 September, Lincoln, anxious not only to avoid foreign involvement but also to regenerate motivation among his own people, issued his Emancipation Proclamation, declaring that with effect from 1 January 1863 all slaves living in those states still in rebellion against the Union would be free men. The war, begun on a point of political principle, had become a crusade. In such circumstances no foreign power would risk association with the Confederacy.

Notes

1. Hooker unintentionally provided the English language with a concise job description. When Washington began to fill up with troops at the beginning of the war crowds of street walkers swarmed into the capital from New York and other cities. The press, aware of the General's fondness for the ladies, maliciously announced the arrival of 'Hooker's Division.' The name stuck.

2. Greene was the son of General Nathanael Greene, a hero of the American War of Independence who, though he rarely won a battle, eliminated the British presence in the South by a campaign of attrition. His own son Dana served as executive officer aboard the ironclad USS *Monitor* during her historic duel with the Confederate ship *Merrimack*.

3. The Federals sustained 550 casualties taking the bridge, the Confederates about 120 in defending it. Had Burnside possessed average abilities he would have located the fords before fighting began. Charles Fair accords him a special place in his study of the consequences of military stupidity, *From The Jaws Of Victory*, a phrase that could aptly be applied to what followed. Toombs, Burnside's opponent, was a political appointee who had been a candidate for the Confederate Presidency. His defence of the bridge marked the high point in a short military career of otherwise dubious value. Both men were lionised by their respective civil populations for their part in the battle.

4. In their youth Ambrose Hill and George McClellan had been rivals for the affections of Miss Ellen Marcy, the daughter of a senior officer. Hill had already won the lady's hand when her parents, hearing a rumour that he had contracted a venereal disease in his cadet days, forbade the match. Miss Marcy then married McClellan. Hill's soldiers knew the story and were aware that he fought with a personal grudge. Whenever he pushed them into a particularly hard-fought action they would shout across to the opposing line: 'For God's sake, Nelly – why didn't you marry him?!' Hill was killed in action on 2 April 1865, one week before Lee's surrender at Appomattox.

4
Captain Fetterman's Disobedience

The roots of the tragedy lay in the fact that the nomadic lifestyle of the North American Plains Indian, depending as it did on hunting and fishing, was not compatible with that of the white settler, who relied upon agriculture and industry to support himself. Even in the vast stretches of virgin land available, conflict had become inevitable by the middle of the Nineteenth Century as more and more settlers took the road West. Understandably, the Indians fought hard to keep the unwelcome newcomers out of their hunting grounds. More often than not, the US Government's attempts to defuse the situation with treaties guaranteeing tribal possession of land were frustrated by the sheer scale of the Westward migration, with the result that for many years conflict along the Old Frontier became a daily fact of life. It might, perhaps, seem curious that the Indians did not make greater efforts to exploit the situation created by the withdrawal of frontier garrisons during the Civil War, until it is remembered that both sides promised them concessions and that the reduced volume of migration in itself eased the pressure a little. Nevertheless, the killing of settlers, the burning of their farms and the ambush of wagon trains continued to take place until, towards the end of the war, the Federal Government re-established the absent garrisons using volunteer regiments of 'galvanised Yankees', recruited from Confederate prisoners of war who had been promised that they would neither be required to serve against their own people nor replace Union troops on the Frontier.

When the war ended the entire situation changed dramatically. Migration soared and the Federal Treasury, having expended a large proportion of its gold reserves, was anxious to replenish them. One source was the Montana goldfields of Virginia City and Helena, which were difficult to reach save by a route that left Fort Laramie, Wyoming, and travelled north-westwards through the Powder River country into Montana. This had been surveyed by a frontiersman named John Bozeman and was variously called the Bozeman Trail, the Virginia City Road and the Montana Road. Unfortunately, the Powder River country contained the best hunting grounds of the Sioux,

Cheyenne and Arapaho, the most warlike tribes of the Northern Plains, who not only regarded certain areas as sacred, but had also been granted possession of the land in perpetuity. In the autumn of 1865 Government commissioners signed a treaty with members of the tribes guaranteeing their rights to all the territory between the Black Hills, the Big Horn Mountains and the Yellowstone River, including the Powder River country, in return for a

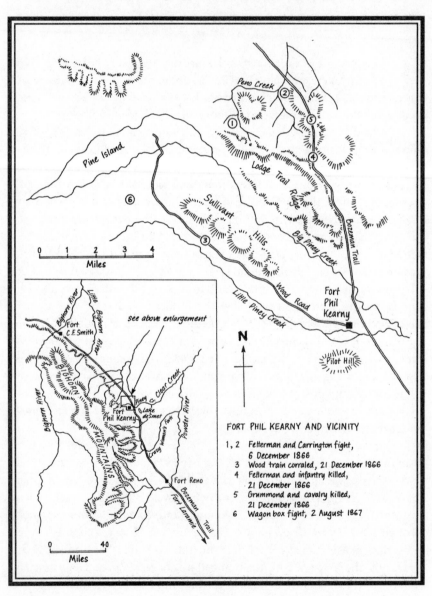

FORT PHIL KEARNY AND VICINITY

1, 2 Fetterman and Carrington fight,
      6 December 1866
3   Wood train corraled, 21 December 1866
4   Fetterman and infantry killed,
      21 December 1866
5   Grummond and cavalry killed,
      21 December 1866
6   Wagon box fight, 2 August 1867

promise that white travellers would be allowed to use the Bozeman Trail in safety. What the commissioners were unaware of was that the Indian signatories, known as Laramie Loafers because they preferred to live on Army handouts rather than hunt, spoke only for themselves. The real voice of the tribes, as expressed in their councils by Chiefs Red Cloud and Man-Afraid-of-His-Horses of the Oglala Sioux, was emphatic that the whites would not be permitted to use the Bozeman Trail. Those that tried did so at their peril and seldom survived, with the result that a growing demand arose for Army protection.

In the spring of 1866 the Government tried again. A new commission was sent to Fort Laramie and opened fresh talks with Red Cloud and the more belligerent chiefs. For a while it seemed that real progress was being made. Then, in an astoundingly tactless piece of bad timing, Colonel Henry B. Carrington marched into Laramie at the head of 700 men of the 2nd Battalion 18th Infantry, with orders to garrison Fort Reno on the Powder River and establish two further forts along the Bozeman Trail between Fort Reno and Virginia City. To the Indians, already distrustful of the white man's word, the obvious inference was that if the newcomers could not obtain the passage they sought by negotiation they would take it by force. It was a challenge so blatant that Red Cloud and his allies could not ignore it and, bitterly angry, they left immediately to prepare for an all-out war in defence of the Bozeman Trail.

Even without the benefit of hindsight it is possible to see that, as far as the Army was concerned, what followed was a disaster waiting to happen. The basic plan of building forts along the Trail, conceived by Major General John Pope, commander of the Department of the Missouri, was flawed for several reasons. From Fort Laramie to Fort Reno on the Powder River was a distance of 100 miles; from Reno to the site of the next fort, to be named Phil Kearny, was 67 miles; and from Phil Kearny to the most northerly fort in the chain, C.F. Smith, was a further long 91 miles. It can thus been seen that in the event of trouble, of which there was plenty a-brewing, none of the comparatively small garrisons were capable of providing mutual support for each other.

Again, given that Carrington's primary task, after the construction of Forts Phil Kearny and C.F. Smith, was the protection of traffic along the Bozeman Trail, he was simply not equipped to carry it out. Only a combination of mobility and firepower would have given him the slightest chance of succeeding, but this he lacked. He possessed sufficient horses for him to mount a small number of men, but the rest were conventional marching infantry, referred to as 'walk-a-heaps' by the Indians. It was, therefore, the latter, mounted on their fast, tough ponies, who possessed the initiative from the outset and dictated the terms of every engagement. Furthermore, with the exception of the 25-strong regimental band, who carried seven-shot breech-loading Spencer carbines, his command was armed with the same muzzle-loading Springfield musket that it had used during the Civil War.

Nor was Carrington himself the ideal man for so inherently hazardous a task. A lawyer by profession, his political connections had ensured that he received a colonel's commission in the days immediately following the bombardment of Fort Sumter, and he had raised the 18th Infantry in July 1861. The regiment had first served in the western theatre of war and then taken part in Sherman's march through Georgia, earning a good reputation and battle honours that included Missionary Ridge, Kenesaw Mountain and Atlanta. Unfortunately, Carrington had not served with it, his talents as an organiser and administrator ensuring that he was engaged in staff duties far from the battlefield throughout the war. He had, therefore, never heard a shot fired in anger, let alone commanded a unit in action, a state of affairs that left him with little in common with those of his officers who had. Sensitive on the subject, he failed to impose discipline on them, was tolerant of insubordination and hesitant in his command decisions, tending to seek compromise when the situation demanded firm handling. Essentially a decent, scholarly man, he proposed resolving any difficulties with the Sioux by means of 'patience, forbearance and common sense.'

Such sentiments struck no answering chord with Red Cloud and his fellow chiefs, who could deploy between three and four thousand mounted braves for attacks on the Bozeman Trail. These warriors, armed with bow, lance, club and axe, fought in ways with which the 18th Infantry, used to the more intelligible battlefields of the Civil War, was totally unfamiliar and to which it was unable to find an adequate response. One method was to mount a decoy attack on a small party in the hope of attracting a much larger reaction force to the scene; it was, of course, the reaction force that was the real target, and the decoys were simply used to lure it onto the main ambush site. Another was to gallop round and round a surrounded party in a diminishing spiral, with the braves alternately discharging their arrows and lying along the blind side of their mounts' necks for cover; when the circle had closed sufficiently, they would mount a sudden, devastating rush from every angle and overwhelm the defenders in a brief, brutal mêlée.

Carrington's command, mercifully ignorant of the ordeals that lay ahead, marched out of Laramie on 17 June. Of the 700 infantrymen in the ranks, only 200 were veterans, the remainder being recruits who had yet to complete their training. There were 226 wagons in the column, containing supplies, portable sawmills and the tools needed to construct the new forts. A large herd of cattle, intended to provide rations on the hoof, plodded along behind. So little did Carrington expect trouble that several of the regimental wives, including his own, accompanied the expedition.

On 28 June the column reached Fort Reno. Carrington dropped off one of his companies to relieve the 'galvanised Yankee' garrison, who were long overdue for release, and, having rested his men, marched on up the Bozeman Trail. On 13 July he set up camp within the confluence of the Big and Little Piney Creeks and began to construct Fort Phil Kearny. In some ways the site selected was excellent, lying as it did on a plateau some 30 feet higher than the surrounding terrain with open fields of fire all round. In one vital respect, however, its situation was less than ideal. Large quantities of timber would be required not only for its construction but also for cooking and heating once it had been built, and the nearest stands lay fully five miles to the west, at the foot of the Big Horn Mountains. The route to this, known as the Wood Road, was overlooked from the north by a range named by Carrington the Sullivant Hills in honour of his wife's family. North-west of the Sullivants and across Big Piney lay a parallel but more broken range known as Lodge Trail Ridge. The only other feature of note on the battlefield was the isolated Pilot Hill, to the south of the fort and across Little Piney, on which Carrington established a lookout post.

Excellent administrator that he was, he quickly had the work of construction in hand. For almost a week axes rang, saws buzzed and hammers banged as the perimeter stockade began to rise. Then the Sioux struck along the length of the Trail, cutting up civilian wagon trains, killing small parties and running off stock under the noses of the garrison. Carrington, unable to respond effectively, single-mindedly pursued his construction programme to the exclusion of his men's training. On 3 August he decided that the work was going sufficiently well for him to fulfil the next part of his assignment and he detached two companies under Captain Nathaniel Kinney to march north and establish Fort C.F. Smith, the site for which was reached nine days later. The effect was to disperse the battalion's presence on the Trail to the point at which it was unable to provide protection for travellers and effectively became prisoners behind its own walls.

Carrington, only too conscious of his mounting problems, wrote a series of alternately alarming and reassuring reports to his immediate superior, Brigadier General Philip Cooke, requesting more men, including a cavalry detachment, breech-loading rifles and more ammunition. As a regular West Point officer, Cooke had little time for political appointees. Together, the continued domination of the Bozeman Trail by the Sioux and items of mess gossip from Fort Phil Kearny quickly destroyed what little confidence he had in Carrington. In particular, it was clear that the attitude of several of the fort's key officers, including Captain Frederick Brown, the Quartermaster, Lieutenant William Bisbee, the Adjutant, and Lieutenant George Grummond, bordered on contempt for their commanding officer. Cooke took the view that it was up to Carrington to become master in his own house and that in any event the problem would solve itself by the end of the year when, under a reorganisation programme, the 2nd/18th Infantry would form the nucleus of the new 27th Infantry and Carrington, who wished to remain with the Eighteenth, would be transferred elsewhere. Nevertheless, what happened on the Bozeman Trail was also Cooke's responsibility and in November he despatched an additional 45 infantrymen and a 60-strong troop of the 2nd Cavalry along the Trail to Phil Kearny.

All, unfortunately, were raw recruits armed with muzzle-loading muskets and the cavalry, commanded by Lieutenant Horatio Bingham, could barely sit their horses, let alone use weapons from the saddle. Several of the 18th Infantry's more experienced officers also reached the fort in November, including Captains William Fetterman and James Powell, who quickly sided with Brown, Bisbee and Grummond in undermining Carrington's authority. Fetterman, whose fine fighting record with the regiment during the Civil War had led to his being rewarded with the brevet rank of lieutenant colonel, soon became the ringleader of this disloyal clique. Plainly, he regarded Carrington as an old woman, scoffing at his inability to come to grips with the Indians; and clearly, the resentment of the battle-hardened veteran commanded by the timid non-combatant was evident in his braggart claim: 'Give me eighty men and I'll march through the whole Sioux nation!' Powell, older and less volatile, simply did not care for Carrington greatly, but, having served on the Frontier in the ranks for thirteen years prior to the war, he was aware of the realities of the situation.

There were, however, one or two present who were not opposed to Carrington. One was Captain Tenodor Ten Eyck, who kept his own counsel and to whom nobody paid much attention. Another was the post's senior scout, Jim Bridger, grown grizzled on the Frontier and still a name to be reckoned with. 'Your men who fought down South are crazy,' he warned the Colonel. 'They don't know anything about fighting Indians.' Nor, at this stage, did many people, but they were learning, and so was Carrington, slowly. He had already established a drill which involved the vulnerable wood trains going into a defensive circle when attacked and holding out until a relief force from the fort arrived; and, when Fetterman and Brown suggested a sweep with 100 men against the numerous Sioux encampments along the Tongue River to the north, he quite rightly told them to go away and come back with a more practical proposition.

By the beginning of December, nevertheless, Carrington had accepted the need to mount active operations both as a means of restoring his command's shaky morale and inflicting a degree of punishment on the enemy. It was, therefore, a great pity that the first of these should have come to grief. When, on 6 December, the lookout post on Pilot Hill signalled that the wood train was once again under attack, Carrington devised a plan intended to ensnare its tormentors. Fetterman and Bingham, with 30 cavalrymen, would relieve the wood train and pursue its attackers along their usual line of retreat round the western end of the Sullivant Hills, across Big Piney and over Lodge Trail Ridge to Peno Creek; simultaneously, Carrington himself would lead 35 mounted infantrymen under Grummond straight up the Bozeman Trail and cut off the Indians in Peno Creek. Unfortunately, the timings of the operation were not coordinated. When the Sioux, about 100-strong, discovered they were running from a force one-third their size, they counter-charged Fetterman and Bingham. The cavalrymen broke and Bingham was cut off and killed. Carrington, held up by the broken terrain on Lodge Trail Ridge, became engaged in a confused fight with another party of hostiles but was eventually joined by Fetterman and some of the rallied troopers. In the meantime, Grummond and three men had recklessly galloped ahead, run into serious trouble and been forced to beat a hasty retreat with seven Indians in hot pursuit. The latter reined in, whooping and shaking their lances, as soon Carrington's party came into view. Grummond, pulling up beside the Colonel, insolently enquired whether 'he was a fool or a coward to allow his men to be cut to pieces without offering help', a remark should have earned him immediate close arrest. It was typical of Carrington's relationship with his officers that he should let it go, and that Powell, back in the fort, should ignore a specific written order for him to bring up reinforcements and an ambulance, detailing a junior officer for the task.

At the end of the skirmish the Indians escaped to the north, taking an estimated ten casualties with them; the garrison's losses amounted to two killed and five wounded, which were remarkably light in the circumstances. The Sioux, delighted that the walk-a-heaps and pony soldiers could now be tempted to venture so far from the fort, decided to set a series of even larger ambushes for them. For his part, Carrington reached the inescapable conclusion that the pursuit of hostiles beyond Lodge Trail Ridge was liable to be dangerous and unprofitable. When, on 19 December the wood train was attacked again, the canny Powell was sent to its relief but refused to be drawn when the Indians feigned flight. The only officers who seemed to have learned nothing from the experience were Fetterman, Brown and Grummond.

21 December dawned bright and extremely cold. The snow from previous falls lay partially melted in frozen sheets where the sun had failed to penetrate the hollows. At 1000 the wood train left the fort. An hour later the lookout post reported that it was under attack and the garrison stood to. Carrington again detailed Powell to lead out a relief force. At this point Fetterman appeared, demanding that he should be given the assignment on the grounds that he possessed greater seniority than Powell. The question of seniority had no bearing on the issue and Carrington should have sent him packing. Instead, he weakly conceded the point, adding that after Fetterman had relieved the wood train his pursuit was not, under any circumstances, to proceed beyond Lodge Trail Ridge. The first element of the relief force, consisting of 49 dismounted infantrymen, moved off at 1115 but had barely reached the gate when they were overtaken by Lieutenant Wands, who repeated Carrington's specific orders. Fetterman nodded and continued on his way. The second element, 27 cavalrymen rearmed with the band's carbines, was already saddling up under Grummond's command. Brown, who was due for posting, hurried up, asking for one more chance to bring in Red Cloud's scalp himself, and Carrington granted him permission to accompany the column, together with two civilians, James Wheatley and Isaac Fisher, both of whom had held commissioned rank during the Civil War and were armed with formidable 16-shot Henry repeating rifles. At 1130, as the troopers were trotting towards the gate, Carrington gave Grummond his orders: 'Report to Captain Fetterman, implicitly obey orders, and never leave him. Under no circumstances must you cross Lodge Trail Ridge'.

It was ironic that at this moment Fetterman had 80 men under his command, just the number with which he boasted he could ride through the Sioux nation. He clearly intended placing the widest possible interpretation on Carrington's orders for, having been overtaken by Grummond's troopers, he directed his march, not towards the wood train but across Big Piney and along the Bozeman Trail behind the Sullivant Hills. Carrington was aware of the fact but believed that he intended to cut off the Indians attacking the wagons, and, at that moment his own attention was absorbed in directing the fire of the fort's howitzers against a party of hostiles hovering near the Bozeman Trail to the north. Fetterman's men became visible again, briefly, climbing the slopes of Lodge Trail Ridge in skirmish order, their progress marked by puffs of powder smoke as they engaged small parties of Indians. Then they disappeared beyond the crest and, at about noon, the sudden outbreak of heavy and sustained firing indicated that they had come under serious attack.

Carrington promptly despatched Captain Ten Eyck with 54 infantrymen and dismounted cavalry to effect a relief. Like any sensible officer venturing into an unknown and certainly dangerous situation, Ten Eyck wanted as much information as possible and for this reason, instead of following the route taken by Fetterman, he forded the Big Piney north of the fort and headed up onto the high ground beyond, from which he could obtain an overall view of the action and plan accordingly. The march was made at the double but by the time the first of the panting men reached the summit the firing had died away to a few isolated shots, and soon ceased altogether. Below, where the Bozeman Trail climbed a feature north of Lodge Trail Ridge, and in the valley between the two, hundreds of Indians were swarming or drifting away to the north; here and there on the feature, subsequently called Ambush or Massacre Hill, were ominous sprawls of white that suggested stripped bodies. Sighting the new arrivals on the high ground, many of the Indians taunted them with challenges to come down and fight. Recognising that this would be tantamount to suicide, Ten Eyck remained where he was and despatched a message to Carrington:

'The valley on the other side of the ridge is filled with Indians who are threatening me. The firing has stopped. No sign of Fetterman's command. Send a howitzer...'

It was now 1245 and Carrington had already despatched another 40 men, together with an ambulance and two ammunition wagons, to join Ten Eyck. He promised the messenger that he would send up a further 50 reinforcements as soon as the recalled wood train came in, but lacked the necessary fit horses to haul a howitzer.

In due course the Indians dispersed northwards and Ten Eyck cautiously led his men off the high ground and towards Massacre Hill. They first came across the bodies of Fetterman's infantry, lying together near a group of boulders; with them were Fetterman and Brown, who had shot themselves through the head. The bodies, riddled with arrows, had been stripped and mutilated so horribly that Carrington's detailed report, quoted below, was suppressed for twenty years.

'Eyes torn out and laid on the rocks; noses cut off; ears cut off; chins hewn off; teeth chopped out; joints of fingers; brains taken out and placed on rocks with other members of the body; entrails taken out and exposed; hands cut off; feet cut off; arms taken out from sockets; private parts severed and indecently placed on the persons; eyes, ears, mouth and arms penetrated with spearheads, sticks and arrows; ribs slashed to separation with knives;

skulls severed in every form, from chin to crown; muscles of calves, thighs, stomach, breast, back, arms and cheek taken out.' Such was the Indians' hatred for the whites that, even after they were dead, they maimed them for the afterlife.

49 bodies were brought into the fort that night; those of Grummond and his cavalrymen were discovered next day, lying further along the hill and beside the Trail.

This mute evidence, together with a few disjointed Indian accounts gathered months later, provided the only clues to what had happened. It seems reasonably certain that Red Cloud himself was not present, although a very promising young warrior named Crazy Horse certainly was and played a prominent part in the fighting. Using perhaps as many as 2000 warriors, the Sioux had set up a major ambush in the broken terrain beyond Lodge Trail Ridge, using decoy parties to attack the wood train and demonstrate north of the fort in order to provoke the soldiers into pursuit. Once Fetterman was seen to be taking a route towards Lodge Trail Ridge the decoys simply led him on, galloping criss-cross ahead and yelling taunts. At this stage, the hot-headed Grummond was in the lead and the probability is that he initiated a headlong pursuit which Fetterman felt obliged to support with his slower-moving infantry. Whatever the truth, the command was already split into three distinct elements by the time it entered the ambush site and the Indians broke from cover, firing thousands of arrows into the blue ranks at close quarters. In the lead were the two civilians, Wheatley and Fisher, and half a dozen troopers, who had quickly found cover and taken a heavy toll of their attackers before they were overwhelmed. Around them was found a ring of dead Indian ponies and 65 pools of congealed blood on the frozen grass; Wheatley in particular seems to have incited the Indians' hatred, for there were no less than 105 arrows protruding from his body. Some distance behind the point, Grummond is said to have decapitated the first of his attackers with a sabre stroke but been killed shortly afterwards. Some of his troopers galloped back to join the infantry, who had come under simultaneous attack, but the rest managed to reach higher ground where they dismounted and formed a defensive circle. The infantry, accompanied by Fetterman and Brown, took up position among some rocks closer to the Trail and did likewise. Within 40 minutes the last survivors had been overrun in a series of rushes culminating in savage hand-to-hand fighting. The last man to die may have been Bugler Adolph Metzger, who used his instrument as a weapon until it was battered shapeless. Maybe it was the fact that he was a small man, still standing defiant and alone among his dead comrades, that touched a chord of admiration among the Sioux, for they did not mutilate his body and even covered it with a buffalo robe. Then, having completed their grisly work elsewhere, they rode off, taking their 70 dead and their wounded with them.

As the afternoon wore on the sky became leaden. That night heavy snow was whipped into a blizzard by a howling wind off the Big Horns and the temperature dropped far below zero. Carrington, severely shaken, kept his garrison stood to but the Sioux did not attack; such an exploitation of their victory would not have occurred to them and in any event the weather kept them pinned within their tepees. He also despatched several couriers to Fort Laramie requesting assistance and, when he went out to recover the remaining bodies next day, gave strict orders that in the event of an Indian attack the women and children were to be moved into the magazine, which was to be exploded if the fort should fall. Thus far, a total of five officers, 91 other ranks and 58 civilians had died in and around Fort Phil Kearny.

The most famous of the couriers, who all risked not only being killed by Indians but also dying of exposure along the way, was John 'Portugee' Phillips, a civilian but an experienced Frontier hand who had been an associate of Wheatley and Fisher. There is little doubt that he was secretly in love with Grummond's pretty wife Frances, for although he had never spoken to her before, he told her before he left: 'I will go if it costs me my life. I will go for your sake.' Carrington gave him a Kentucky thoroughbred grey and watched him ride through the fort's water gate into the whirling darkness.

Phillips' 236-mile ride to Fort Laramie was an astonishing epic of endurance that has become one of the legends of the Old West. In conditions that amounted at times to a total white-out, obliterating all landmarks, he reached Fort Reno. There was, however, no help to be had there for the post did not possess a telegraph and the garrison was too small to do anything more than look to its own defences. He continued on his way, being forced to fight his way through a war party during the second day, and on the morning of Christmas Eve reached Horse Shoe Station, 190 miles from Fort Phil Kearny. Here he managed to pass the gist of his message to a telegraph operator but, troubled by fully justified doubts that it would get through, decided to ride the remaining distance to Laramie. He arrived shortly before midnight on a dying horse, icicles hanging from his buffalo coat and beard. Nothing could have been more dramatic than the sudden appearance of this frozen, exhausted figure in the midst of the Officers' Christmas Ball, gasping out its dreadful news before crashing unconscious to the floor. Because of the prevailing weather conditions there was little that could be done for the moment other than advise higher authority, but on 1 January four companies of 1st Battalion 18th Infantry marched out of

Laramie, followed by two companies of 2nd Cavalry two days later, reaching Fort Phil Kearny on 16 January to find the garrison unexpectedly alive and the post intact.

With the column came Lieutenant Colonel Henry Wessels, bearing orders from Cooke to assume command of Fort Phil Kearny in place of Carrington. This was simply part of the regimental reorganisation referred to above, but its timing carried with it the implication that Carrington was being held responsible for the recent disaster, an inference that he bitterly resented.

The arrival of reinforcements, while reassuring, placed an added strain on the fort's resources. The garrison remained captive within its own walls, the remaining horses died for want of fodder and were eaten, an unbalanced diet which resulted in an outbreak of scurvy, and the supply of firewood ran out long before the winter ended. Nothing whatever had been heard from the even more isolated Fort C.F. Smith, far to the north. With the coming of spring, notwithstanding the resumption of the Indians' harassing attacks, a strong column was despatched along the Bozeman Trail to discover whether anyone was left alive, or indeed if the fort was still standing. To the disgust of the would-be rescuers, they found its occupants snug, warm and in better physical condition than themselves, thanks largely to the efforts of the cook sergeant, who had laid in an extensive stock of vegetables purchased at mining camps.

Nevertheless, as spring turned to summer, the Sioux and Cheyenne kept the Bozeman Trail firmly closed. That the Fetterman Massacre provoked nothing like the same public outcry as that of Lieutenant Colonel George Armstrong Custer and part of the 7th Cavalry ten years later is hardly surprising; after the recent Civil War, in which thousands of citizen soldiers died in every major battle, the death of 80 regulars in an obscure frontier skirmish was regarded as regrettable but part of the price that must be paid for national expansion. The Army, however, faced with unfinished business, demanded weapons appropriate to the scale of the task and during the summer redesigned Springfield rifles, adapted for breech-loading, began reaching the garrisons along the Bozeman Trail.

These were first used when approximately 500 Cheyenne attacked a hay cutting party two-and-a-half miles north-east of Fort C.F. Smith on 1 August. Here a 100-foot-square enclosure, constructed from logs and willow boughs, had been prepared as a mule pen and as a refuge in case of attack. When the Indians appeared, the party, consisting of twelve civilian workers and nineteen soldiers commanded by Lieutenant Sigismund Sternberg, immediately took cover in the enclosure and opened fire. The

Cheyenne, expecting to be confronted by nothing more serious than the older muzzle-loading musket, closed in for what seemed to be an easy kill. Instead, they were met by a steady withering fire that thinned their ranks and were forced to draw off in surprise. Arrows began to thud into the timbers and Sternberg was shot through the head. A civilian named Colvin, armed with a Henry repeating rifle, took charge. After two more mounted attacks had been beaten off the Cheyenne changed their tactics, crawling towards the enclosure, covered by sniper fire. Once more they were stopped and had finally begun to shred away from the field when, somewhat late in the day, a relief force accompanied by a howitzer finally arrived from the fort to speed them on their way with a few shells. In what subsequently became known as the Hayfield Fight, the haycutters and their escort sustained the loss of three killed and two wounded; estimates of Indian losses vary but were undoubtedly much heavier.

Next day a very similar engagement took place near Fort Phil Kearny. Red Cloud, accompanied by 1500 braves, swooped down on the wood train yet again. At first the Indians had some success, shooting down four of the loggers and running off the mules. In command, however, was the steady ex-ranker Powell, who had also constructed a refuge nearby, consisting of fourteen loopholed wagon boxes laid in an oval with grain sacks and logs in the spaces between. Into this tumbled the remainder of the party, including Powell himself, Lieutenant John Jenness, 26 soldiers and four civilians. Powell allocated three of the new breech-loaders to each of his best shots, gave the order to fire only on his word of command, and detailed the rest of the men to act as loaders.

Red Cloud could be seen on a nearby hill, just out of rifle range, signalling the first attack on the enclosure. Led by Crazy Horse and American Horse, some 500 mounted Sioux and Cheyenne surged forward in a wild gallop that threatened to ride over the flimsy defences. When the range closed to 50 yards Powell gave the order to fire. Some Indians went down but the rest, supremely confident that once the whites had fired a volley some 30 seconds would elapse while they reloaded, thundered on. To their amazement, the loopholes continued to spit flame. Its centre shot out, the charge parted to circle the wagon boxes, but still braves and their mounts crumpled and crashed to the ground under the impact of the .50 calibre slugs. Those who attempted to close in suddenly found themselves facing an increased volume of fire as loaders snatched up Colt six-shooters and the civilians banged away with their Henry carbines. Their attack broken and in disarray, the Indians streamed back whence they had come, leaving the ground littered with dead and wounded.

Red Cloud ordered four more similar attacks, alternating with sniper fire, and each was broken up before it could do any damage. He then ordered a dismounted attack en masse, but his braves, unused to fighting this way, bunched together and provided a fine target for Powell's marksmen; even so, some of them were killed within five feet of the defences before the rest broke and ran.

Fighting had begun at 0700 and it was now approximately noon. The Indians began gathering up such of their dead and wounded as they could, the last of them being chased off into the hills when, right on cue, a relief force arrived from the fort. Powell estimated that about 60 of them had been killed and 120 wounded; his own losses amounted to five killed, including Jenness, and two wounded.

Together, the Hayfield Fight and the Wagon Box Fight, as Powell's engagement became known, went some way towards evening the score for the Fetterman Massacre, and they restored the morale of the garrisons along the Bozeman Trail. Yet, surprisingly heavy though his losses had been in these comparatively minor actions, they did not diminish Red Cloud's resolve. Nor, indeed, did they make any difference to the overall strategic situation; the Trail remained shut save to strongly escorted military traffic.

By the end of 1867 it was apparent that the plan for opening up Montana Territory by means of the Bozeman Trail had proved to be an expensive failure. Besides, the Army was needed elsewhere; the Union Pacific Railroad, for example, had made it clear that unless adequate military protection could be guaranteed, construction work would be suspended. National priorities, therefore, resulted in the negotiation of a fresh treaty with the Sioux, recognising their right to the disputed land 'so long as the buffalo range there in numbers'. Red Cloud had won his war, but he refused to sign the treaty until the military presence on the Bozeman Trail had been removed. On 19 May 1868 the order was given to abandon Forts Reno, Phil Kearny and C.F. Smith. They were burned to the ground by the triumphant Indians as soon as the garrisons had marched out.

Red Cloud's people would enjoy their land for a further ten years, but their old lifestyle was doomed by the apparently innocuous reference to buffalo in the peace treaty. Lieutenant General William Sherman, responsible for pacifying the West, was well aware that the vast herds provided the tribes with food and hides for clothing and tepees, and he saw to it that they were hunted to within a hair's breadth of extinction. No longer able to survive, the Red Man was forced to submit, but before he did so he won his last victories on the Powder and Little Big Horn Rivers in 1876.[1]

Carrington devoted the rest of his life to justifying his actions on the Bozeman Trail. His contemporaries were inclined to shrug and regard him as a man wrongly posted, although the view of Twentieth Century historians has tended to be more sympathetic. His wife Margaret, author of the best-selling *Absaraka, Home of the Crows*, which recounted her experiences on the Frontier, died in 1870, the same year that Carrington left the Army.

Portugee Phillips did not marry Frances Grummond, the young widow he worshipped from afar. After he had recovered from his ordeal the Government rewarded him with a grant of $300 (£75 at the prevailing rate of exchange), which could hardly be described as generous. Nevertheless, he married and settled down to raise cattle, only to have the vengeful Sioux run off much of his stock. When he died in 1883 the Government, perhaps regretting its previous miserly attitude, paid his widow $5000 as compensation for the loss.

The Carringtons had been extremely kind to Frances Grummond when her husband was killed and remained in contact with her after they had all left Fort Phil Kearny. In due course she became the second Mrs Carrington and in 1912 produced a book of her own entitled *Army Life on the Plains*.

The Fetterman Massacre was to claim one further victim, and that was Captain Tenodor Ten Eyck. Whispers suggesting that he should have marched straight to Fetterman's assistance – a course of action that would simply have added to the death toll – evolved into implications of cowardice. Already isolated, he turned increasingly to the bottle for comfort. Once on this slippery slope his descent was rapid. Sometimes drunk to the point of being incapable of performing his duties, he was court-martialled and found guilty of conduct unbecoming an officer and a gentleman. General Grant, the Army's senior officer, was not unsympathetic and ordered the findings to be set aside. By now, however, Ten Eyck's health had broken down and, having endured years of slanderous accusations in silence, he left the service in 1871.

Notes

1. See *Last Stand!* Chapter 4.

5
Stricken Field: Maiwand, 27 July 1880

In November 1878 Great Britain once again found herself at war with Afghanistan, for precisely the same reason that she had gone to war in 1839, namely the elimination of Russian influence within that country. When Dost Mohammed died in 1863 he was succeeded by his son Sher Ali. The succession was opposed by the latter's nephew, Abdur Rahman, who progressively gained the upper hand in a protracted dynastic struggle. Despite British warnings that the invocation of Russian assistance would be regarded as a hostile act, Sher Ali unwisely opened negotiations with the Tsar's representatives. British troops therefore crossed the frontier at three points, those under the command of Major General Sir Frederick Roberts defeating an Afghan army at Peiwar Kotal on 2 December. When Sher Ali fled his son Yakub, acting as Regent, negotiated a treaty under the terms of which a British Resident with wide-ranging powers was to be installed in Kabul, in exchange for a £60,000 subsidy. Ostensibly, this seemed to defuse a potentially dangerous situation; in reality, it merely created the conditions in which a major explosion became inevitable.

The British Resident, Sir Louis Cavagnari, arrived in Kabul on 24 July 1879. In some respects he was an ideal choice, being charming, intelligent and thoroughly versed in Frontier politics; in others the reverse was true, since he was also arrogant, impetuous and intensely ambitious. Above all, his part in negotiating the recent treaty had ensured that he was not personally welcome for, whatever their internal differences, most Afghans bitterly resented any form of foreign intervention and regarded his imposed presence as a humiliation.

Cavagnari was accompanied only by his personal secretary, Mr Jenkyns, a surgeon named Kelly and, because Yakub had personally undertaken to guarantee his safety and he himself did not wish to provoke the Kabulis with a display of force, a deliberately small escort consisting of 25 cavalrymen and 50 infantry of the Corps of Guides under the command of Lieutenant Walter Hamilton, who had recently been awarded the Victoria Cross for an action in the early days of the war.

Before proceeding further, it is worth mentioning that the Guides were a very unusual regiment indeed. When the First Sikh War ended in 1846 the British occupied the Punjab and found themselves in permanent contact with the ungovernable Pathan tribes inhabiting the frontier zone. Fortunately, the East India Company's army at this period contained a number of energetic individualists, including John Nicholson, William Hodson and the brothers George and John Lawrence who, by assuming responsibilities far beyond their rank and years, were able to keep a difficult situation under control, notwithstanding the as-yet uncertain loyalties of the Sikhs. At Peshawar, George Lawrence ordered his assistant, 25-year-old Lieutenant Harry Lumsden of the 59th Bengal Native Infantry, to assemble a unit of men who were personally familiar with the vast, tangled terrain of the new Frontier. Lumsden went even further, recruiting 'trustworthy men who could at a moment's notice act as guides to troops in the field and collect intelligence beyond as well as within the border....men notorious for desperate deeds, leaders in forays, who kept the passes into the hills and lived amid inaccessible rocks.' By sheer force of personality he knocked a very wild bunch into shape, producing a regiment that not only contained both cavalry and infantry sub-units but also, for the first time, adopted a khaki uniform for easier concealment. In addition, Lumsden applied the principle of selective recruitment so that service in the Guides became a much sought after honour. Great store was set on personal initiative, individual responsibility and loyalty. For any member of the regiment found wanting the ultimate disgrace was to be told to hand in his weapons and uniform and leave. In due course competition to join the Guides, who can be regarded as a forerunner of modern elites such as the SAS, was intense, so that in addition to Pathans the ranks would include Sikhs, Dogras, Gurkhas and others who were able to reach its exacting standards.

For a few weeks Cavagnari and his escort remained unmolested in the sullen atmosphere of Kabul. Then, at the end of August, several Afghan regiments from Herat arrived on a routine rotation of postings. They jeered openly at the Kabuli regiments for allowing themselves to be defeated by the British at Peiwar Kotal and, their pay being seriously in arrears, were beyond the control of their officers. On the morning of 3 September they paraded and were given a portion of their back pay. They demanded the balance but were told that there was no more money available. Someone shouted that the British had money and they rushed to the Residency. Some started looting at once but were driven out when the sentries opened fire.

The Heratis returned in force with their weapons, accompanied by the mob. The Residency lacked a perimeter wall and was overlooked from several directions, but Hamilton did what he could to organise defences. Three of his men were out cutting forage for the horses; a fourth was buying flour; and three more were detained when Cavagnari sent them in rapid succession in vain attempts to enlist the Amir Yakub's promised protection. These seven were the only inhabitants of the Residency to survive.

As to the fate of the rest we have only fragmentary evidence on which to rely. Under incessant fire from which there was little protection, the Guides fought back, their numbers decreasing by the hour. One after another, Cavagnari, Kelly, Jenkyns and Hamilton were killed. The Afghans brought up a gun and began to pound the buildings at point blank range. Several sorties were made, driving the enemy back for a while, but the respite they won was only temporary. Frequent promises that the garrison's Muslims would be spared were scornfully rejected. By evening, the Residency was ablaze. The last few men on their feet, led by a Sikh, Jemadar Jewand Singh, made a final charge into the armed mob and died fighting; as the spirit of the regiment demanded, they had remained true to their salt and each other. In and around the smouldering shell of the Residency lay approximately 600 Afghan bodies.

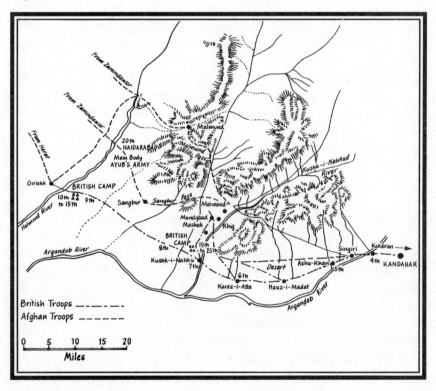

Later, the British commissioners investigating the incident submitted their conclusions, writing in the third person: 'They do not give their opinion hastily, but they believe that the annals of no army and no regiment can show a brighter record of bravery than has been achieved by this small band of Guides'. The entire escort was awarded the Indian Order of Merit. The battle honour 'Residency, Kabul' was to have the same significance for successive generations of Guides that 'Camerone' held for members of the French Foreign Legion.[1]

A punitive expedition under Roberts defeated the Afghans at Charasia on 6 October, then occupied Kabul, where the ringleaders of the attack on the Residency were tried and hanged in front of its ruins. Yakub, now thoroughly frightened, had already sought Roberts' protection and indicated that he wished to abdicate, claiming that 'he would rather be a grass-cutter in the English camp than rule Afghanistan'. Despite this, the impression of 'shiftiness' received by Roberts was fully justified, for Yakub remained in constant contact with the anti-British elements among his former subjects.

It was decided that Roberts' army would remain in Kabul over the winter. The troops occupied the partially fortified Sherpur cantonment a mile to the north-east of the city, strengthening the defences with abattis and barbed wire entanglements. It was as well that they did so, for the mullahs had begun preaching a holy war against the foreign infidels and daily thousands of resentful Afghans began to converge on Kabul. On 14 December a sortie ended badly and the enemy, thus encouraged, laid siege to Sherpur. Shortly before dawn on 23 December they attempted to rush the walls. Potentially, the garrison was in serious danger, for the defenders were thinly spread along a perimeter four-and-a-half miles long. On the other hand, Roberts possessed something of a secret weapon in that his mountain batteries had a supply of the new star shells. To their astonishment, the dense Afghan masses suddenly found themselves illuminated against the snow, then raked through and through with sustained volley firing. Ignoring their heavy losses, they continued to surge forward until 1000. An hour later they came on again, but with less enthusiasm. They were then shelled as they attempted to form up again and at 1300 began streaming off the field. Roberts sent out the 9th Lancers, Guides Cavalry and 5th Punjab Cavalry, who quickly turned the enemy's defeat into an utter rout. Of the estimated 100,000 Afghans who had attacked Sherpur, over 3000 had been killed or wounded; Roberts' losses amounted to just three killed and 30 wounded.

Although the country remained in a thoroughly unsettled state, some consideration could now be given to the question of who would become the next Amir of Afghanistan. The final choice fell on Abdur Rahman, who was acceptable to the British and many Afghans. Unfortunately, he was not acceptable to Yakub's brother Ayub, the governor of Herat, who felt that he had a right to the throne. Becoming the focus both of internal discontent and anti-British feeling, he quickly attracted a large following and in June 1880 took the field, intending to consolidate his hold on southern Afghanistan. British intelligence, however, reached the conclusion that he planned to march across the country through Kandahar to Kabul, defeat Abdur Rahman and assume the crown. This set the scene for one of the most serious defeats ever sustained by the British Army in India.

Kandahar was held by a divisional-sized force, consisting of one cavalry and two infantry brigades, commanded by Lieutenant General J.M. Primrose. Also present were some 6000 Afghan troops under the command of Abdur Rahman's local governor, another Sher Ali, who had been armed and equipped by the British as a gesture of goodwill.

At the end of May 1880 it became clear that Ayub was on the point of leaving Herat. As his army had to cover 350 miles before it reached Kandahar there was plenty of time in which to make preparations. Nevertheless, Sher Ali, believing that a show of force would discourage local dissidents from joining the rebels, marched out with his provincial troops and established a blocking position at Girishk on the Helmund river, approximately 80 miles west-north-west of Kandahar. Unfortunately, he was already damned in his countrymen's eyes for cooperating with the British and his presence, far from overawing the local tribesmen, merely annoyed them. When signs of disaffection began to appear in his own ranks he despatched a message to Primrose asking for his assistance. The request was approved by the latter's political and military superior on the grounds that Sher Ali must not be seen to fail for want of British support and on 4 July a column, consisting of one infantry and one cavalry brigade, was despatched to Girishk.

In overall command as well as being commander of the infantry brigade was Brigadier General George Burrows. At the age of 55 he might have been considered a little elderly for a field command, especially as he had last seen active service during the Mutiny, almost a quarter of a century earlier and had been employed continuously on staff duties since 1872. His Second-in-Command, and also commander of the cavalry brigade, was Brigadier General Thomas Nuttall, who was a year younger. He had also fought during the Mutiny, and again ten years later in Abyssinia, but had never served in a cavalry regiment.

The infantry consisted of the 66th (later Royal Berkshire) Regiment, which was considered to be steady and dependable, less two of its eight companies stationed at the outpost of Khelat-i-Ghilzai, 80 miles north of

78

Kandahar; the 1st Bombay Native Infantry (Grenadiers), a regiment of great seniority and good reputation which had, however, only experienced a brief period of active service in Aden since the Mutiny; and the 30th Bombay Native Infantry (Jacob's Rifles), which had seen no active service at all and included a high proportion of young recruits whose weapon training was incomplete.

The cavalry brigade consisted of the 3rd Light Cavalry and the 3rd Sind Horse, both of which had served in Abyssinia, while the latter had thus far given an excellent account of itself in the present campaign; and E/B Battery (E Battery of B Brigade) Royal Horse Artillery, originally raised as an East India Company unit and absorbed into the British service after the Mutiny, with six 9pdr muzzle-loading guns.

Also under Burrows' command was a half company of Bombay Sappers and Miners, giving him an approximate overall strength of 2300 men plus, of course, an unknown number of followers and civilian transport drivers.

By the time Burrows' column reached the Helmund on 11 July Sher Ali's troops had become so seriously unsettled by Ayub's approach that it was agreed they should be marched back across the river and disarmed. Unfortunately, before this decision could be put into effect all save the cavalry mutinied and set off to join Ayub. Burrows pursued them and after a brisk exchange of fire forced them to relinquish their artillery, consisting of six smoothbore muzzle-loading weapons, four of which were 6pdr guns and two 12pdr howitzers. This acquisition would ultimately prove to be of very dubious value, for the mutinous gunners not only escaped on the team and ammunition wagon horses but also cut up the harness before they left. By using E/B Battery's lead horses the guns could be moved and in due course fresh harness and teams were sent up from Kandahar. As no horses could be spared for the captured ammunition wagons, Burrows' decision to burn them was understandable. Less so was his order that, with the exception of 52 rounds per gun, the rest of the ammunition would be dumped in the Helmund, since much of it could have been transported on the fifty camels that had also been captured. Herein lay one of the seeds of disaster.

The captured guns were formed into a Smoothbore Battery under the command of Captain J.R. Slade, E/B's battery captain, who was joined by two Royal Artillery officers, Lieutenants T.F.T. Fowle and G.S. Jones, and Lieutenant G. de la M. Faunce of the 66th. E/B also provided drivers and NCOs to act as the Number Ones of the gun detachments, consisting of forty-two men of the 66th, who were trained in gun drill.

Following the disintegration of Sher Ali's army, Burrows was aware that he would be unable to hold the line of the Helmund, which at this season of the year was fordable for much of its length. In addition, there were no supplies to be obtained in the immediate vicinity, so he withdrew to the Khusk-i-Nakhud river where he could cover the direct approach to Kandahar. This retrograde movement, coupled with the defection of Sher Ali's

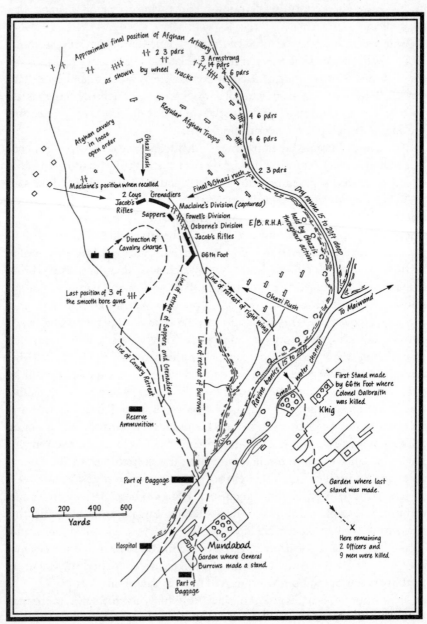

men, convinced the local tribes that their best interests lay with Ayub and they began to flock to his standard in very large numbers.

At this point Burrows received a despatch from the Commander-in-Chief Afghanistan, forwarded by General Primrose from Kandahar.

'You will understand that you have full liberty to attack Ayub, *if you consider you are strong enough to do so*. Government consider it of the greatest political importance that his force should be dispersed, *and prevented by all possible means from passing on to Ghazni*.[2] In the aftermath of his defeat, Burrows said that he interpreted this as a definite instruction to take the offensive. To some extent he was the prisoner of a long-standing tradition that, whatever the odds, the British in India had always attacked and generally emerged victorious. Again, experience had revealed that an Afghan attacked was far less formidable than an Afghan attacking. The problem was that Burrows was unaware of Ayub's real strength. Somewhat hazy intelligence sources put it at ten regular Kabuli and Herati infantry regiments with about 6000 men, some 4000 cavalry and 36 guns of which three were breech-loading 14pdr Armstrongs, far more powerful than anything Burrows possessed. The unknown factor was the number of tribesmen and ghazis who had joined Ayub during his march. This was growing constantly so that, by the time the two forces met, Burrows was probably confronted by an army of not less than 25,000 men; some sources actually put the figure as high as 35,000.

Another aspect of the despatch that profoundly influenced Burrows' thinking was the reference to Ghazni, a town two-thirds of the way along the road between Kandahar and Kabul. This suggested that Ayub planned bypassing Kandahar and marching directly on the capital. Such, in fact, was not his intention, but it was an option Burrows could not afford to ignore.

On 20 July Ayub began crossing the Helmund at Haidarabad. By the 23rd the opposing cavalry screens were in contact and the following day it became apparent not only that the British were outnumbered many times, but also that Ayub was heading for Maiwand. This would place him fifteen miles closer to Kandahar than Burrows, and also offered him a direct route to Ghazni. In these circumstances Burrows was forced to act but, perhaps recognising that he was facing a moment of truth, he delayed issuing the necessary orders for two days. This was unfortunate, for Ayub's army was less encumbered with baggage and therefore travelled faster than his own column. It took almost the whole night of 26/27 July to pack up the camp at Khusk-i-Nakhud so that it was an already tired force that began marching north at 0700 the following morning; some of the men had eaten no breakfast and others were denied the chance to refill their water bottles.

The force was screened by an advance guard consisting of most of Nuttall's cavalry and two two-gun divisions of E/B Battery. The main body marched in parallel columns with the baggage on the right, then in succession the 66th, the Rifles, the Smoothbore Battery, the Sappers and Miners and the Grenadiers. Bringing up the rear were a squadron of the Sind Horse and E/B's remaining section. It was already extremely hot, with the morning heat haze already giving way to mirages, clear visibility being limited to about 1500 yards; it would become much hotter still, with the temperature exceeding 120 degrees in the shade, had there been any.

By 1030 the column was moving along the eastern side of a dry ravine 50 to 100 feet wide and between 15 and 25 feet deep. It reached a village named Mundabad, consisting of a few houses and mud-walled gardens, three quarters of a mile beyond which lay the very similar village of Khig. At about this time the cavalry and their guns crossed the ravine and began probing across an area of grey-brown sandy desert covered with flinty stones and scattered scrub. Away to the north, dense clouds of dust could be seen through the heat haze, extending from west to east. Closer inspection revealed that these were being raised by masses of marching men, the leading elements of which had already reached Maiwand. In due course, when Afghan horsemen emerged from the mass to watch the watchers in turn, it became clear that Ayub's army was already moving across Burrows' front.

Ayub and Burrows now faced an unexpected encounter battle. Ayub's object was simply to destroy the British force hovering on his flank and then continue his advance. Burrows, too, had the bones of a plan, namely to lure Ayub across the arid plain and, using the ravine and Mundabad as defences, wear down his army until it had lost its offensive capacity. That, however, was not the way in which he allowed the battle to develop.

E/B Battery, commanded by Major G.F. Blackwood, was first into action, supported by the cavalry. On the right Lieutenant N.P. Fowell's division halted 500 yards from ravine, opening fire at about 1050. On the left, Lieutenant H. Maclaine's division galloped a mile from the ravine before opening fire a little later. Blackwood then called up his third division, commanded by Lieutenant E.G. Osborne, from the rearguard and, with Burrows' approval, concentrated all his guns in a battery position 2000 yards from the ravine and the same distance from what he judged to be the centre of the enemy army. By degrees, the rest of the column came up and aligned itself on E/B. The infantry regiments, leaving one company each to guard the baggage near Mundabad, deployed with the 66th and the Rifles to the right of the guns and the Grenadiers to the left, while the Sappers and Miners, having been detailed as the battery's close escort, dug in immediately behind. Initially, the Smoothbore Battery took position on the left of the Grenadiers, fronting north, and Nuttall withdrew his cavalry behind the left flank.

Six weeks later, a defeated general seeking to justify his actions, Burrows claimed that his hand had been forced by the length of Maclaine's initial advance from the ravine: 'I was compelled to send the cavalry and artillery in support at once and hasten on the infantry. Thus the whole affair was precipitated and I had lost the opportunity of reconnoitring the enemy and selecting the position in which I would give battle.'

That a general officer should seek to attribute his troubles to a dead subaltern reflects no credit whatever on the former. Maclaine certainly possessed a thrusting, independent spirit and was inclined to be awkward, but he was not out of control and he moved across into the main battery position as soon as he received Blackwood's order to do so. Burrows' point regarding reconnaissance is, however, worth considering, for opposite Khig the main ravine was joined by a subsidiary branch which ran from north to south approximately parallel to and between 600 and 900 yards from the British position, providing the enemy with excellent cover. Again, the plain, stretching away towards mountains to the north and west, was by no means as level as it looked and contained numerous undulations that were not immediately apparent, especially in the heat haze. Having said that, Burrows could see that, as he had anticipated, the whole Afghan army was wheeling ponderously towards him and also that, such was its size, both his flanks would be turned if he remained where he was. This was surely the moment when, having trailed his coat successfully in front of Ayub, he might have ordered a measured withdrawal to the better positions offered by the ravine and Mundabad. Unfortunately, he did not and at noon the comparatively short British line remained completely exposed in the open. Behind the infantry the spare ammunition mules waited patiently and along the ranks went the regimental bhistis with their waterskins, giving some men what was to be their last drink and others the last that they would enjoy for very many hours.

Both British batteries were now firing steadily, their shells bursting among the still distant but visibly advancing ranks. The weight of the Afghan reply, however, was mounting and it was no comfort to the British crews that, for various reasons, Ayub had been forced to leave six of his guns behind, for they and the infantry were forced to endure the fire of 30 assorted 3pdrs, 6pdrs and 14pdrs, deployed in a great arc around them. The Afghans, too, were handling their guns very cleverly, using depressions in the ground to push them forward and close the range. At this stage, neither side was doing the other a great deal of damage, for the intense heat, reflected from the baking ground, was producing an impenetrable shimmer that made accurate range estimation impossible. Subsequent examination of the battle-field, for example, revealed that one target, estimated to lie between 500 and 600 yards from the muzzle was, in fact, barely 400. The result was that, while some rounds were striking their targets, most of the opposing fire was high. Yet, in due course even this was to have an adverse effect on the British conduct of the battle. The bhistis, having refilled their skins at Mundabad, could see the shellbursts fountaining across the plain between themselves and the fighting line, ammunition wagons burning and horses knocked down, and they refused to go forward again. Later, this same nervousness gripped the ammunition resupply parties of the two Indian regiments, so that some of their British officers, already too few in number, had to be diverted to supervise the task.

The first of Burrows' infantry to open fire was the 66th, which enjoyed some protection by having been deployed in a shallow, dried-out water-course. Typical of any of the Widow of Windsor's British line regiments, the 66th, commanded by Lieutenant Colonel James Galbraith, had a highly developed esprit de corps and believed that it was just that little bit better than the rest. Its ranks, the average age of which was about 22, contained men from many different backgrounds, including agricultural labourers, the scrawnier products of urban slums and, as was usual with many English and Welsh regiments of the day, a fair proportion of Irishmen. Not many of those present had arrived with the regiment in India ten years previously, for every year since a number of time-expired men had left for home and been replaced by recruit drafts from the depot, together with men from regiments returning home who preferred to continue serving in India. Straightforward in outlook, they possessed a mental and physical toughness stemming from far lower expectations than those fashionable today. Their conversation, well-larded with oaths, took place in a mixture of English and Urdu.[3] They were, in short, the sort of men so well understood and immortalised by Rud-yard Kipling, their daily business being to fight the Empire's hundred for-gotten wars in the farthest corners of the earth, all for a shilling or so a day and their keep. Excluding the two detached companies, those serving with the baggage guard and the Smoothbore Battery, the 66th had fifteen offi-cers and 364 other ranks in the fighting line.

The regiment was armed with the Martini-Henry breech-loading rifle, firing a .45-calibre round. British musketry techniques were currently under-going a period of revision, with the result that in the Bombay Army, from which Burrows' troops were drawn, simultaneous volley firing had, for the moment, been replaced by continuous firing from the right in the manner of a feu-de-joie, with each man squeezing his trigger immediately after his right-hand neighbour. Firing still took place standing up, but attention had been paid to the lessons of the American Civil War and the Franco-Prussian War, and to reduce casualties loading was carried out lying down, an awkward and tiring movement that involved rolling onto the left side to work the breech lever properly.

By noon dense swarms of ghazis had begun to converge on the regiment's position from the direction of Maiwand. Galbraith waited until he was satisfied that they were close enough, then verified the range with company volleys. A few of the enemy fell but the dust kicked up ahead of their serried ranks indicated the creation of a dense beaten zone. He handed over control to his company commanders and firing became continuous as the range shortened. From right to left, the ghazis' leading ranks were being shot down like rows of skittles, but always there were others ready to pick up the fallen banners and, screaming imprecations, maintain the impetus of the attack. Although held frontally at the approximate line of the subsidiary ravine, several thousand more of them surged into the yawning space between the regiment and Khig. To meet the threat, Galbraith swung round his right hand company and, at the suggestion of one of his staff, Burrows sent two of the Smoothbore Battery's guns across to cover the threatened flank. Thus, when the moment came for the ghazis to deliver what they believed would be their final annihilating rush, they ran straight into a blizzard of Martini-Henry rounds and case shot, being shot down in scores. As the attack collapsed, many of its survivors sought easier prey by pressing on along the line of the main ravine towards Mundabad and the baggage.

It was now a little after 1230. The 66th had every reason to feel pleased with themselves and indeed would not be troubled again for some time. When the Afghans opened an inaccurate, long-range fire on them, Galbraith ordered them to lie down. With the distractions of action past, most men became even more aware of the brazen heat beating down upon them and the growing thirst aggravated by the absence of the bhistis. Sweat-soaked khaki drill had dried out, indicating that bodies were retaining what fluid they could. Old hands, conscious of the precious contents of their water bottles, took the smallest possible sips, rinsing them round several times before swallowing them.

Having effectively turned Burrows' right flank, Ayub now began to turn his left, using his cavalry and Herati irregulars. Burrows responded first by wheeling two Grenadier companies to the left, then prolonging the line with two companies of Rifles and the Smoothbore Battery's two howitzers. The weakest links in this prolonged chain, now bent back like a fish hook, were the semi-trained Rifle companies, whose only British officer, 21-year old Lieutenant D. Cole, had only been with the regiment for two months.

Approximately a quarter of a mile behind the left flank Nuttall's cavalry were simultaneously being outflanked to their left by a horde of Afghan horsemen, riding in loose order. Too few in number to mount a decisive charge, yet unable to withdraw because they were now effectively protecting the rear of the British battle line, they were forced to remain as static targets for much of the battle, losing approximately one third of their horses. Yet, somehow, by presenting a bold front and using their carbines, they managed to keep the Afghan horsemen in check.

The baggage guard, too, was coming under simultaneous pressure from two directions. 'Cavalry were hovering about twelve hundred yards from our left flank, and cavalry and infantry on the right, much nearer, in gardens,' wrote Major Ready of the 66th. 'I could not see our line, but saw the enemy's guns, many of them, on a rise. We formed up the baggage guards in a ^ shape across the head of the baggage, Quarry and the Grenadiers on the left on the edge of a small nullah, Jacob's Rifles and a few Grenadiers on the right. Shells and round shot came up to the baggage. The ghazis and the cavalry pressed on the right. Colonel Malcolmson (of the Sind Horse) told me to retire the baggage. Did so, into the nullah at first, then beyond. One section of Quarry's company sent to extreme right to hold gardens....I left my horse behind Quarry's company and went to the right. Found Bray and a few men hotly engaged with men behind walls, high ones, and shooting cavalry and others trying to work round towards our rear. At this time there was a large body of ghazis, villagers and cavalry in the nullah (main ravine), about 500 yards up, waiting to try and rush. Our cover was not good, the walls running mostly towards the enemy. However, we held on for a long time'.

By 1300 it was clear that the fate of Burrows' force was already sealed. Whatever plans may he have had about retiring to Mundabad and fighting a defensive battle counted for nothing once he had allowed his troops to become closely engaged so far out in the open. His tiny fighting line of just over 1700 men was surrounded on three sides by an army at least ten times stronger, with a tenuous line of retreat to the south-west being held open by the baggage guard. Simultaneously, Ayub was steadily pushing forward his guns to batter the British line while his regular infantry closed in to deliver the final assault. In the circumstances he could hardly lose, although the price he was to pay would be harsh.

Among the criticisms subsequently heaped on the unfortunate Burrows was that, as a former infantryman, he concentrated on the infantry battle to the exclusion of his other arms. This is, perhaps, a little excessive for, having once allowed himself to be mesmerised into immobility, he became a prisoner of events. Positioned behind the centre of his line he watched E/B and the Smoothbore Battery firing away steadily against the enemy's slowly approaching infantry and guns. There was a suspicion that one Afghan battery was forced to limber up and make for the rear, and that another gun was knocked out, but in the shimmering heat one could not be sure and it seemed to make little difference to the volume of enemy artillery fire. There was a slow but steady trickle of casualties from the infantry, the walking wounded hobbling over the baking plain towards Mundabad, the more seriously injured being carried to the field dressing station that had been set up a little way behind the line.

Shortly before 1300 Ayub's principal line of attack became apparent and Burrows ordered Lieutenant Colonel H.S. Anderson of the Grenadiers to take his regiment forward a distance of 500 yards and, with Cole's two companies of Rifles covering his left, break up the enemy's concentration with volley fire. This apparently desperate measure was, in fact, the only chance he had of saving his command, and numerous precedents existed proving that such an unexpected, aggressive response could change the entire complexion of a battle.

The Grenadiers had already covered one hundred yards before the Afghans awoke to what was happening and concentrated the fire of their guns against the advancing line. Despite its volume, this caused comparatively few casualties, although they were enough to alarm Burrows, who halted the advance, believing that the regiment would be torn to pieces if it continued.

What might have happened had it continued was demonstrated during the next few minutes. The Afghan regulars, Herati regiments opposite the Grenadiers and Kabulis supported by ghazis opposite the main body of the Rifles, completed their preparations and began to move forward behind their banners. The Indian regiments, armed with the Snider .577in breech-loading rifle, firing a heavy round calculated to bowl over the most dedicated fanatic, set their sights and came up into the aim. At 800 yards they let drive, supported by the British guns. The Heratis were ripped apart, rallied and attempted to come on again through the leaden sleet, then turned and fled out of range, leaving the ground carpeted with their dead. The main body of the Rifles, fewer in number than the Grenadiers, also succeeded in halting the Kabulis, although the latter went to ground and began to snipe at long range.

Observing that the Heratis were beginning to drift towards his left, Burrows decided to lay back his flank again. The movement revealed that Cole's two Rifle companies had become seriously unsettled. By 1330 the Smooth-bore Battery had expended the ammunition in its limbers and, being an ad hoc unit without proper transport to bring up fresh supplies, Slade sent it back to Mundabad to replenish, then moved across to take over command of E/B Battery from Blackwood who, seriously wounded, needed urgent medical attention. The sight of half the British artillery limbering up and heading for the rear further demoralised Cole's companies, and it provided the Afghans with the encouragement they needed, as did an aborted charge by some of Nuttall's cavalry into the area between the 66th and Khig. They began working their way forward again, cleverly using the folds in the ground until by 1400 they had ten guns within 300 and 600 yards from the British line while their infantry was within 600 yards. Casualties began to rise sharply. Thirty per cent of the Grenadiers had already been killed or wounded, a higher proportion than the experts predicted a native regiment would tolerate, yet they were still fighting. The Rifles' losses were smaller but still amounted to 23 per cent of their strength and when Cole was killed by a roundshot, command of his two detached companies passed to a single jemadar. Secure in their dry watercourse, the 66th had barely been touched. E/B and the Smoothbore Battery, however, had already lost about a quarter of their manpower and over half their horses. Nuttall's cavalry regiments, having been under constant exposure to artillery and now rifle fire, had also begun to lose men and horses at an alarming rate.

The physical and mental condition of Burrows' hard-pressed little force was beginning to deteriorate, too. Heat exhaustion was reducing the men's reactions to those of automata. Water had become the paramount thought in most minds. Rifles, too hot to hold, had begun to blister hands. The thundering Afghan artillery, and the reply of their own guns, was concussive in its effect.

When, at about 1430, the Afghan gunfire died away, the comparative silence was almost tangible. Spirits rose briefly in the hope that the enemy had expended his ammunition, but Ayub had merely completed his preparations and had given the order for a renewed assault. Suddenly, with a great roar, the Afghan horde surged forward against the British line, knives, swords and bayonets flashing in the sun. Hundreds went down as the 66th, the Rifles and the Grenadiers responded with tearing volleys and E/B Battery's shells burst among the running ranks. The attack staggered and seemed to be on the verge of collapse: then, with bewildering speed, disaster struck.

It began on the left where the two isolated companies of Rifles, deprived of artillery support, their British officer dead and held in place with difficulty by a jemadar and a few older hands, found themselves swamped by an attack in overwhelming strength from their front and left. Their nerve snapped and they fled to the right, into the rear ranks of the Grenadiers, with large numbers of the enemy in pursuit. Sensing victory, the Afghan attack swept forward again. The Grenadiers attempted to form square but were unable to close the rear face and into the gap crowded the remnants of the Rifle companies and scores of blood-crazed ghazis, hacking and stabbing at will.

Simultaneously, E/B Battery had switched to case shot as the battle came to close quarters. It was, however, clear that while the Afghans were being cut down in large numbers they could not be held and Slade ordered the teams forward to limber up. As Fowell had been wounded earlier he brought out the centre division himself. On the left, Maclaine either did not hear the order to retire or chose to fire one round too many into the enemy's faces. His guns were overrun and a brief, vicious fight took place around them, rammers and sponge staves against a whirlwind of flashing Khyber knives and slashing swords. Most of the gunners were killed although Maclaine managed to save one team, thanks to Sergeant Patrick Mullane, who smashed his galloping horses through the ranks of the triumphant ghazis, pausing only to lift the terribly wounded Driver Istead onto his limber. The two guns of the battery's right-hand division were got out only with difficulty. Their commander, Osborne, charged straight into the ghazis and cut down several who were attacking a British officer, thereby saving his life. He then dismounted to help his few remaining gunners to hook on but was shot dead as the teams moved off. Covered by the Sappers and Miners, who fired three volleys into the enemy before retreating, Slade pulled back for 400 yards and dropped into action again. By then, however, it was apparent that the overall situation was beyond saving and, picking up three guns of the Smoothbore Battery for which a little ammunition had been found, he retired across the ravine to Mundabad and again came into line to cover the remnants of broken units now streaming off the battlefield.

Burrows attempted to ease the situation by ordering Nuttall's cavalry to charge. It was no easy matter to get the troopers to bucket their carbines, draw sabres and turn their backs on the Afghan horsemen, nor was it clear whether they were intended to relieve the struggling Grenadiers or recapture E/B's two lost guns. They charged willingly enough, but at the critical moment Nuttall himself swerved off to the right, claiming later that he intended to clear his brigade's front. Understandably, many of his troopers followed, although others rode on to cut down those Afghans attacking the rear of the Grenadiers, so giving the regiment a brief respite in which to reorganise itself. After this Nuttall's men, their will eroded by their long ordeal under fire and their confidence sapped by the fiasco, could not be persuaded to charge again and trotted off the field to Mundabad.

With the reduction in pressure, the Grenadier officers were able to exert their authority. It is uncertain quite what happened next, but the grisly archaeology of grave examination weeks after the battle suggested that elements from three or more companies probably formed a square and that this almost certainly absorbed the attention of the victorious Afghan right wing for some time. What is certain is that the troops attempting to reform in Mundabad did not come under immediate pressure for some time, and that the bodies of 70 Grenadiers were found together halfway between their original position and the ravine. Again, although the story was not endorsed by Lieutenant Colonel Anderson, one of the regiment's officers recorded that hundreds of the enemy had been killed in attempts to wipe out a stubborn knot of Grenadiers, and the weight of evidence tends to support such a claim.

Other Grenadier companies, however, had moved off to their right and become mingled with the Sappers. Shaken by the sudden collapse of everything on their left, the Rifles also broke. Burrows did what he could to direct his Indian regiments towards Mundabad but a mob of fugitive Grenadiers, Rifles and Sappers charged into the dry watercourse occupied by the 66th in such numbers that the regiment was forced out into the open. Those of the enemy immediately opposite, having already been taught a healthy respect, thought that they were about to be counter-attacked and ran as soon as the long line of jostling helmets appeared.

The moment was brief. Galbraith had no alternative but to conform to the general retreat, although, being now on the wrong side of the watercourse, the regiment was approaching Khig rather than Mundabad. Some details of this phase of the engagement are uncertain, but it seems probable that until now bayonets had not been fixed. Likewise, it seems likely that while the Colours were in or near the line, they had not been uncased. What is certain is that the heat had reduced the men to a torpor from which they emerged slowly and that their company ranks were swollen and disordered by the fugitives. It is also certain that the withdrawal to the main ravine was conducted at a walk since nothing more would have been physically possible. The regiment, too, was simultaneously required to fire to its front and rear, driving ahead of itself those ghazis who had infiltrated into the space between its right flank and Khig, and holding off the Afghans who, having recovered something of their courage, were following up its retreat, never daring to come within 25 yards but shooting into the men's backs the while. Some 80 soldiers, British and Indian, were killed before the main ravine was reached, including two of the 66th's company commanders, Captains Garrett and Cullen.

It was, perhaps, of Maiwand that Kipling was thinking when he penned the following lines in *The Young British Soldier*; the scene he sets, indeed, has such a terrifying authenticity that he may well have drawn his inspiration from survivors of the battle.

> When first under fire an' you're wishful to duck,
>   Don't look nor take 'eed at the man that is struck,
> Be thankful you're livin', and trust to your luck,
>   And march to your front like a soldier....
>
> If your officer's dead and the sergeants look white,
>   Remember it's ruin to run from a fight,
> So take open order, lie down and sit tight,
>   And wait for supports like a soldier....
>
> When you're wounded and left on Afghanistan's plains,
>   And the women come out to cut up what remains,
> Jest roll to your rifle and blow out your brains,
>   An' go to your Gawd like a soldier....

The Afghans had left their womenfolk behind, but the men were nearly as handy with their knives and obviously the wounded provided better sport than the dead for the wholesale mutilations that were taking place across the field.

The 66th lost what remained of its internal order when it reached the main ravine, the ranks breaking apart as the men were forced to tumble down the 20-foot banks and claw their way up the other side. Those on the right made their way to Mundabad, where chaos reigned. Slade's guns were banging away, Burrows was struggling to put together a rearguard and frantic efforts were being made to get the wounded away on carts, horses, camels and mules. The civilian transport drivers, seeing which way the wind blew, had already left in droves with their animals, cutting their loads free. Some of the 66th came across their abandoned officers' mess stores and slaked their desperate thirst with anything to hand. The predictable effect of alcohol on already dehydrated bodies was to leave many incapable of being assisted; obviously, any criticism is best left to those who have survived a similar ordeal.

On the regiment's right Galbraith succeeded in effecting a rally on the south bank of the ravine. He did so by uncasing one of the Colours, the symbols of the regiment's honour, and may have been wounded at the time as he was seen to be kneeling. Instinctively, his own officers and soldiers closed in to protect it, together with some Grenadiers, Rifles and Sappers, until the group was about 200 strong.

They were, of course, doomed from the outset, but the manner of their deaths was recorded first by a wounded officer of the 66th, Lieutenant H. Lynch, who was being assisted to the rear and witnessed the beginning of the end, and by the Afghans themselves who, however vicious their way of war might have been, were deeply impressed by the subsequent display of supreme courage.

The group, in an untenable position, was quickly surrounded and became the focus of the enemy's fire. Galbraith was killed and Lieutenant Barr was shot dead across the broken staff of the uncased second colour. Men began to fall steadily but, firing the while, the group retired slowly through Khig to a mud-walled garden where a second stand was made. By now, its numbers had dwindled to about 130; by now, too, it is possible that regimental pride had led to both Colours being unfurled, although this is pure conjecture. For a while the walls of the little enclosure flamed defiance but when the Afghan artillery arrived the end was in sight. Here died Major Blackwood, the wounded commander of E/B Battery, and Lieutenant Henn, commanding the Sappers and Miners. Lieutenant Heywood, holding a Colour above his head, rallied the dwindling numbers of the 66th with a shout of: 'Men! What shall we do to save this?' When he fell his place was taken by the Adjutant, Lieutenant Raynor, but he too was mortally wounded. For a while he was protected by the regiment's big drummer, Darby, who obstinately refused orders to save himself and was shot down. In turn, the Colours passed through the hands of Second Lieutenant Olivey and Sergeant Major Cuppage until they died; then they were borne in succession by sergeants, corporals and private soldiers. At length, they finally fell under a wild ghazi rush, going down in a bloodstained welter of struggling khaki uniforms and white robes.

Of the 66th, there remained only two officers, Lieutenants Chute and Hinde, and nine men still on their feet. Recognising the impossibility of recovering the Colours, they decided to try and fight their way out and had covered about 300 yards before they were surrounded by cavalry and forced into a tight knot, fighting back to back. Weeks later, when the site was examined, dead horses still ringed the spot where the regiment's Last Eleven had died.

Even in the full flush of victory, the Afghans were awed by the end of the 66th. 'Surrounded by the whole of the Afghan army, they fought on until only eleven men were left, inflicting enormous loss on the enemy,' wrote one of Ayub's senior artillery officers. 'These men charged out of the garden and died with their faces to the foe, fighting to the death. Such was the nature of their charge, and the grandeur of their bearing, that although the whole of the ghazis were assembled round them, no one dared to approach to cut them down. Thus, standing in the open, back to back, firing steadily and truly, every shot telling, surrounded by thousands, these officers and men died; and it was not until the last man was shot down that the ghazis dared to advance upon them. The conduct of these men was the admiration of all that witnessed it.'

It was not, however, just the soldiers of the 66th who fought and died at Maiwand. A regiment is a family, a family has its dogs, and dogs will attack those who attack their people, doing a great deal of damage in the process. Captain McMath and his dog were killed together near the ravine. When, fearing reprisals, the Afghans finally buried the British dead, they flung the animal into his master's grave, intending to insult; the irony was that, unashamed sentimentalists as they were, the Victorians would have regarded the gesture as touchingly appropriate. A second dog, Bobbie, fought to the end and survived. Nondescript, white and woolly with a flat head, brown ears and mask, he was typical of the dogs that adopted entire British regiments abroad, although mostly he was Sergeant Kelly's dog. Bobbie remained with the Last Eleven until the end and was evidently still full of fight when the ghazis closed in, for he received a sword cut for his trouble. At length, when the Afghans decided that there had been fighting enough for the day and went off to loot the British baggage, he picked himself up and hobbled after the remnants of his regiment.

For the survivors of Burrows' column the long retreat to Kandahar was an ordeal that was even worse than the battle itself. Only the artillery and the former baggage guard managed to preserve their unit discipline, halting from time to time to keep the Afghan pursuit at bay.

'All over the wide expanse of desert are to be seen men in twos and threes retreating,' recalled Slade. 'Camels have thrown their loads; sick men, almost naked, are astride of donkeys, mules and camels; the bearers have thrown down their dhoolies and left the wounded to their fate. The guns and carriages are crowded with helpless wounded officers and men suffering the tortures of the damned; horses are limping along with ugly wounds and men are pressing eagerly to the rear in hope of finding water. The distant booming of cannon is still heard;[4] the hordes of irregular horsemen are to be seen amongst our baggage animals, relentlessly cutting one and all down and looting. The survivors of the Battle of Maiwand owe their lives to the looting that took place in the retreat. A few alone remain with the General to try and turn the rout into an orderly retreat. And so it goes on for five or six miles, till the sun begins to sink serenely into the horizon. The cries for 'Water! Water!' become more frequent and louder and louder. Men can hardly speak, the wounded open their mouths and show a dry parched tongue and with a sad expression convey to your mind but a glimpse of their intense suffering. After a long search in the dead of night a deep well full of muddy water is found in the village of Hauz-i-Madat. There is just sufficient to satisfy the wounded and those who are fighting round the well for dear life, but none can be spared for the already worn out and exhausted horses. Everyone's hand is against us. Villagers from all sides creep up behind the low mud walls and fire on us, and many a gallant fellow who had battled against the trials of the night fell victim to the jezail. At last the River Argandab is reached; it is 11 a.m. and 32 miles from the battlefield. With what joy and delight do the unfortunate men and horses, who have not wetted their lips during the night, welcome the sight of it!'

As the horses became more and more exhausted, Slade was forced to abandon all but one of the Smoothbore Battery's now useless guns and employ the remaining strength of their teams, plus conscripted chargers, to haul E/B's guns and limbers. During the night Maclaine, searching for water, was captured and beaten up by villagers; later, he was handed over to the Afghan regulars, who treated him well. With the coming of dawn, sniping at the column increased. Grabbing his carbine, Gunner Collis, began stalking the snipers themselves, deliberately drawing their fire on himself until the last of the wounded and stragglers had staggered past.

Some of Nuttall's troopers had reached Kandahar with news of the disaster during the early hours of the morning. Primrose had wasted no time in sending out a relief force which met the head of Burrows' weary column near Kokeran and then assisted Slade in covering the withdrawal. Water had done much to restore discipline, and, as Slade put it, 'Although we still had to fight our way from stone to stone, our troubles and hardships were practically at an end.' By 1500 on 28 July, after 33 hours' marching and fighting on practically empty stomachs and little water, the rearguard passed through the gates of Kandahar.

Of the 2565 men present at Maiwand, 962 were killed, including a party of 150 Grenadiers and Rifles who lost their way during the retreat and were surrounded and massacred; only 161 wounded survived the battle and the retreat. The 66th sustained 288 casualties from a strength of 473, the Grenadiers 427 from 649, the Rifles 268 from 624, E/B Battery 34 from 146, the Smoothbore Battery 15 from 43, the Sappers 25 from 46 and the cavalry 64 from 575. Seven guns had been lost or abandoned. Over 2000 horses and transport animals had been killed or captured together with large quantities of ammunition and equipment.

Primrose immediately informed the Commander-in-Chief of the disaster and, believing that Ayub would waste no time in closing in on Kandahar, put his defences in order. Yet the fact was that, whatever criticisms might be levelled at Burrows for his tactical handling of the battle, he achieved his strategic objective. It took Ayub a week to clear the field of his own dead, which included 1500 of his regulars and between three and four thousand ghazis. More of his men left for home with the bodies of their kinsmen. When he resumed his advance he was forced to leave 1500 seriously wounded behind in Maiwand.

His desultory siege of Kandahar does not form part of this story, nor does the epic march of Roberts' army from Kabul to Kandahar, still quoted as a triumph of logistic planning. When, on 1 September, Roberts forced a battle on Ayub outside the city, the latter's army had shrunk to about 15,000 men and he was decisively defeated, losing all his artillery, including the two guns captured from E/B Battery. Maclaine, a prisoner in his camp, was murdered by a ghazi as the Afghans fled. This engagement marked the end of the war and, having seen Abdur Rahman firmly established on the throne, the British left Afghanistan the following year.

Ayub rebelled again in 1881 and this time succeeded in capturing Kandahar. He was, however, defeated when Abdur Rahman personally took the field against him, and fled to Persia. Burrows received sympathetic consideration and left the Army as a major general in 1886. Nuttall returned to the staff and retired as a lieutenant general in 1890.

Slade, made a Companion of the Bath for his achievements, was subsequently knighted and in due course became Commander-in-Chief Egypt. E/B Battery as a whole was awarded the Honour Title 'Maiwand'. Two of its members, Sergeant Mullane and Gunner Collis, were awarded the Victoria Cross. Unfortunately for Collis, the original Victoria Cross Warrant contained a clause to the effect that the award became forfeit following conviction of any infamous crime and in 1895 his decoration was withdrawn when he committed bigamy. Understandably, the incident provoked great indignation. When Edward VII came to the throne he rescinded this part of the Warrant and is said to have commented that, in his opinion, any man who had won the VC could wear it on the scaffold, if it ever came to that!

The loss of the 66th's Colours, following so close upon the temporary loss of one of the 24th Regiment's Colours at Isandhlwana the previous year,[5] confirmed that such objects of veneration had no place on a modern battlefield and henceforth they were laid up by regiments proceeding on active service. The Afghans themselves evidently prized the captured Colours, which were originally lodged in the fort at Karan, for in 1883 an escorted party of the Afghanistan Boundary Commission was forbidden to approach within 100 yards of the building. Ten years later the Colours were said to have been moved from Karan for safekeeping elsewhere, but for more than a century nothing more has been heard of them.

The 66th returned home in 1881 and were presented with new Colours. Bobbie went with them and, suitably dressed in a scarlet jacket trimmed with imitation pearls, was presented to Queen Victoria at Osborne House. The Queen listened to his remarkable story, examined his wound and pinned the Afghan War Medal to his collar. For Bobbie, however, garrison life in England was not the same as soldiering in India. He became bored, began to stray and was finally run over and killed by a hansom cab in Gosport in October 1882. Today, still wearing his medal, he can still be seen in the regimental museum, a great deal cleaner and tidier than the night when, his coat matted with blood and dust, he staggered into Kandahar citadel to flop down beside the exhausted survivors of the 66th after one of the bitterest battles in the Army's history.

Notes

1. See *Last Stand*, Chapter 3.
2. Author's italics.
3. Although 50 years have passed since the end of the Raj, India was so deeply embedded in the Army's consciousness that even today many Urdu words remain a normal part of its speech. A few of the more obvious examples are: *jaldi!* (get a move on!); *dhobi* (laundry); and, of course, *char* (tea).
4. The guns heard by Slade were almost certainly those engaging the last remnants of the 66th.
5. See *Last Stand*, Chapter 5.

The Defence of Hougoumont
Above: The First or Grenadier Guards defending the South Gate at Hougoumont. A painting by Simkin. (By permission of the Regimental Lieutenant Colonel, Grenadier Guards, photograph supplied by the National Army Museum)
Below: R. Gibb's painting of the closing of the Main or North Gate of Hougoumont by members of the Coldstream and Third Guards. This was achieved only after a party of the enemy had burst their way into the interior of the defences. Colonel Macdonell and Corporal Graham can be seen with their shoulders to the left-hand gate. Wellington was later to remark that the successful outcome of Waterloo depended upon this incident. (Courtesy, The Coldstream Guards)

Jellalabad

Above: The last stand of the 44th (later Essex) Regiment at Gandamak, painted by W.B. Wollen. Captain Souter is on the right of the group with drawn sword and the Regimental Colour tied round his waist in the manner of a sash. One of the men is searching a dead comrade's cartridge box for ammunition; the body in the right-foreground is that of an officer in the Bengal Horse Artillery. Even after the 44th had expended the last of their ammunition several Afghan charges were required to overwhelm them. (Copyright the Essex Regiment Association; photograph supplied by the National Army Museum, London)

Below: Lady Elizabeth Butler's famous painting *The Remnants of an Army*, showing the wounded Dr Brydon approaching the reconstructed walls of Jellalabad. His horse, shot through the spine near the tail, died shortly after. Despite the myth created by the painting, Brydon was not the only survivor of the Kabul garrison. (Somerset Military Museum Trust)

Antietam

Above: Union infantry advancing into The Cornfield during the early stages of the battle. (ASKB)

Below: French's Division closing in on Roulette Farm. The Sunken Lane is on the left of the picture. (ASKB)

Bottom: When, eventually, Burnside resumed his advance, only a thin line of infantry and guns barred his way into Sharpsburg, the church tower of which can be seen in the distance. It was at this juncture that Hill's division, having force-marched from Harper's Ferry, attacked his flank and forced him to retreat. (ASKB)

Left: Ambrose P. Hill, photographed in lieutenant general's uniform towards the end of the Civil War. His hatred for McClellan remained a driving force as long as the latter held command. At Antietam he took his revenge on his former rival. (Massachusetts Commandery Military Order of the Loyal Legion and the US Army Military History Institute)

Right: Major General George McClellan and his wife Ellen. McClellan's instinctive caution was another factor which denied him a decisive victory over Lee at Antietam. In their youth Ellen had been courted simultaneously by McClellan and Ambrose Hill and actually been engaged to the latter. The engagement was broken after a campaign of rumours questioned Hill's morality and she married McClellan. Hill never forgave either of them. (Massachusetts Commandery Military Order of the Loyal Legion and US Army Military History Institute)

Captain Fetterman's Disobedience
Above: The Wagon Box Fight. Captain James Powell and his men take cover in their improvised defences. The troops were equipped with new Springfield breech-loading rifles which Powell concentrated in the hands of his best shots, employing the rest of the men to act as loaders. This action, together with the Hayfield Fight the previous day, restored the morale of the Army on the frontier. (US Department of the Army)

Maiwand
Below: Although the charge of Nuttall's cavalry brigade did not achieve its object, it did clear the enemy from the British rear and enable the withdrawal to begin. (Courtesy of the Director, National Army Museum, London)

Above: E/B Battery Royal Horse Artillery coming out of action at Maiwand. (Courtesy of the Director, National Army Museum, London)

Below: The last stand of the 66th (later Royal Berkshire) Regiment at Maiwand. Sergeant Kelly's dog Bobbie remained with the men to the end then, despite a sword-cut across the back, followed the remnants of the force for 40 miles until it reached Kandahar. (The Royal Gloucestershire, Berkshire and Wiltshire Regimental Museum, Salisbury)

Mafeking
Above: A painting by Frank Feller showing Baden-Powell during one of the first sorties from Mafeking. (Courtesy of the Director, National Army Museum, London)
Below: The armoured train with its crew of British South Africa Police. Two Maxim machine guns are visible, one on a ground mounting and the other on a field carriage. (Courtesy, The Scout Association)

Above: Home-made artillery and ammunition at Mafeking. The Wolf was built in the railway workshops. Baden-Powell is on the extreme left of the picture. (Courtesy, The Scout Association)

Peking
Below: The International Gun, otherwise known as Betsy or the Dowager Empress. (Courtesy of the Director, National Army Museum, London)

Above: US Marines beside the fortified ramp leading to the top of the Tartar Wall behind the American Legation. As the Tartar Wall overlooked the entire Legation Quarter, there was much bitter fighting on this sector of the defencesand at one stage the Chinese held the ramp on the right of the right of the picture. (Royal Marines Museum)
Below: Large areas of Peking were devastated during the fighting. (US National Archives)

The Lost Battalion
Above; The difficult hillside position held by the 'Lost Battalion'. The location is given as the Bois de la Buironne, near the foot of Mont de Charlevaux, approximately one mile north-east of Binarville, Meuse. (US Army Military History Institute)

Tebourba
Below: Wrecked German tanks litter the woodland where they were knocked out by 2nd Hampshires and supporting artillery units. (Trustees of the Imperial War Museum, London)

Above: The presence of Tigers in North Africa was not suspected until the Battle of Tebourba. (Trustesy of the Imperial War Museum, London)

Right: Lieutenant Colonel J.M. Lee, DSO, commander of 2nd Hampshires at Tebourba. (Courtesy, The Royal Hampshire Regiment Museum)

Tebourba
Above: Terence Cuneo's painting of Major H.W. Le Patourel winning his Victoria Cross on Point 186. (Courtesy, The Royal Hampshire Regiment Museum)

Kohima
Below: The area of the DC's bungalow and tennis court showing numerous bunkers and trenches. (Trustees of the Imperial War Museum, London)

Right: A pre-war photograph of Lance Corporal John Harman, VC. (Courtesy, The Queen's Own Royal West Kent Regiment Museum)

Below: Charles Stadden's painting of Lance Corporal Harman winning the Victoria Cross at Kohima (By courtesy of the artist and The Queen's Own Royal West Kent Museum)

Mortain
Above: The town of Mortain after the battle. (US Army Military History Institute)
Below: Panzergrenadier halftrack and other vehicles knocked out by anti-tank guns near L'Abbaye Blanche, north of Mortain. (US Army Military History Institute)

Iwo Jima

Above: An aerial view of Mount Suribachi, the broken slopes of which were honeycombed with defensive positions. (Trustees of the Imperial War Museum, London)

Right: View from the summit of Mount Suribachi across Iwo Jima, showing the northern plateau in the distance. (US National Archives)

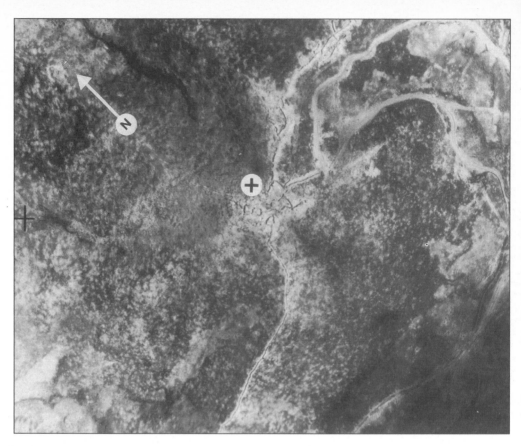

Pork Chop Hill
Above: Air reconnaissance photograph showing Pork Chop Hill on the left of the picture. The Chow Bunker was positioned in the re-entrant approximately in line with the + and beneath the N. On the right of the picture are the lower slopes of Hill 200, forming part of the main American defence line. By now the entire terrain has been torn up by shellfire. (US Army Military History Institute)
Below: Casualty evacuation from Pork Chop Hill. (US Army Military History Institute)

6

The Place of Stones: Mafeking, October 1899 – May 1900

'I want you to go to South Africa.' The speaker was Field Marshal Lord Wolseley, Commander-in-Chief of the British Army, the victor of numerous colonial campaigns and a byword for efficiency.

'Yes, sir,' replied the officer he was addressing, a short, spare man with shrewd, intelligent eyes, a well-trimmed military moustache and a rapidly receding hairline.

'Well, can you go on Saturday next?' asked Wolseley.

'No, sir,' answered Lieutenant Colonel Baden-Powell after a moment's thought.

'Why not?' asked the Commander-in-Chief sharply.

'Because there's no ship on Saturday – but I can go on Friday!'

It was the summer of 1899 and the possibility of war between the British Empire and the Boer Republics of the Transvaal and the Orange Free State was daily becoming a probability. What Wolseley required of Baden-Powell was that he should raise an irregular regiment of mounted infantry – later increased to two – in Rhodesia and Bechuanaland and with this invade the northern Transvaal when war broke out. There he would tie down Boer forces that could otherwise be employed against the comparatively small number of British troops in Cape Colony and Natal until reinforcements could arrive from the United Kingdom and India. The idea, while superficially attractive, discounted what had happened four years earlier when a political adventurer, Dr Leander Starr Jameson, had mounted a raid into the Transvaal from Mafeking, hoping to provoke a rising among the many Uitlanders (foreigners, mainly of British extraction) living there and so put an end to the various injustices to which they were subject. The rising had not materialised and after three days the Boers had simply rounded up Jameson's 500 followers and forced them to surrender. Naturally, the fact that the raid had been mounted from British territory further aggravated relations between the Boers and the Empire, as well as alerting the former to the dangers inherent in leaving Mafeking untaken in the event of open hostilities. Now, the dangers present in Baden-Powell's projecting himself into this hornets' nest with less than one thousand newly-raised men were only too obvious.

Robert Stephenson Smyth Baden-Powell, however, was not altogether a conventional soldier, and Wolseley knew it. He had been commissioned into the 13th Hussars without passing through Sandhurst and served with the regiment in India. At first he had seemed little different from the average cavalry subaltern of the time, devoting much of his time to polo and pig-sticking. Socially, his sense of humour and talents as an artist, mimic and actor made him a popular figure. Yet, as his career progressed, it became clear that he had an above average interest in his profession and in 1885 he published his book *Reconnaissance and Scouting*. He first encountered the horrific aspects of war when his regiment provided escorts for those investigating the disaster at Maiwand, noting on the site of the 66th's stand that the Afghans' ideas of burial consisted of pushing down the mud walls onto the bodies. Real active service, nevertheless, eluded him for many years and his thoughts continued to focus on the value of intelligence gathering. With this in mind, he had once attended the summer manoeuvres of the Imperial German and Russian armies in an unofficial capacity and been arrested for his trouble. He had better luck while serving in Malta, successfully spying on the French in North Africa and the Austrians in Bosnia, where he ingeniously concealed the details of a fortress within a drawing of a butterfly. During the Ashanti War of 1895 he led a force of 800 unruly native pioneers whom he kept in order by sheer force of personality, reinforced with prompt use of the lash whenever the occasion demanded it. The following year found him serving on the staff in Matabeleland, an appointment that did not suit his temperament at all. He frequently vanished on scouting missions which led to the rebellious tribesmen being tracked down in very difficult country that had long been considered impenetrable. Had they been able to lay hands on him, the Matabele would have put an end to him on the spot and they took to calling him 'Impeesa', meaning The Hyena Who Slinks Through The Night. Baden-Powell, an expert in projecting his own image, put about the more complimentary translation of The Wolf Who Never Sleeps, and it was this which caught the imagination his contemporaries, black and white alike, and has been quoted ever since. On the conclusion of the Matabele War he was given command of the 5th Dragoon Guards, then in India, and it was while he was enjoying a spell of home leave that he had been appointed to his present assignment.

Arriving in Cape Town, he was obstructed by the authorities at every turn. There were only 7000 British troops in Cape Colony and a further 3000 in Natal, facing a probable invasion by a total of 40,000 Boers. The atmosphere was uncannily similar to that which was to prevail in Singapore 42 years later, in that sensible defensive measures were discouraged in case they might provoke the enemy. Baden-Powell was allocated guns and ammunition, but denied the horses and transport with which to move them; furthermore, he was not permitted to recruit in Cape Colony. At length an enterprising Mafeking merchant, Mr Benjamin Weil, undertook to supply the necessary rations, fodder and clothing upon receipt of a personal promissory note in the sum of £500,000, issued by Major Lord Edward Cecil, Baden-Powell's Chief of Staff and son of the Prime Minister, Lord Salisbury. On 28 July Baden-Powell left the politically convoluted atmosphere of Cape Town for Bulawayo, Rhodesia, where a sharper perspective existed. Here, the British South Africa Police agreed to supply him with rifles and he commenced a recruiting drive which lasted throughout August and September.

The recruits themselves came from every walk of life. There were labourers, carpenters, electrical engineers, masons, engine drivers, musicians, cooks, chemists, and waiters; there was a tripe-dresser, a florist, and a barber; several had seen military service before, including a German who had been present at the Siege of Paris and a Turk who had been present at the Siege of Plevna, and there were a number who had previously served in the Royal Navy. When, at length, the Army condescended to supply unschooled horses, it was found that many of the recruits were unable to ride. Inevitably, several days of chaos ensued until riders and mounts reached an understanding. Nevertheless, by mid-September both of the new regiments had reached their designated strength of 450. The Rhodesia Regiment, commanded by Colonel (later Field Marshal) Herbert Plumer, was based in Bulawayo, with the tasks of defending Rhodesia and keeping open the supply lines of the Protectorate Regiment, commanded by Lieutenant Colonel Charles Hore, which was given the task of defending Bechuanaland and conducting forays into enemy territory. At first, the Protectorate Regiment was based at Ramathlabama in Bechuanaland, some sixteen miles north of Mafeking, which lay across the border in Cape Colony. Thanks to the meddling of the Cape Town bureaucrats, the Colony was technically out of bounds to Baden-Powell, but when stores began piling up at Mafeking, thanks not only to Cecil's purchase but also to further enterprise on the part of Mr Weil and the interception of consignments bound for Rhodesia, they agreed to his suggestion that a guard should be placed over the stockpile. Unfortunately for them, they did not specify the size of the guard and before they knew it Baden-Powell had moved in the whole of the Protectorate Regiment. Some historians have criticised him for thus tying down his force in a static defensive role, but he had been quick to appreciate that his make-believe mounted infantrymen would be no match for the hard-riding, sharpshooting Boers on the open veldt; and again, he was convinced that the accumulation of stores at Mafeking would in itself act as a magnet for a considerable body of the

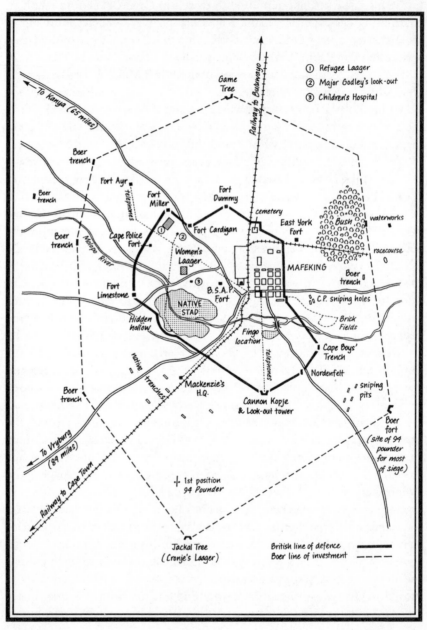

enemy, whom he could tie down in a protracted siege and so carry out the primary requirements of Wolseley's directive.

Mafeking was situated close to a point where the frontier of Cape Colony met that of the Transvaal, to the east, and Bechuanaland Protectorate, to the north. It lay on the Cape Town – Bulawayo railway, 890 miles from the former and 500 from the latter. The town itself was positioned just north of the Molopo river in the centre of a shallow saucer, six miles across and bounded by low hills. Consisting in the main of single-storey mud-brick buildings roofed with corrugated iron, from a distance it resembled an American Wild West township, an impression enhanced by the mule-drawn stage coach that met the trains and carried passengers across the border to destinations in the Transvaal. It was a prosperous little place with its own Mayor, Town Council, Resident Commissioner for Native Affairs and Resident Magistrate. In addition to houses and shops, it possessed a railway station, a court house, a hospital with 40 beds, three hotels, two schools, several small churches, a bank, a library, its own newspaper, a recreation ground, a brickfield, a racecourse with a tin-roofed grandstand, and a convent run by the Irish Sisters of Mercy. The town's major employer was the railway, with sidings, goods depots, engine sheds and workshops to the west of the main line. To the south-west of modern Mafeking, which dated only from 1884, lay the much older native township or Stad, straddling the Molopo and inhabited by Baralong tribesmen and their families. Nearby was a hillock from which protruded a number of strangely shapen rocks that the troops would call Stonehenge; they were, in fact, the origin of the town's name, meaning The Place of Stones.

To defend this large area Baden-Powell had very limited resources, even after he had enrolled all the able-bodied local men willing to serve, including two veterans of the Crimean War. The active elements of his garrison consisted of the as-yet untried Protectorate Regiment, with 21 officers and 448 men; Captain B.W. Cowan's company of the locally recruited Bechuanaland Rifles with five officers and 77 men; Colonel J.A. Walford's contingent of the British South Africa Police, with ten officers and 81 men; and a contingent from the Cape Police with four officers and 99 men under the command of Inspectors Brown and Marsh. This gave a total strength of 745 first line troops, of whom only 576 were armed with modern Lee-Metford magazine rifles and the remainder with obsolete Martini-Henry single loaders. In an emergency another 450 men of the Railway Volunteers, the Town Guard and the half-caste Cape Boys, all recruited from the townspeople and given elementary training, would be used to man inner defences with an assortment of weapons; of these, the Cape Boys were to play a particularly distinguished part in the coming siege. Officially, British and Boers alike had let it be known that this was to be a white man's war in which the native population had no part, save in self-defence, and with this loophole in mind Baden-Powell issued arms to the Baralongs, who assumed responsibility for defending their stad and thus an important sector of the outer perimeter.

The question of heavy weapons was one which gave Baden-Powell serious anxiety. He had been issued with two ancient muzzle-loading 7pdr cannon. Cape Town had promised him two modern 5in howitzers, but in their place sent two more elderly 7pdrs. The wooden carriages of all four guns had begun to rot through age but, thanks to the efforts of the local wagon builder, Mr Gerrans, they were put into a serviceable condition and became the responsibility of Major F.W. Panzera, a former Royal Artillery officer, who reflected ruefully that the maximum range of his charges was something less than 2000 yards. In addition, Baden-Powell had seven Maxim machine-guns, a Hotchkiss one-pounder quick-firer and a Nordenfeldt heavy machine-gun; the last, being a naval weapon, was manned by a crew of former seamen.

Work on the defences started in mid-September. These took the form of an outer and an inner ring, the former consisting of makeshift forts constructed at suitable points, the more important being connected to Baden-Powell's command post in Dixon's Hotel by field telephone. Lacking the manpower to hold trench lines between these strongpoints, Baden-Powell resorted to guile. He laid extensive dummy minefields, using boxes filled with earth, around which he posted warning notices. Well aware that the town contained Boer sympathisers, he announced that there would be a test firing in the minefields and instructed the civilians to stay indoors. He then laid a real mine which he exploded by remote control and was rewarded by the sight of a man peddling a bicycle along the Transvaal road as fast as he could go. Subsequently, these dummy minefields seriously inhibited the Boers' conduct of operations. Barbed wire would normally have been incorporated into the defences but, having very little of it, he resorted to another form of bluff, extending long lines of string over which the troops were instructed to step with exaggerated care – this, too, was duly noted by the Boers' spies, who were kept well away from the fortified positions, some of which were actually dummies intended to absorb some of the enemy shellfire. Two armoured trains were constructed, each consisting of an engine covered with boilerplate and loopholed trucks protected with rails and a splinter-proof iron roof. These were able to provide cover for the northern, southern and western sectors of the defences from the main line, but the town itself masked their fire to the east and to solve this problem a special spur was constructed. As the war clouds began to gather refugees, both white and black, began to arrive from the Transvaal. Understandably, Baden-Powell had no wish to feed more mouths than he had to and he advised them, and as many townspeople as wished, to leave while the railway was still open. Some did so, although a large number of families refused to leave their menfolk and for them a camp was set up west of the town, within the perimeter but away from any obvious military target.

Late on 10 October the garrison was informed by telegraph of the Boers' declaration of war. The next day was spent strengthening the defences and at noon on the 12th the last refugee train steamed off to the south. Shortly after, the chattering telegraph key fell silent. At 1500 the train returned with news that the line had been cut 24 miles to the south. Of one armoured train, sent to collect two more field guns, there was no news whatever; in fact, in the first action of the war it had been ambushed and forced to surrender after an hour-long fight against overwhelming odds. It was now apparent that Mafeking was cut off. As the Boers could clearly be expected very soon, Baden-Powell had the troops paraded in the town square and gave them a simple message:

'All you have to do is sit tight and when the time comes shoot straight.'

During the afternoon a railway ganger came in and reported that a party of Boers was lifting rails some five miles to the south. Next morning the armoured train went out and dispersed them, killing one. When a second party was reported to be cutting the track to the north Baden-Powell sent out an engine pushing two trucks packed with dynamite, of which he had so much in store that it represented a real danger. On sighting the Boers the driver halted, uncoupled the trucks and then shunted them at speed towards the enemy before putting his engine into reverse. The Boers, believing that they were under attack from an armoured train, opened a brisk rifle fire. The resulting explosion was heard for miles around. When the real armoured train approached the site that afternoon it engaged several Boers gathered around the crater, presumably looking for their vanished comrades.

Baden-Powell's scouts reported large bodies of the enemy crossing the line south of the town and more approaching from the north-east. In fact, the capture of Mafeking was one of the Boers' primary objectives, not simply because of the large quantity of stores accumulated there, but because they hated the place. It was from Mafeking that the Jameson Raid had been mounted; and Mafeking was also home to the Baralongs, who had worsted them in years of sporadic warfare over land rights before British rule was imposed. Altogether, the commandos trotting west from the Transvaal border numbered between 6000 and 8000 men under the command of two of the best Boer generals, Piet Cronje and Koos de la Rey. With them came thirteen field guns of various weight, most of them outranging the British artillery by a wide margin. A quick and easy victory was anticipated over the tin-pot township and its rag-bag garrison of part-time soldiers.

On the morning of 14 October one of Baden-Powell's patrols, commanded by Captain Lord Charles Bentinck, surprised a Boer laager northeast of the town. With the enemy in hot pursuit, Bentinck withdrew towards the railway, on which the armoured train was moving north to spring the trap. The Boers, some 400 in number, rode straight into the fire of two Maxims, the Hotchkiss and the 50 troopers of the BSAP forming the crew. At first, they disregarded their losses, believing that the train was at their mercy, especially as they were being supported by a Krupp field gun and a 1pdr pom-pom from higher ground to their rear. Rifle bullets and shell splinters clattered off the armour, adding to the din of continuous firing within, and made speech impossible. The Hotchkiss, concentrating on the enemy guns, made them change position twice and finally silenced them. At this, the Boers began to shred away, leaving their casualties behind. The direction of their retreat took them out of the leading truck's arc of fire and, seeing this, the train commander, Captain A.P.W. Williams, gave the order to reverse around a curve until the guns would bear again. The Boers, mistakenly scenting victory, rallied and began to press home their attack afresh, only to be beaten off with further casualties.

It was now approximately 0715 and the sound of continuous heavy firing for the preceding 45 minutes had given rise to such concern that Baden-Powell sent out troops from his small central reserve to support the train. These consisted of the Protectorate Regiment's 50-strong D Squadron, commanded by Captain Charles Fitzclarence, a Royal Fusilier descended from the liaison between King William IV and Mrs Jordan, followed by one troop of A Squadron. Fitzclarence began pressing the Boers back towards their laager, but in so doing entered the area between their quarry and the train, forcing the latter to cease firing. Observing this, the Boers began working round the right flank of the by-now heavily outnumbered squadron. Baden-Powell, informed by telephone of the potentially serious situation that was developing, sent out Bentinck's troop again, accompanied by one of the 7pdrs under the command of Lieutenant K. Murchison, another ex-Royal Artillery officer. Murchison quickly burst three rounds of shrapnel above the heads of the Boer flanking force, which then galloped off when Bentinck charged them, firing from the saddle. Discouraged, the rest of their commando ceased firing and withdrew out of range.

The first round had unquestionably gone to the garrison, whose morale soared. During the four-hour action over 60 Boers, including four field-cornets, had been killed, and 150 wounded. Baden-Powell's losses amounted to four killed, fourteen wounded and one missing.

Cronje opened a correspondence with Baden-Powell the following day, during the course of which it was agreed that there would be no fighting on Sundays. Thinking, no doubt, of the mysterious explosion of the two railway trucks, and heedful of the many warning notices around the perimeter, the Boer general claimed that the use of mines contravened the Geneva Convention. Baden-Powell replied that their use was a recognised adjunct of land and sea warfare and was not prohibited by the Convention in any way.

On the morning of 13 October the town was shelled for the first time and one of the dummy forts took a pounding. On average, about 70 shells per day landed within the perimeter throughout the siege, but only rarely were the Boer guns concentrated against a single target in this way. Much of their fire was spread indiscriminately across a wide area, thereby reducing its effectiveness. The women's camp, the hospital and the convent were hit regularly. Baden-Powell's protests that the Red Cross flag was being disregarded were acknowledged courteously enough, but shells continued to land in what should have been safe areas. For the sake of morale, Baden-Powell put up a notice describing the effects of the first day's bombardment:

Killed – one hen

Wounded – one yellow dog

Smashed – one hotel window

Most people were encouraged but were still urged to take the precaution of digging themselves a 'bomb-proof' dugout roofed with rails and sandbags. Surprisingly, the garrison and the townspeople alike settled down very quickly to a siege routine with growing confidence that any Boer assault could be repelled. Such moves as the enemy did make were frustrated by the armoured train, while at night the Boers suddenly found themselves brilliantly illuminated by searchlights shining from different sectors of the perimeter. These were the invention of Sergeant Moffat, who had discovered a stock of carbide, used then as a fuel for bicycle lamps, and installed burners inside highly polished reflectors made from shaped biscuit tins. They annoyed the Boers considerably and greatly impressed the Baralongs, who saw them as a clear demonstration of 'Impeesa''s incredible powers.

By the evening of 20 October Cronje had decided that Mafeking could only be taken following a sustained bombardment and gave Baden-Powell formal warning of what was to follow. A 94-pound Creusot siege gun, named Gritje by the Boers and Creechy by the garrison, was brought up from the Transvaal and opened fire on the 24th. Surprisingly, it caused little damage, although one shell demolished a couple of storage sheds and started a fire in which most of Sergeant Moffat's precious stock of carbide was consumed.

Next day a determined attack was launched along the Molopo valley against the Baralong stad. It was first contained by machine-gun fire from the neighbouring forts and the Baralongs themselves, then decisively repulsed by a counter-attack force consisting of two squadrons of the Protectorate Regiment, 40 Cape Boys and one 7pdr, under Major Alexander Godley, commanding the western sector of the defences. Observing the activities of the Boer ambulances that evening, the garrison estimated that it had inflicted approximately 80 casualties.

Meanwhile, the Boers had been pushing their own trenches closer to the town, especially on the eastern sector. To put an end to the menace of long-range sniping, Fitzclarence's D Squadron, supported by the Cape Police, mounted a trench raid on the night of 27 October. The raid was thoroughly prepared, two lamps in line above the town indicating the direction that D Squadron would take to the objective; the Cape Police, split into two parties, were to operate on the raiders' flanks and only open fire when the Boers raised the alarm. Fitzclarence's men, instructed to use only the bayonet, crept stealthily forward until the dull glow from an oil lamp indicated that they were close to the enemy trench. The continued mutter of conversation from below indicated that they had not been observed. Drawing his sword, Fitzclarence gave the order to charge. The line surged over the parapet like a wave, smashing down the flimsy roof, and went to work with their bayonets. Some of the occupants fled, others managed to get off a round or two before they were killed. The Cape Police immediately opened fire on the enemy lines opposite. The Boers responded, shooting down the dim line of running fugitives from the captured trench. Fitzclarence, having run through four of his opponents, climbed onto the parapet and blew the recall signal on his whistle.

Next morning a truce was arranged to recover the dead and wounded. The Boers, who regarded the bayonet as a barbaric weapon, were bitter and claimed that, one way or another, they had sustained nearly 100 casualties. Cronje, who had deliberately trivialised his casualties thus far, reported the loss of only three men. Fitzclarence, who was to receive the Victoria Cross for this action and that thirteen days earlier, believed that about 40 Boers had been killed or wounded in the trench and that perhaps a dozen more had been shot down by their own people. His own losses amounted to six killed, nine wounded and two missing.

It had now become essential that Cronje should do something to restore the flagging spirits of his men, and he decided to attack Cannon Kopje on the southern edge of the perimeter. This, the weakest link in the chain of fortified posts surrounding Mafeking, was held by Colonel Walford and 45 BSAP troopers with one 7pdr and two Maxims. No trenches could be excavated from the solid rock, so the garrison had been forced to build a breastwork from loose stones, topped with a layer of sandbags spaced to provide loopholes and embrasures. In front of this was the framework of an old windpump, adapted to serve as a lookout post. Nearby was Walford's tiny command post, dug into a pocket of earth only three feet deep. Some 40 yards behind the hill the garrison's quarters were located in a reinforced dugout.

Before dawn on 31 October five of the Boer guns focused their fire on Cannon Kopje, which had been regularly shelled for several days. There was, however, an intensity in the volume of fire that made Walford order all save three of his men back to their dugout, taking the Maxims with them.

As the light grew stronger Trooper von Dankberg, a German soldier of fortune, climbed the lookout post, disregarding the flying shards of metal from bursting shells, splinters of shattered rock and snipers' bullets that plucked at his uniform and smashed his telescope. He reported large numbers of held horses to the south and south-west, indicating that their riders were approaching on foot. This was confirmed by movements in a wide belt of high grass that extended to within 300 yards of the breastwork. More Boers were working their way around either flanks and snipers could be seen settling into shallow scrapes. Walford, realising that the enemy would soon launch their assault, ordered his men up from their dugout and had just informed Baden-Powell of the situation when the telephone line was cut by shellfire. Baden-Powell sent out two 7pdrs under Murchison, followed by the reserve squadron, doubting whether these reinforcements would reach the fort in time.

The Boer guns maintained their fire until the last possible moment, as did the snipers. Within a minute of so of the breathless garrison reaching the breastwork it had been decimated. Captain Marsham was hit twice by a sniper, the second time fatally. Captain Pechell fell with a bullet through his head. A shell hit the breastwork and burst beyond, killing Sergeant Majors Upton and Counihan and Corporal Lloyd. More men, struck by bullets or shell splinters, were going down around them. For a few seconds the troopers showed signs of wavering. Then, the shelling ceased abruptly and the Boers broke cover, heading up the hill's forward slope at a run. A spluttering, rapid rifle fire broke out along the breastwork, punctuated by the banging of the 7pdr. On either flank, belts were snaking their way into the Maxims as they scythed their deadly way across the enemy ranks. The attack was broken up just 200 yards short of the breastwork and the Boers turned and ran for cover. In the sudden silence the garrison became aware of Murchison's two guns thumping away behind them. Murchison's shooting was described as 'brilliant', and for five minutes he burst shrapnel over the heads of the Boers attempting to outflank the fort until they, too, broke and fled.

Cronje had employed a minimum of 700 men in the attack and, had it succeeded, he could have advanced straight into the town with little to stop him; after that, the various elements in Baden-Powell's command would have been forced to surrender or be rounded up and defeated in detail. He could then have ridden south with his entire force, where his arrival at this critical time would almost certainly have resulted in the fall of Kimberley and a march on Cape Town itself. As it was, losses amounting to approximately 100 killed and wounded had been incurred to no purpose. Walford's casualties included eight killed, five seriously wounded and more with lesser injuries, about one-third of those involved. The result had been far too close for comfort and that night, having ridden out to congratulate the survivors, Baden-Powell sent out reinforcements, supplies and material to render Cannon Kopje more defensible. Next day, the Boers began to mass opposite the position but dispersed again after an hour, evidently having thought better of making another attack.

Apart from the daily shelling, and a sortie to beat up a Boer laager on 7 November, very little occurred for almost three weeks. Then, on 18 November, large dust clouds were seen heading south from the Boer lines. Cronje was going, taking more than 4000 of his men with him, leaving behind Commandant J.P. Snyman to continue the siege with the rest and five or six guns, including Creechy.

The Boer lines of investment had never been so complete that messengers could not get in and out at will. Baden-Powell was well aware that the war in South Africa was going badly for the British. Kimberley and Ladysmith were both under siege and would clearly not be relieved for some time: in such a context Mafeking would obviously have to wait much longer so that, despite the departure of Cronje, his own troubles were far from being ended. On the other hand, as the local area commander, he could be satisfied at having fulfilled his strategic mission by personally tying down as many as 8000 Boers who would have been better employed elsewhere during the past five weeks, while to the north Plumer's Rhodesia Regiment was making a sufficient nuisance of itself to absorb the attention of a further 2500.

If Cronje's conduct of the siege could hardly have been said to be vigorous, Snyman's bordered on the indolent. Day by day, week by week, month by month, he continued to shell the town but made no further attempt to take it. All around the siege lines the Boers remained passive, save in the Brickfields sector to the east of the town. Here they were opposed by the Cape Boys and some Fingo refugees from the Transvaal. Hatred was mutual and of such intensity that a continuous grudge fight developed. Once again, the garrison's ingenuity paid dividends. Grenades, made from jam tins filled with dynamite, were flung across into the Boer trenches, even the remoter of which were not safe from one man who used a fishing rod and line to hurl them into the middle distance. Baden-Powell, keen to keep the enemy on edge at night, hit on the idea of megaphones made from tin boxes, through which orders appropriate to a raiding party would be given and clearly heard by the Boers; in the Brickfields in particular the command 'Fix bayonets!' always provoked a terrific fusillade from the trenches opposite. In the end, the Cape Boys triumphed, pushing enemy back steadily and blowing up several kilns used by his snipers. Baden-Powell admired them greatly and changed the title of their unit to the Colonial Contingent.

The fact remained that a very long siege lay ahead. Baden-Powell's primary concern was to maintain the morale of his troops and the townspeople, and in this respect he was the ideal man for the job. Hearing of the 9th Lancers' successful charge at Elandslaagte on 21 October, and knowing that the Boers hated the lance even more than they did the bayonet, he had the railway workshops make a quantity of them. These were not for active use – it took a very long time to train a lancer to professional standards – but to bluff the enemy yet again. Every so often a squadron of the Protectorate Regiment would be armed with the weapons and, like a stage army, would appear behind different sectors of the defences, pennons fluttering. This in itself caused some alarm in the enemy ranks, and not a little bewilderment. How on earth had a lancer regiment managed to work its way through the siege cordon? Such is the power of suggestion that one man believed he had heard the 'new arrivals' trotting through the dark, and another claimed to have come across their spoor. Another ruse was to erect dummy figures, dressed in uniform, at various points around the defences. By mechanical means the dummies could be made to nod, wave a flag or raise an imitation pair of binoculars. They acted as a magnet for the Boer snipers, who not only wasted much ammunition but also disclosed their own positions. To confuse the enemy's artillery, Baden-Powell frequently changed the positions of his few precious guns, leaving replicas in their place. At one stage he enraged Snyman by having leaflets distributed to the Boers under a flag of truce, informing them that their generals were liars, that they were losing the war and that they had better surrender by a given date to save their farms from confiscation. Morally, Baden-Powell was on top and he intended to stay there.

The town's food supplies had been consolidated at the beginning of the siege and strict price controls introduced, thereby ensuring that everyone was dealt with fairly. Black marketeering, hoarding and misappropriation were dealt with severely. When the Boers began pilfering the Baralongs' cattle, the latter's armed 'cattle guards', referred to as The Black Watch, were encouraged to raid the Boers' herd, and did so with considerable success. When, despite the imposition of rationing, food supplies began to run down during the last months of the siege, it became necessary to slaughter the Protectorate Regiment's horses, Baden-Powell set up a factory producing sausages, brawn and other by-products. To reduce the strain on stocks the black refugees were encouraged to leave, but only after arrangements had been made for Plumer to establish food depots in safe areas. Many did leave, although those caught by the Boers were turned back if they were lucky and murdered if they were not. For those who remained, soup kitchens were set up.

There was no aspect of the town's life which Baden-Powell did not mobilise for the common good. From 1 November a newspaper, the *Mafeking Mail*, began to appear daily, 'shells permitting', at the weekly subscription rate of one shilling (5p). This kept everyone fully informed of events as they occurred and included contributions from those journalists present – Vere Stent of Reuter's, Angus Hamilton of *The Times*, Major F.D. Baillie, late 4th Hussars, of *The Morning Post*, E.G. Parslow of the *Daily Chronicle*, J.E. Neilly of the *Pall Mall Gazette* and G.N.H. Whales of the *Cape Press*.

Baden-Powell was determined to make the best possible use of all his resources. While commanding the 5th Dragoon Guards in India he had given his younger troopers far more responsibility than was the custom at the time, a policy that had produced excellent results. Now, permanently young at heart himself, he observed the town's boys playing and realised that he could simultaneously make good use of their energy and keep them out of trouble. Issued with forage caps, uniform tunics and crossbelts, they were formed into a Cadet Corps and made responsible for the delivery of messages, either by bicycle or on foot. Although often forced to work under fire, they never let him down.

When hard currency became scarce, Baden-Powell, with a rare insight into economics, issued siege banknotes and restored circulation. Special postage stamps were also issued. At first these were simply British Bechuanaland stamps overprinted with 'Mafeking Besieged'. As supplies ran out Godley, Cecil and the postmaster agreed on a new issue showing Baden-

Powell's head, taken from a photograph. The garrison commander, fearing a charge of lèse majesté would result from the substitution of his own head for that of Queen Victoria, was horrified and ordered the issue withdrawn, too late to prevent several sheets going into circulation or private collections. A fresh design, showing one of the Cadet messengers on his bicycle, was hurriedly introduced.

It was during the Sunday truces that Baden-Powell worked hardest to maintain morale. The band played and for those not on duty there were cricket or football matches on the recreation ground. There were also, while enough fit horses remained, gymkhanas and carriage parades. There were baby competitions, photographic competitions, and every other sort of competition that human ingenuity could devise. In the evening there was usually a variety concert in which Baden-Powell caused much mirth with his comic impersonations.

On Monday mornings it was back to the grim business of war. Baden-Powell, referred to as B-P by his officers and the Colonel by the townspeople, was playing to win. He could often been seen on the observation post above Dixon's Hotel, studying the Boer lines for long periods, turning over in his mind what the enemy's intentions were and how he could frustrate them. At night he would disappear, entirely alone, on some scouting mission, returning while it was still dark to snatch an hour or two's sleep.

The siege, however, had not degenerated into the fun-packed adventure described by left-wing historians. Week by week, soldiers and civilians were blown apart or died by the sniper's bullet. Burial parties remained a common sight. The hospital wards were filled with the wounded and maimed. Sickness combined with a steady trickle of casualties to reduce the garrison's active strength. In the claustrophobic atmosphere it was not surprising that personalities should begin to grate on one another. Baden-Powell himself was on poor terms with Hore, commanding the Protectorate Regiment, Cecil, his own Chief of Staff, and the town's Medical Officer. Murchison, though an outstanding artilleryman, was a dangerously unstable character. During a heated argument with Parslow he shot the journalist dead. After being convicted of murder by a court martial he was sentenced to death, although after Baden-Powell had considered representations on his state of mind he recommended clemency. This could only be granted by the Commander-in-Chief South Africa, with whom Baden-Powell was not in contact, and in the meantime Murchison was placed in close arrest.

It was over the Christmas period that Baden-Powell made his one serious mistake of the siege, although sheer bad luck, or possibly careless talk and treachery, may also have played a part.

111

The garrison had become restive and was anxious for another crack at the Boers. Game Tree Hill, situated to the north of the town just west of the railway, offered a suitable opportunity, as its possession would deny the enemy the gun position from which they had been shelling the hospital and also bring an area of good grazing within the perimeter. The fact that the Boers had begun strengthening their defences on Game Tree added a degree of urgency to the planning.

The intention was that during the early hours of Boxing Day the armoured train would steam very quietly to a point beyond Game Tree; two squadrons of the Protectorate Regiment (C under Captain Ronald Vernon and D under Fitzclarence) would move up to a point level with Game Tree; and Major Panzera, with two 7pdrs and a Maxim, was to move into a position from which he could bring the objective under fire from the south. At first light the Boer trenches, under fire from front and rear, would be stormed with the bayonet. Major Godley would be in overall command of the operation.

From the start, almost everything went wrong. The armoured train moved soundlessly up the line at two miles per hour until, just short of Game Tree, the speaking tube from the leading truck shrilled urgently. A voice reported that the track ahead had been broken and the driver slammed on the brakes. The two squadrons conformed and lay down in the grass well short of their intended assault start line. Panzera, with muffled harness, dropped the trails of his guns in their allotted position and waited.

It was now high summer in the southern hemisphere and first light began to show before 0400. Since it revealed that the train and the assault squadrons were out of position, Panzera, unaware of the reason, delayed opening fire until 0428. By then the sun was rising and the British were clearly visible to the Boers. Nevertheless, the squadrons rose from the grass and began to advance on the objective.

What should have been a short flanking attack with ample fire support had become a frontal assault over 1400 yards of open country with very little fire support, as Panzera's gunners and the armoured train were soon compelled to cease firing for fear of hitting their own men. The attackers were cut to pieces. Those who did reach the summit found themselves confronted with a loopholed blockhouse with head cover consisting of sandbags laid over rails. A few managed to fire into the loopholes but by then Godley, watching from the train, observed parties of mounted Boers circling round the flanks to cut them off and had the recall signal blown on the locomotive whistle.

Casualties amounted to 26 killed, including Vernon, 23 wounded, including Fitzclarence, and three missing, approximately half of those involved. Boer losses came to three killed and ten wounded. The only bright spot in the unrelieved gloom was the award of the Victoria Cross to Sergeant H.R. Martineau and Trooper H.E. Ramsden, both of whom, though wounded themselves, brought in wounded men under fire.

Yet, if the events of 26 December caused morale to fall, on 3 January there was a development which caused it to rise again. One morning in December Godley had ridden into Rowland's Farm and noticed a peculiar gatepost, half-buried and overgrown. When dug out it proved to be a bronze 16pdr ship's cannon. When it was cleaned up the words BP & Company became evident on the barrel and taken to be a good omen; they stood, in fact, for Bailey and Pegg, cannon founders of Staffordshire. The gun was taken to the railway workshops where, under Panzera's direction, it was refurbished and mounted on a carriage produced by Gerrans. Once balls had been cast and powder charges prepared, it was taken out for test firing on 3 January and aimed at a Boer laager 3000 yards away. Its ball reached the target without the slightest difficulty, sailing through the parked wagons in a series of bounces. Such was the consternation caused that the Boers inspanned and pulled back three miles.

The gun, named Lord Nelson for obvious reasons, was then taken to engage Creechy, the enemy's 94pdr siege gun. Creechy's crew, alarmed by the incredible bouncing missiles, ran for cover. Believing that an attack was imminent, the Boers massed a force of horsemen nearby, only to have this raked with shrapnel by the 7pdrs. Whenever Creechy's crew returned to their weapon, they were sniped at and treated to a clip of the Nordenfeldt's little shells, one of which, bursting within the gun position, killed the gunlayer and wounded several more. Creechy would continue to kill, maim and cause damage, but because of this sort of harassment its position was regularly changed, each move giving the garrison a respite of a day or so.

Although the siege of Mafeking had long since fulfilled its strategic purpose, at the psychological level it had begun to assume even greater importance. The self-confidence of the British public had been seriously shaken by the defeats at Stormberg (10 December), Magersfontein (10-11 December) and Colenso (15 December), known collectively as Black Week. It was worried by the Army's apparent inability to come to grips with the situation, and by the fact that thousands of regular troops had allowed themselves to be passively besieged in Kimberley and Ladysmith. Yet, in sharp contrast, here was a tin-pot town on the outer edge of the back of beyond, held by a few hundred amateurs under the command of an obscure colonel who was repeatedly making fools of the Boers. Baden-Powell himself set the tone in one of his earliest despatches:

'All well. Four hours' bombardment. One dog killed.'

The public loved his self-deprecatory sense of irony, the more so because the copy filed by the Mafeking press corps described the real fighting in such detail. There was a universal feeling that as long as Mafeking held out all would come right in the end. Baden-Powell became hero, his picture pasted in shop windows and projected by magic lantern in theatres all over the country, always to prolonged cheering. He himself remained unaware either that he had become a celebrity or that the events of the siege were being watched anxiously throughout the Empire. Then, on 12 April, a runner worked his way through the Boer lines with a personal telegram from the Queen Empress:

'I continue to watch with confidence and admiration the patient and resolute defence which is so gallantly maintained under your ever resourceful command. Victoria RI'

It was a considerable boost to morale at a period when the garrison had not only begun to feel abandoned, but was also estimating how long their declining food stocks could last. They were aware that Kimberley had been relieved on 15 February, that their old enemy Cronje had been forced to surrender with 4000 of his men at Paardeberg on 27 February, and that the siege of Ladysmith had been raised the following day, but their own relief seemed as remote as ever.

In many ways, this placed an even greater strain on Baden-Powell. His own position was far from secure, yet he was reluctant to make demands on Lord Roberts, now Commander-in-Chief South Africa, at a time when the latter was planning the invasion of the Transvaal and the Orange Free State.

Since the failure at Game Tree, he had mounted only small scale operations, although these succeeded in dominating No Man's Land and rendering some of the Boers' forward outposts, including that at Jackal Tree Hill to the south of the Baralong township, untenable. Panzera busied himself mixing stable artillery charges from such materials as blasting powder and shotgun cartridges. With the assistance of the railway workshops, he also produced another gun, named The Wolf. This consisted of a 5in steam pipe upon which an outer jacket of iron railings was shrunk for reinforcement. Bronze trunnions and a breech were cast in the foundry and Gerrans produced a carriage from the chassis of a threshing machine. Horseshoes, now sadly in plentiful supply, were melted down with all sorts of scrap metal to produce 18-pound shells that were filled with Panzera's own explosive. The Wolf was test fired on 26 February, achieving a range of 2300 yards. It was sited in the Brickfields sector, where it gave good service throughout March until an attempt to increase the range by using a heavier charge ended in

114

irreparable damage to the breech. This loss was more than balanced when, on 11 April, Creechy fired off the last of its 94-pound shells and was dismantled for the journey back to Pretoria.

If the danger to Mafeking seemed to be decreasing, the reverse was actually true. As Boer fortunes continued to decline, President Kruger, now desperate for some good news to give his people, decided that it should be the fall of the hated dorp that had defied him for so long. His grandson, Field Cornet Sarel Eloff, who had commanded the post at Game Tree Hill for a while, was sent back to Mafeking with reinforcements that included 40 or so French and German volunteers and orders to capture the town regardless of cost.

Eloff was as vigorous as Snyman was apathetic, and he had a sense of humour. On 30 April he sent in note to Baden-Powell, commenting that he had heard that the garrison played cricket on Sundays and offering to bring in a team of his own. As 200 days had passed since the siege began, Baden-Powell replied that the garrison had already scored 200 not out against the bowling of Cronje and Snyman. Eloff is said to have been amused by the response, remarking that it was 'tough, but true enough'.

The Boers had became more active after Eloff's return from Pretoria and an attack was anticipated. When, at 0350 on 12 May, heavy firing broke out opposite the eastern perimeter, Baden-Powell, knowing that this was the strongest sector of the defences, recognised that it was a feint but nevertheless had the alarm sounded and the reserves stood to in anticipation of the real attack, wherever it might come.

The firing died away as the moon set and by 0515 had ceased altogether. At that moment Eloff was leading almost 250 men along the bed of the Molopo from the west, heading towards the Baralong township; behind, a similar number were being held back until he had broken through the perimeter defences. Guiding him was a Trooper E.J. Hay (some accounts give the name as Hayes), who bore a grudge against an officer and had deserted to the Boers. Hay had already told all he knew about the dummy minefields and make-believe wire entanglements, and he was able to pinpoint the position of the British outposts. Before anyone knew it the Boers had broken into the Baralong township, chasing the tribesmen and their families into the darkness and setting fire to the straw roofs of their huts.

Hay now advised Eloff to head for the British South Africa Police Fort, lying just to the west of Mafeking itself. The term fort was purely nominal, as it consisted solely of a house used by Colonel Hore as the headquarters of the Protectorate Regiment, and some mud-brick barrack buildings, none of which had been prepared for defence. The twenty or so defenders, assuming

115

that the figures emerging from the smoke-filled half-light were their own men falling back, were quickly overwhelmed and captured by the 150 Boers accompanying Eloff. Hay, strutting about girded with Hore's sword and gold watch, suggested that the prisoners should be lined up on the veranda when British fire began hitting the building, but Eloff would have none of it.

The Boers had now penetrated to within 800 yards of the town centre. Baden-Powell, prepared for such an emergency, calmly ordered the appropriate counter-measures, observed with sincere admiration by Edward Ross, the local auctioneer:

'He stood there at the corner of his offices, the coolest of cucumbers possible, but his orders rattled out like the rip of a Maxim. He had taken in the position without a moment's thought or hesitation, and when his outposts had been passed through by the enemy, within twenty minutes he had formed an inner line of defence right across the front of the town, with men and guns in sufficient numbers to mow down any number of the enemy that would dare to attempt to cross the clear open space still remaining between where the enemy were and the town. You could not realise his commands if put down in cold black and white. It was his tone, his self-possession, his command of self, his intimate knowledge of the defences, where everything at that moment was, and where it was to be brought and put to, showed us the ideal soldier....'

One of Baden-Powell's counter-measures was to despatch Fitzclarence's D Squadron to the area of the native township where the Baralongs, furious at the destruction of their homes, had been rallied by Captain C.F. Marsh and were already pressing the intruders back. Snyman had delayed pushing reinforcements through to Eloff for too long, and with the coming of full daylight it was no longer possible for them to get through the withering fire that would inevitably be put down by Godley's unsubdued forts on the western perimeter. The result was that the 100 or so Boers remaining in the area of the township were soon penned into two groups, one in a mud-walled cattle kraal and the other on the summit of the boulder-strewn kopje. Shortly after noon one of the 7pdrs was brought up and Marsh gave a shouted order for bayonets to be fixed. At this a white flag was waved and 27 survivors emerged from the kraal with their hands raised. Had it not been for Marsh's strenuous intervention the Baralongs would have massacred them on the spot.

Marsh then turned his attention to the kopje. After the 7pdr burst half-a-dozen rounds of shrapnel above the summit some 50 men bolted down the slopes into the bed of the Molopo, hoping to escape by the same means they had arrived. They found their path barred by D Squadron until Baden-

Powell, unwilling to feed more prisoners' mouths than he had to, ordered Fitzclarence to let the fugitives through.

By mid-afternoon only the Police Fort remained in Boer hands, the focus of a half-circle of flickering rifle fire. The tin roof was riddled and the water tank was deliberately punctured by snipers. As casualties began to mount the Boers' high spirits gave way to depression; only the French volunteers remained cheerful, having slaked their thirst on cases of captured wine. Eloff, now aware that he would not be reinforced, remained philosophical but gradually he lost control of his men. As dusk was gathering they held an angry meeting, after which about 60 of them, including Hay, made their escape into the gathering shadows. Recognising that the end was now inevitable, Eloff surrendered to Hore at 1800 and was marched with his remaining men into the Market Square, where Baden-Powell greeted him with a genial invitation to dinner at Dixon's Hotel.

It was estimated that about 50 Boers had been killed and the same number wounded. Some of those attempting to escape from the Police Fort were caught by the vengeful Baralongs and never seen again, including the traitor Hay. The garrison's losses amounted to twelve killed and twenty wounded, of whom eight of the dead and half the wounded were Baralongs.

The attitude of the 108 prisoners varied. The Boers hovered between sullen acceptance and despair. A German officer requested immediate release on the grounds that his leave had almost expired. The French were more tongue-in-cheek about their reasons for being in South Africa. One declared that his most cherished ambition was to learn English, but failed to explain why he had travelled so far to do so. The prize undoubtedly went to the man who claimed that his beloved in Paris was an avid philatelist and that all he wanted was a set of siege stamps.

For the moment, however, Eloff knew several things Baden-Powell did not, namely that a relief column under Colonel Brian Mahon, consisting of cavalry and mounted infantry, was advancing rapidly north from Kimberley; that this had reached a point only 60 miles from Mafeking; and that Plumer's force, which had itself been reinforced with a battery of Royal Canadian Artillery, was on the point of joining it. In the circumstances, therefore, his own attack on the town had been made as a matter of urgency.

It was not until Tuesday 15 May that Baden-Powell received confirmation of Mahon's presence. Next day there was the sound of gunfire away to the north-west as Mahon and Plumer engaged a Boer covering force under De La Rey. There were signs, too, that Snyman's wagons were breaking laager and heading for the Transvaal border. Then, during the late afternoon, a distant heliograph winked across the veld:

117

'From Colonel Mahon's Force – How are you getting on?'

At 1900, with the moon rising, an unfamiliar mounted patrol wearing the ostrich feather of the Imperial Light Horse in their turned-up slouch hats, passed through the defence lines and entered the town. The patrol's commander, Major W.D. Davies, asked directions to Baden-Powell's headquarters, outside which he and his men were quickly surrounded, 'besieged with questions, clapped on the back, shaken by the hand and generally welcomed'.

The rest of Mahon's force entered the town at 0330 the following morning. With them was the journalist Filson Young of the *Manchester Guardian*, who wrote: 'No art could describe the hand shaking and the welcome on the faces of these tired-looking men; how they looked with rapt faces at us commonplace people from the outer world as though we were angels, how we all tried to speak at once, and only succeeded in gazing at each other and in saying, "By Jove!" "Well, I'm hanged!" and the like senseless expressions that sometimes mean much.'

Next day Mahon's troops and such of the garrison as still retained its mobility went out and saw off the few remaining Boers in a half-hour engagement. There followed a ceremonial march-past by the relief column and the garrison during which Baden-Powell displayed his emotion for the only time in the siege. Later, there was a memorial service for those who had given their lives in defence of the town. Half the 44 officers originally present had been killed, died of disease or been wounded, as had 304 of their men and 182 non-combatants; deaths alone among the Baralongs and the native refugees amounted to 264. No figures exist for the Boer casualties, but a figure of 500 dead has been suggested, including a high proportion who had died of their wounds.

If, in Mafeking itself, the celebrations were modest enough, in London and elsewhere throughout the United Kingdom they approached the proportions of a riot. Earlier in the week unconfirmed reports, inspired by one of Reuter's men who had witnessed the early success of Eloff's attack, had appeared in the international press describing in lurid details the fall of Mafeking. Then, at about 2100 on the Friday evening, the news vendors began a totally unexpected clamour – Mafeking had been relieved! One special edition after another began pouring off the presses. Theatrical performances and formal dinners alike were abruptly terminated by the news. The occupants of music halls, public houses and private homes swarmed into the streets, laughing, shouting, singing patriotic songs and cheering. Duke and dustman shook hands for sheer joy. Bunting appeared as if by magic. Flag sellers did a roaring trade. Soon, every major thoroughfare and open space between the City and Park Lane was jammed with rejoicing crowds, leaving horse buses and carriages stranded like islands. They surged down the Mall to Buckingham Palace and gathered in dense masses outside the house near Hyde Park Corner where Baden-Powell's mother lived, cheering lustily whenever she appeared on the balcony. The crowds grew and grew throughout the night. The good-natured uproar continued all through Saturday and on into Saturday night. Only with the advent of Sunday did comparative tranquillity begin to return.

Inevitably, Mafeking Night generated its own hangover. Nothing like it had ever been seen before. Sober minds reflected that the successful ending of the siege was a comparatively minor success rather than a great victory, pondering whether the wild scenes were a symptom of national decadence. Yet, they were not.

Understanding of the psychological aspects of war was as yet in its infancy. The ordinary citizen had simply identified himself very closely with Baden-Powell. It was Baden-Powell who had preserved the national honour in the war's darkest days and Baden-Powell who, having fulfilled the mission he had been sent out to perform, had continued to fight on, alone and apparently regarded as expendable, long after the fortunes of war had swung Great Britain's way. He was, in British eyes, a hero who had been the plucky under-dog from the beginning; he deserved to win, he had won, and that was all there was to it. Similarities exist in the welcome extended by Berliners to General Paul von Lettow-Vorbeck following his remarkable campaign in East Africa during the First World War.

It was equally inevitable that, once the euphoria had died away, professional jealousies should seek to minimise Baden-Powell's achievements. Mafeking, it was whispered, would have fallen to any general only slightly more competent than Cronje and Snyman; in reply, it could be said that, with the exception of Baden-Powell, every British commander in South Africa at the time would undoubtedly have lost it.

Baden-Powell's rewards were another congratulatory telegram from the Queen and immediate promotion to major general, after which he took part in the invasion of the Transvaal. Yet it was not his military career that was to earn him a peerage and renown, but his founding of the Boy Scout movement. The boys of the Mafeking Cadet Corps had fully vindicated his ideas and, of course, being a national hero opened many doors to him. The movement had enormous popular appeal and quickly became international in its scope. Since then, countless millions of boys and girls all over the world have benefited from the ideals that were conceived in a little, tin-roofed town, besieged and sweltering under a hot sun on the African veld. Baden-Powell, who took greater pleasure in his title of Chief Scout than the fame he had won at Mafeking, died peacefully at his home in Kenya in 1941.

7

Boxers and Bannermen: The Siege of the Peking Legations, June – August 1900

Throughout its vast length and breadth the ancient empire of China was dying, the victim of a totally corrupt administration within and ruthless exploitation from abroad. Local officials, mandarins and provincial governors all extracted a varying degree of squeeze from those who required them to perform the duties for which they were already drawing pay; and, in order to retain possession of their lucrative appointments, these men in turn paid squeeze to their superiors in the central administration; who, for identical reasons, passed on suitable sums to those members of the Imperial family and court officials who could best serve their interests. By 1900 it had become apparent that the ruling Manchu dynasty only retained political power because of the iron will of one woman, the Dowager Empress Tzu Hsi, who implacably swept aside all who dared oppose her.

Fifty years earlier, Tzu Hsi had become the favourite concubine of the Emperor Hsien Feng. She had born him a son who succeeded to the throne in 1861, only to die three years later. Having secured the loyalty of the Household troops and the influential palace eunuchs, the Dowager Empress experienced no difficulty in having herself proclaimed regent for her infant nephew, Kuang Hsu. When the latter came of age in 1889 he attempted to introduce a series of much-needed reforms. The Dowager Empress, infuriated by the threat to the dynasty's absolute rule, promptly staged a coup and placed him under house arrest; only the intervention of a powerful body of provincial governors, supported by the Peking diplomatic corps, saved the Emperor's life, but thereafter he amounted to nothing more than a figurehead.

Nevertheless, even the Dowager Empress had to agree that reforms were urgently needed in the armed services, which sustained one humiliating reverse after another during the short war with Japan between July 1894 and April 1895. Such reforms, however, meant higher taxes, the burden of which inevitably fell upon the poor peasant farmers, who were already over-burdened with squeeze, unfavourable trading conditions and natural disasters. Yet, pay they must, or suffer cruel physical punishment; many such men, forced into the clutches of moneylenders, remained forever in debt or lost their land.

However, so thoroughly poisoned was the Chinese system that only a small proportion of funds thus raised were used for their stated purpose. For example, huge sums apparently destined for the Navy were spent on constructing an ornate marble boat on a lake in the Imperial Gardens. The Army fared even worse, for although large quantities of modern equipment, notably machine-guns and artillery, were purchased abroad, the real beneficiaries were the government officials placing the orders, who received a percentage of the cost as commission from the manufacturers. Few of the weapons themselves were issued to the troops; most remained locked in their arsenals, partly to conceal the scale of fraud and partly to prevent their use by any one of the self-seeking factions that intrigued for power at the court of the Dowager Empress.

This simply emphasised the official attitude that the Army was a necessary evil that must never be allowed to become powerful enough to threaten the internal status quo. It consisted of three major elements, the first of which were the Manchu Bannermen, some 460,000 strong, who provided the Household Guard and various other divisional-sized forces including the Peking Gendarmerie. A curious feature of the Banners, as these formations were known, was that they were hereditary, being descended from the Manchurian units that had brought the ruling dynasty to power two centuries earlier. Anyone between the ages of 16 and 60 who was eligible for membership of a Banner could draw pay and rations and thus had a vested interest in preserving the power of the ruling family. In this sense the Banners could be regarded as completely reliable insofar as palace politics were concerned, but in the overall military context they were all but useless.

Much the same could be said of the Green Flag regiments, which approximated to a gendarmerie raised locally by provincial governors. These may have numbered as many as 500,000 men, although mandarins and senior officers undoubtedly drew the pay of soldiers who existed only on paper. The best men in these units were creamed off into what were known as the New Formations, which were better armed and considered second only in status to the Bannermen. There were, however, difficulties in getting these troops to serve outside their own provinces and to resolve this problem the Regular Army contained a further element, the 30,000-strong Fighting Braves, recruited mainly from Moslem volunteers in Kansu Province, whose primary function seems to have been the suppression of civil disorders; in the opinion of many, they were little better than a rabble of armed bully-boys.

Finally, a Tibetan and Mongolian militia of unknown strength was available to support and reinforce the regular troops. Although, in theory, the Imperial Government could field some 1,750,000 men, it was incapable of maintaining anything like that number.

After the debacle of 1895, attempts were made by some of the more conscientious army commanders, notably those of the Guards, the Self-Strengthening, the Pacification and the Tenacious Armies, to create balanced formations of infantry, cavalry, artillery and engineers, uniformed and trained along European lines. To this end, Western instructors were engaged, only to find they faced an impossible task. Soldiering was regarded as a despised profession, so it was hardly surprising that the junior commissioned ranks were lazy, incompetent, more interested in their privileges than their duties, and as corrupt as the system that produced them. Some formations had been issued with modern artillery and machine-guns, while others had not; it mattered little, since the budget did not allow for live ammunition training anyway. The range of personal weapons extended from halberds, swords and bows to muskets and the latest Mauser rifles, with little attempt at standardisation. The men themselves, ill-disciplined and disinterested, simply reflected the manner in which they were led and their conditions of service. The irony was that the Chinese, properly led, made excellent soldiers; the British-officered 1st Chinese Regiment, raised to protect the Royal Navy's base at Wei-hai-wei in 1898, was highly regarded for its drill, turnout and standard of marksmanship.

The fact was that ever since the Opium Wars of 1839 and 1856, it had become clear that the Imperial Chinese Army was incapable of fighting a modern war. The Powers of the time, which by 1900 included Great Britain, France, Germany, Austria-Hungary, Russia, Italy, the United States and Japan, used the Empire's weakness to extract one concession after another in a highly competitive game. As far as trade was concerned, this meant that they could purchase raw materials at very favourable prices and simultaneously flood the Chinese market with their own goods, causing deep resentment among local manufacturers. The Treaty Ports swarmed with adventurers and soldiers of fortune from all over the world, eager to exploit the system and amass fortunes in the process. Even the construction of railways, though a symbol of progress, had adverse effects, since it deprived thousands of boatmen and carters of their traditional living. What undoubtedly annoyed the Chinese most, however, were the activities of Christian missionaries, on whose behalf their respective governments had secured still more concessions. On its own, the sight of well-meaning Anglican, Roman Catholic and Protestant missionaries locked in a vigorous contest for converts, yet apparently preaching the same Gospel, might have appealed to the Chinese sense of humour. The truth was, however, that Christianity, while admittedly benevolent, was not compatible with such Confucian concepts as ancestor worship; and no one who had climbed a rung or two on the complex ladder of the Chinese Establishment was inclined to favour a creed preaching equality.

It was ironic, therefore, that a situation had arisen in which the Dowager Empress's government could largely gloss over its own shortcomings and attribute all China's ills to foreign influences. Such excuses were accepted by a large proportion of the population, and especially by an extreme nationalist secret society called the I Ho Ch'uan or Fists of Righteous Harmony, better known in the West as the Boxers because of the nature of the callisthenic exercises that formed part of their rituals. Even today, very little is known about their origins, although the society may have developed as part of a clandestine resistance movement to the Manchus, who, despite their long tenure of the throne, were regarded by most Chinese as foreigners. By the end of the Nineteenth Century the Boxers' hatred had been extended not only to all foreigners, but also to Chinese Christians and any Chinese in foreign employ, these categories being defined respectively as First, Second and Third Class Devils. The movement's greatest appeal lay among peasant farmers and discharged soldiers. Violence formed an essential part of its philosophy, its followers believing that their rituals gave them an immunity against the weapons of their enemies. Very little is known about its numbers, although they were clearly extensive, or of its hierarchy and organisation, or of its links with the Imperial Court and the Army, which obviously existed. The Dowager Empress's attitude to the Boxers was ambivalent, but by the end of 1899 she had evidently decided that, unofficially at least, they could be used to render the presence of foreigners in China as unpleasant and dangerous as possible. In this respect she was undoubtedly influenced by Prince Tuan, the father of the Heir Apparent, who was in turn opposed by General Jung Lu, the Commander-in-Chief of the Northern Armies, on the grounds that armed intervention by the Powers to restore order would have disastrous consequences for the Dynasty. For the moment, however, it was the arguments of Prince Tuan that prevailed.

Murderous attacks on Christian missionaries and their converts began almost at once, accompanied by widespread destruction of foreign property, including the hated railways. By the spring of 1900 the Boxers were in control of large areas of the countryside and were converging on Peking. At first the diplomatic corps in the city, used to the unsettled state of the country, was complacent and merely lodged protests with the Tsungli Yamen, the

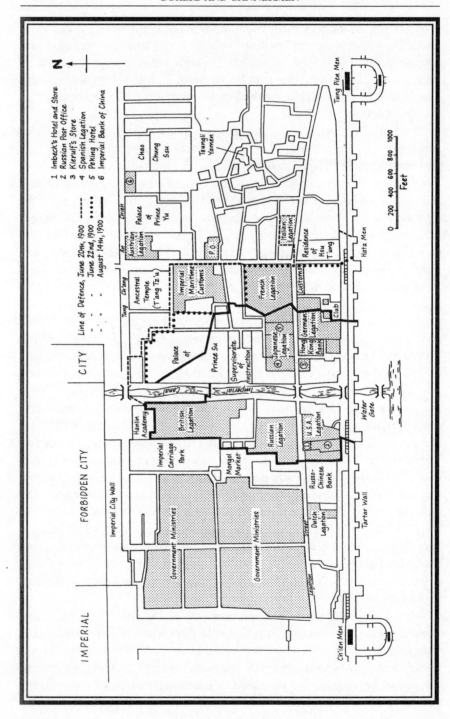

Chinese Foreign Ministry, confident that the outbreak would either burn itself out or be brought under control. The outrages, however, became more widespread and on 26 May the legation ministers, having consulted their own governments, asked the Yamen's permission to summon guards from their respective warships lying off the mouth of the Pei-ho River in the Gulf of Chihli. The Yamen's response was that such a step was not necessary and a few young Bannermen were despatched to the Legation Quarter. Understandably, these were not considered to be adequate protection and on 30 May the ministers repeated their request. Reluctantly, the Yamen consented, specifying that no more than 30 soldiers would be permitted at each location, a restriction with which the Powers had no intention of complying. The largest contingent, consisting mainly of marines and sailors, arrived on the evening of 31 May and was followed by a smaller party on 3 June. The legations now had 452 men, including 22 officers, available for their defence, this total consisting of 37 Austrians, 78 French, 52 Germans, 81 British, 41 Italians, 25 Japanese, 81 Russians and 56 Americans.

As yet, the troops had no common purpose and tended to regard each other with the same suspicion as their political masters. The British contingent, for example, was to have been 100 strong but was reduced to the same number as the Russians to save the face of the latter's commanding officer. Of those present, only the US Marines, fresh from the war in the Philippines, and the few Japanese who had served in the recent war against China, had any experience of active service. The Royal Marines brought with them an elderly four-barrelled Nordenfeldt that jammed during every cycle, the Austrians had a 1pdr Maxim for which there were only 120 rounds, and the Americans had a Colt Model 1895 light machine-gun, efficient but inclined to overheat and run away after sustained firing. The Russians, conforming to the contemporary standard of Tsarist bumbledom, reached Peking with a quantity of 9pdr shells only to discover that the gun itself had been left behind on the platform at Tientsin railway station. All in all, this was not an ideal force with which to defend an area that was basically indefensible, the less so when a French and an Italian officer, with 30 French and eleven Italian marines, were detached to defend the Roman Catholic Peit'ang Cathedral on the other side of the city.

Peking at this period consisted of not one but several walled cities, the major portions of which were the contiguous Chinese City to the south and the Tartar City to the north, the latter being surrounded by a thick battlemented wall some 40 feet high. Inside the Tartar City was the Imperial City and inside this was the Forbidden City, containing the Emperor's palace. The Legation Quarter, approximately 1500 yards square and bisected by a canal running from north to south, lay between the southern walls of the Imperial and Tartar Cities.

Meanwhile, the situation in and around Peking continued to deteriorate rapidly. On 9 June the Boxers burned down the grandstand and other buildings at the racecourse. Sir Claude MacDonald, the British Minister, telegraphed Vice Admiral Sir Edward Seymour, the senior naval officer with the warships off the Pei-ho, requesting the immediate despatch of reinforcements. Seymour quickly assembled a 2000-strong multi-national force and left Tientsin by rail the following morning, expecting to complete the 90-mile journey to Peking that evening. Repeatedly delayed by deliberately damaged track and clashes with large groups of Boxers, he had only reached Lang Fang, 40 miles short of Peking, by nightfall on the 11th. Warned by his scouts that resistance ahead was stiffening, he decided to remain where he was for the moment and send back one of his trains for further supplies. The train returned empty on the 15th with news that the track between Yangts'un and Tientsin had again been destroyed. Seymour, now hampered by wounded and running short of food and ammunition, was therefore compelled to conduct a difficult retreat through hostile territory in which units of the Imperial Army had now begun to side openly with the Boxers. The trains had to be abandoned at Yangts'un, where the railway bridge over the Pei-ho had been seriously damaged. The withdrawal continued on foot and by commandeered junk until it reached the Imperial arsenal at Hsiku, just short of Tientsin, on 22 June. Here, having driven out the small Chinese garrison, Seymour decided to halt and await relief, taking advantage of the stored arms, ammunition and rations.

Much had happened in Tientsin since he left for Peking. On 15 June the Boxers occupied the Chinese quarter of the city and two days later they mounted a sustained attack on the International Settlement. Offshore, the senior Allied naval officers had already agreed that possession of Tientsin was essential to future operations and on 17 June the Taku Forts, covering the mouth of the Pei-ho, were bombarded and stormed by landing parties. By 23 June the Allies had fought their way up-river to relieve the International Settlement. In the meantime, an Englishman, James Watts, and three Cossacks had made an extremely courageous ride from Hsiku to Taku on 20 June, passing through the entire enemy army, and informed the Allies of the plight of Seymour and his men. On 26 June a Cossack relief force broke through to Hsiku but, in the light of China's formal declaration of war on the 21st, no further attempt to reach Peking could be made before the arrival of the international reinforcements now converging on the Gulf of Chihli.

126

Very little of these events was known to those in the Legation Quarter at Peking, for on 10 June contact with the outside world was severed by the cutting of the telegraph line. The following day Mr Sugiyama, the Japanese Chancellor, left the Quarter for the railway station, hoping to meet the first of Seymour's trains. On the way he was dragged from his cart and hacked to death, almost certainly by Chinese regular soldiers. On 15 June the Boxers began rampaging through the Chinese City, setting fire to every shop that transacted business with foreigners. Very soon, the conflagrations raged out of control, dense clouds of black smoke billowing over the Tartar Wall. Several sorties were made by legation guards to rescue trapped Christians, leading to armed confrontations with the Boxers, a number of whom were killed. Despite this, the attitude of the Imperial Government remained placatory and even apologetic; the hooligans, it claimed, would soon be dispersed and all would return to normal. Then, on 19 June, the Minister at each Legation was handed a note from the Tsungli Yamen, now headed by the fervently nationalist Prince Tuan. It stated that, because of Allied aggression at Taku, the Imperial Government could no longer guarantee the safety of the diplomats and demanded that they, their staffs and the legation guards should vacate Peking by four o'clock the following afternoon and proceed under escort to Tientsin. The reference to Taku, of course, meant nothing to the Ministers but after prolonged discussion they despatched a reply agreeing with the demand in principle but requesting a meeting with the Tsungli Yamen next morning to arrange a delay in their departure. Only the German Minister, Baron Klemens von Ketteler, a former soldier, brave but impatient and blunt to the point of rudeness, was for rejecting the note.

The proposed meeting was to have taken place at 0900 but, no reply to the Ministers' response having been received 30 minutes after that time, von Ketteler decided to visit the Tsungli Yamen himself, contrary to the advice of his colleagues. His chair was stopped by a Bannerman who shot him dead, snatched his watch and disappeared into the crowd. One curious aspect of the murder was that it was reported in Chinese and European newspapers several days before it took place, which in itself suggests a planned assassination and widespread foreknowledge. Whatever the truth, the effect was to inject some iron into the Ministers' decision-making. It was unanimously agreed that the as the Yamen's proffered safe conduct clearly amounted to nothing more than an invitation to their own massacre, those in the Legation Quarter would remain where they were and fight it out until help arrived. Promptly at 1600 the Chinese opened fire.

Until this moment comparatively little had been done to prepare the Legation Quarter for war. It possessed no obvious defensive features save the adjacent sector of the Tartar Wall, the loss of which would render the entire area untenable. In other respects, the garrison would be forced to rely on makeshift barricades constructed from carts, barrels and sandbags, and loopholed walls covering every approach. The various national contingents each had their own areas of responsibility, although in emergencies troops from any of them could be rushed to a threatened point. The British and French defended their respective legations and, together with the Austrians, provided a mobile reserve. The Americans, Germans and Russians also defended their own legations as well as the vital Tartar Wall. The responsibility of the Japanese and Italians was the Su Wang Fu, the palace and grounds of a Chinese nobleman, broadly occupying the north-eastern sector of the defences. Four Legations, those of Austria, Belgium, Holland and Italy, lay outside the chosen perimeter and were abandoned at once.

Large numbers of European and Chinese Christian refugees had been reaching the Legation Quarter and the Peit'ang Cathedral for some time. Of these approximately 125 men, of whom more than half had had some previous military experience, volunteered to serve with the troops. Civilian males were drafted onto committees that had been formed to regulate such diverse matters as rations, fuel, water, sanitation, fire defence and Chinese labour. Simultaneously, their womenfolk established a nursing service and used their sewing machines to manufacture thousands of sandbags from sacking, blankets and even dress material. There were plenty of fresh water wells and, thanks to the presence of two commercial stores within the Quarter, and the discovery of 230 tons of government grain in a warehouse, food was never to be a problem, save for the 2700 Chinese refugees, who received little or no rations and were ultimately forced to feed themselves on dogs, rats, rubbish and roots. Despite this, the Chinese, most of whom squatted in the Su Wang Fu, were expected to earn their sometimes dubious protection by providing burial and working parties.

The question of command almost resulted in a disaster before the siege was three days old. Captain von Thomann, commander of the Austrian cruiser *Zenta*, was the senior serving officer present and claimed overall command as his right. Unfortunately, whatever his merits as a seaman may have been, he was no soldier. During the morning of 23 June he misinterpreted an increase in the volume of Chinese fire as a prelude to an all-out attack and issued orders for all contingents to fall back to the last line of defence in the British Legation. The withdrawal was made quietly and without panic, and it was probably for this reason alone that the Chinese did not follow it up and administer the coup de grâce. The troops were chased back to the perimeter by their own horrified Ministers who then unanimously agreed that Thomann had lost his head and should be relieved at once. In his place they appointed Sir Claude MacDonald as Commander-in-Chief, partly because of his pre-eminent position in the diplomatic corps and partly because of his previous military experience, which included the 1882 campaign against Arabi Pasha in Egypt and the hard-fought battles of Tamai and El Teb during the Dervish Wars.

The appointment was not universally popular. The Americans thought that his manner was far too superior, a contemporary criticism often levelled at the upper class British abroad, but obeyed his orders through their own officers. Lieutenant Baron von Raden of the Russian contingent, jealous of Russian standing in relation to the British, was far from pleased by the appointment but, being seriously outranked, was forced to accept that it was necessary. In the event MacDonald exercised command with tact and understanding, appreciating that his own experience counted for little in the sort of brutal, bloody street fighting that was taking place, yet offering the moral support of an older soldier to the permanently tired junior officers and NCOs who commanded detachments around the perimeter.

The fighting from 23 to 25 June was some of the fiercest of the entire siege. Boxers and Chinese regulars pressed their attacks all round the perimeter, the former being identifiable by the red headbands or sashes that served them in lieu of uniform. They quickly realised that massed headlong assaults served only to pile up casualties in the confined streets and resorted to advancing behind movable barricades in the shelter of which they erected more permanent structures, slowly tightening their grip on the core defences. It was fortunate that, thanks to its lack of training, the Chinese artillery was largely ineffective, most of its shells passing over their intended targets. On the 23rd the Chinese, taking advantage of a strong northerly wind, sought to render the British Legation untenable by setting fire to the adjacent Han-lin Library, containing thousands of irreplaceable manuscripts. The flames spread to neighbouring houses but the legation itself was saved by the incessant work of bucket chains, labouring under constant fire.

The 24th was marked by a series of successful Allied counter-attacks. Attacking westwards along the 52-foot wide Tartar Wall the Americans pushed back the Chinese the better part of a half-mile. To the east the Germans went in with the bayonet, killing an entire unit of Bannermen, whose bodies were left lying in the street as a warning to anyone else who wanted to try conclusions. In the Fu the Japanese and Italians feigned a retreat which drew crowds of exultant, screaming Boxers onto a killing ground where they were shot down in droves. Nearby, a seven-strong party of Royal Marines, led by Captain Lewis Halliday, made a sortie to tackle Boxers who were attacking the western wall of the British Legation. In an alley the party suddenly came face to face with five Boxers, all of whom were armed with rifles. In the exchange one of the Marines was mortally wounded and Halliday was shot through the left shoulder and lung at close range. He responded by shooting four of his opponents with his revolver, the fifth escaping round a corner when the weapon misfired. A second sortie, this time in greater strength, captured and demolished a small building from which the Boxers had been firing, and in so doing cleared the field of fire from the legation wall. For his part in the action Halliday, whose wound kept him in hospital for the remainder of the siege, was awarded the Victoria Cross.

After a week's fighting the garrison's casualties amounted to a score of men killed and the same number wounded, a rate of attrition that obviously could not be sustained for long. This in itself was cause for serious concern, especially as all hope of Seymour's column reaching the city had long since evaporated. On the other hand, the morale of the troops had actually risen. They had seen the sort of treatment accorded by the Boxers to their prisoners and knew that they were fighting not only for their own survival but also for that of the Legation Quarter's women and children; if they needed any reminder, it was provided by the head of a Professor James, a civilian captured during the first days of the siege, which stared blankly at them across the lines from the top of a pole. The various contingents, too, had begun to develop a mutual confidence in each other as day followed day.

Disaster came close to striking on 1 July. A surprise attack forced the Germans off the eastern end of the Tartar Wall and the Americans, taken in rear, were forced to conform. Once again, the Chinese failed to follow up their success. During the day Captain J.T. Myers, the American commander, was able to recapture his own position with a combined American, British and Russian force, and construct a barricade to protect its rear. Simultaneously, the French were almost forced out of their legation but recovered it with a counter-attack, while in the Fu an Italian sortie to capture an enemy field gun failed with some loss of life.

At the western end of the Tartar Wall the Chinese had begun building a timber tower which would enable them to fire down into the American sector. This was captured during the early hours of 3 July by British and American marines. Myers was wounded in the attack and command of the American contingent devolved upon his Second-in-Command, Captain N. Hall, who is described as being neither effective nor popular with his men.

On 7 July the defenders had a stroke of luck. Some Chinese Christians, digging a trench, uncovered a small muzzle-loading rifled cannon, a relic of the Second Opium War, of more or less the same calibre as the Russians' 9pdr shells. These were already being used by two ingenious artificers, Armourer's Mate Thomas, Royal Navy, and Gunner's Mate Mitchell, US Marines, to refill the Italians' expended 1pdr shell cases, which were then topped-off with scrap metal to create an elementary but effective canister round. Now, the two devoted their attention to modifying the 9pdr shells to fit the bore of their latest acquisition, for which the Italian weapon's spare carriage had been brought into service. This involved splitting the composite round and loading the propellant first, followed by the projectile. The gun, referred to variously as Old Betsy, The Dowager Empress or the International Gun, went into action next day against a Chinese battery 300 yards distant. Her first round was high and actually burst in the Imperial City, an event that must have caused considerable pleasure in the Legation Quarter; her second was short; but her third was exactly on target.

By now the Chinese had accepted the futility of further frontal assaults and resorted to continuous sniping and tunnelling under the perimeter defences to plant explosive mines. Their snipers were surprisingly efficient and began to notch up an unacceptable tally of kills. On the night of 12 July Hall positioned one of his marines, Private Dan Daly, in an advanced position on the Tartar Wall with the specific task of containing this menace while a working party strengthened the defences. Daly had only joined the Marine Corps a year earlier but he was a crack shot and a born fighter with a strong killer instinct. During the first hour he shot eight of the enemy. For 30 minutes there was silence, then six Boxers charged out of the darkness towards him. He dropped three, butt-stroked one and bayoneted two. Settling down, he methodically surveyed the enemy position for signs of movement and picked off three more. He was then attacked by four men, three of whom fell to his rifle and the fourth to his bayonet. Altogether, Daly was attacked eight times during the night and in the intervals between he continued to shorten the lives of those behind the Chinese barricade. Curiously, the Boxer attacks were made with swords, spears and knives; only once was a firearm used – its owner missed and was not given a second chance. By dawn, the American working party had finished its task and Daly crawled back to the shelter of the Marine barricade, leaving the Wall littered with bodies. His achievement was rewarded with the Congressional Medal of Honor. Yet it was not for this, nor for a second Medal of Honor he won in 1915 in Haiti, that he is best remembered in the US Marine Corps' Hall of Fame. It was for a shouted command given when, as a hard-bitten sergeant, he led his platoon into action in the teeth of German machine-gun fire at Belleau Wood in June 1918: 'Come on, you bastards – d'you want to live forever?'

On 13 July the Chinese exploded a mine beneath the French Legation, killing two sailors and starting a fire. Three days later Captain B.M. Strouts, commanding the Royal Marines, was killed while some of his men were relieving the exhausted Japanese in the Fu. This steady trickle of casualties continued to erode the strength of the garrison; MacDonald, depressed by the loss of Strouts, doubted whether they could hold out until the end of the month. Had he but known it, the British press had already published a sensational account of the Legation Quarter's last hours, and *The Times* went so far as to print his own obituary. Nor, isolated as he was from the outside world, could he have known that sufficient Allied troops had been landed for the native city of Tientsin to be finally stormed.

This caused serious alarm within the Imperial Government, where disillusion with the Boxers had begun to take root. Obviously, grave miscalculations had been made and corrective measures must be taken as a measure of urgency. The same afternoon that MacDonald began to ponder how much longer the defence could last, he and the other ministers received conciliatory notes from the Tsungli Yamen. The following day a cease-fire was agreed by MacDonald and representatives of General Jung Lu.

During the truce a series of messages was received from the Tsungli Yamen, simultaneously threatening yet expressing concern for the ministers and their staffs, who were again urged to depart for the safety of Tientsin. These invitations were declined. The garrison's spirits rose when a Japanese agent worked his way through the lines with details of the Allied victory at Tientsin and the promise that a strong column was marching to the relief of the Legation Quarter. They fell again when, as day followed day, the column failed to appear. A trade in eggs, fruit and tobacco developed between the besiegers and the besieged and at one point the Dowager Empress sent in several carts containing rice, melons and ice.

The ambivalent attitude of the Chinese began to harden as the days passed without any sign of an Allied advance from Tientsin. The reason was that, because of the destruction of the railway, the relief force would have to rely on its own transport and it was taking far longer than had been expected to round up the necessary carts and pack animals. Cease-fire violations became more frequent as time passed, accompanied by the usual expressions of venomous courtesy. The Imperial Government, for example, having learned of the death of the then Duke of Edinburgh, sent MacDonald its formal note of condolence; barely had he finished reading this when his bedroom was wrecked by the explosion of a Chinese shell!

The apparent inactivity of the Allies at Tientsin strengthened the hand of the war party in the intrigues that surrounded the Dowager Empress, the result being the beheading of some of the moderate mandarins who had been instrumental in arranging the cease-fire. When, on 4 August, the relief force finally left Tientsin, the enraged reactionaries evidently attempted to save face by ordering the destruction of the Legation Quarter. Fighting was renewed at once and raged with increasing ferocity in the Fu, around the gutted Han-lin Library, and in the Mongol Market to the west of the British Legation.

The relief force, commanded by Lieutenant General Sir Alfred Gaselee, contained over 18,000 men (approximately 2900 British, Indian and Chinese, 2200 Americans, 9000 Japanese, 2900 Russians and 1200 French) and 70 guns. It fought its way through one Chinese position at Peits'ang on 5 August, and then another at Yangts'un the following day. After that, the enemy's resistance seemed to crumble, although the intense heat in which the march was conducted began to take its toll. By 8 August a handful of courageous couriers had succeeded in establishing contact between the relief force and the defenders of the Legation Quarter. That evening MacDonald received an encouraging message from Gaselee saying that the latter had reached Tsai Tsun, approximately halfway between Tientsin and Peking. Of greater operational use was the message sent by the commander of the Japanese division, Major General Fukushima, to Colonel Shiba, commander of the Japanese Legation guards, since it estimated that the relief force would reach Peking on 13 or 14 August. Simultaneously, Gaselee received a map of Peking drawn by MacDonald, showing the Allied positions in the Legation Quarter and the points at which entry to the city could be best effected. The question of national prestige having already begun to intrude upon inter-Allied cooperation, Gaselee decided to keep this information to himself as long as possible.

On 12 August those on the Tartar Wall observed large numbers of Chinese troops leaving the city. Despite this, the assault on the Legation Quarter was renewed with unparalleled ferocity the following day. Thus far, anxious to preserve his ammunition stocks, MacDonald had placed strict limitations on the use of automatic weapons, but with relief so close and the defences coming under intense pressure, he was obviously not inclined to grant the enemy an eleventh-hour victory. The Americans' Colt and the Austrians' Maxim were therefore allowed to rattle away until the Chinese guns had been neutralised; they may, too, have contributed to a noticeable reluctance on the part of the enemy infantry to mount their usual frenzied attacks.

The sounds of the battle around the Legation Quarter were clearly audible as the relief force closed in on Peking from the east. A plan had been agreed for the assault on the Tartar City, but the details of this were quickly submerged when, eager for the prestige of being the first to enter, the national contingents surged forward during the early hours of 14 August. The Americans, French, Japanese and Russians immediately became involved in heavy and prolonged fighting around the various gates on the eastern and southern sections of the Tartar Wall. The British, however, had the benefit of Gaselee's map and a returned businessman to guide them through the warren of the Chinese City. As soon as they came within view of the walls one of the garrison's sailors was seen signalling with semaphore flags: 'Come in by the water gate'. This was the opening through which the canal bisecting the Legation Quarter left the Tartar City. At about 1430 some 70 men of the 7th Rajputs dashed across the moat under sporadic fire from the Hata Men Gate to their right. With the assistance of the American Marines within,

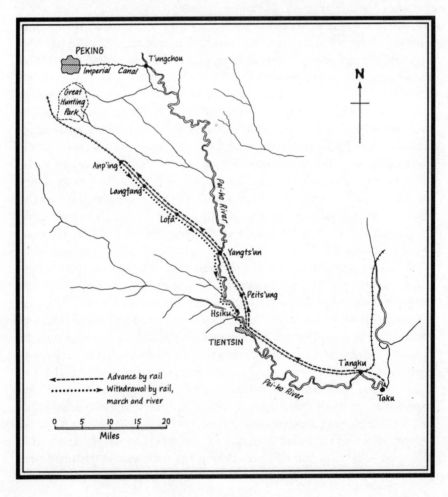

they broke through the grating covering the entrance and, wading through the mud, slime and sewage, clambered up the banks of the canal to the cheers of the Europeans and delighted applause from the Chinese refugees. The Americans and French broke through an hour later but elsewhere the Japanese and Russians both incurred over 100 casualties overcoming determined resistance that lasted until nightfall.

Few had expected that the isolated Peit'ang Cathedral, containing 3900 refugees guarded by only 43 French and Italian sailors, would survive the siege, yet day after day those in the Legation Quarter had listened to the continued sounds of battle from that direction. The soul of the defence had been a young French naval officer, Ensign Paul Henry, who had conducted a most aggressive resistance. Perpetually short of ammunition, he insisted that his men made every round count and such was the force of his personality that during one Boxer attack two volleys, amounting to 58 rounds, left 43 of the enemy sprawled dead in front of the barricades. Throughout the siege the Chinese shelled the enclosure heavily, and they exploded several mines beneath the defences, one of which killed 136 people. From time to time Henry tried to establish contact with the Legation Quarter but all of his Chinese Christian messengers were caught, their heads being derisively exhibited on poles for his benefit. He had not expected to survive the siege and was killed by a sniper on 30 July. Command devolved on an even younger Italian officer, Midshipman Olivieri, who was buried alive for several hours by the explosion of a mine on 12 August. To the annoyance of the French, the Peit'ang enclosure was relieved by the Japanese on the morning of 16 August.

By then, the Imperial Family had considered that the wisest course of action would be to leave Peking. On the 15th they left the Forbidden City on what was called, for the sake of face, a Tour of Inspection, and did not return until January 1902. Prior to leaving, the Pearl Concubine, the Emperor's favourite, had the temerity to suggest that she and the Emperor should remain in Peking. Hard though times might suddenly have become for the Manchus, the Dowager Empress was as intolerant of argument as ever and ordered the palace eunuchs to fling the unfortunate woman down a well.

The defence of the Legation Quarter and the Peit'ang cost the various Allied detachments 64 killed and 156 wounded, which might be regarded as modest in the circumstances. The heaviest loss fell on the French, with 16 killed and 45 wounded, but casualties among the 25-strong Japanese contingent actually exceeded 100 per cent with five killed and the remainder wounded, some more than once. Of the civilian occupants of the Western and Japanese legations, twelve were killed and 23 wounded. No record exists of casualties among the Chinese refugees, which may have been as high as 1,000, including deaths caused by enemy action, starvation and disease. Likewise, it is impossible to assess the losses inflicted on the Boxers and the Imperial Army, although these were undoubtedly severe.

To Chinese eyes, the Allies did everything possible to justify their reputation as savage barbarians, thoroughly looting Peking and holding their victory parade in the Forbidden City. At the end of September, having been joined by the German East Asia Brigade, the Allies marched through northern China eliminating the last pockets of Boxer resistance. The Germans, encouraged in an unfortunate speech of the Kaiser's to behave as the Huns had done, spread terror wherever they went and thus handed their opponents in future wars a propaganda victory. The Chinese authorities, having found the Boxers useless, had no further use for them and either decapitated them themselves or handed them over to the Allies for execution; undoubtedly, many old scores were paid off in this way, and many who died had no connection with the Boxers whatever.

In December formal peace negotiations began. At a diplomatic dinner even those whose professional stock in trade was ringing insincerity must have choked on their port to hear the Imperial Government's representative thank the Allies for their timely assistance in its hour of need. In the end, further humiliating concessions were extracted from the Chinese, who were also required to pay the Allies a total indemnity of £67.5 million.

The defence of the Legation Quarter and its relief was a unique and brief episode of rare international cooperation necessitated by force of circumstances. As soon as the so-called Boxer Rebellion was over, the Powers resumed their previous stance of intense rivalry. In 1904 Russia and Japan became involved in an all-out war; ten years later most of the Powers who had fought as allies in China were at each others' throats.

Of the principal players in this strange episode, the Dowager Empress and the Emperor died mysteriously within a day of each other in 1908. Aged two, Pu Yi, the new Emperor, clambered briefly onto the throne of his ancestors but following a revolution in 1911 China became a republic. Sir Claude MacDonald was rewarded with the post of Ambassador to Japan; when he died in 1915 *The Times* used verbatim sections of the premature obituary it had printed in 1900. Halliday became a full general and was at one time the oldest surviving holder of the VC. Seymour, despite the failure of his expedition, later became an Admiral of the Fleet. Many of the minor players would achieve fame in later life. The defences of the International Settlement at Tientsin, for example, were laid out by a young American engineer named Herbert Hoover who would one day become President of the United States. Serving as Seymour's Chief of Staff was a Captain John Jellicoe who would command the Grand Fleet at the Battle of Jutland. Also present with the Seymour expedition was another future commander of the Grand Fleet, Commander David Beatty, who had recently commanded a Nile river gunboat at the Battle of Omdurman; and, commanding the destroyer HMS *Fame* in the Gulf of Chihli was Lieutenant Roger Keyes, who was to lead the raid on Zeebrugge in 1918 and become Chief of Combined Operations in the Second World War.

8

The Lost Battalion: the Argonne Forest, 2–7 October 1918

By the autumn of 1918 the Allied armies had begun to advance steadily all along the Western Front. All, save one, were utterly wearied by four years of continuous slaughter and were very close to the limit of their manpower resources, their understrength ranks being filled with older men and young conscripts. The French, driven too far, had mutinied the previous year and the British, sickened by the bloodbaths of the Somme and the Ypres Salient, had developed a deeply cynical attitude towards their leaders. At last, however, victory seemed to be within their grasp and this spurred them to make one final, decisive effort that would put an end to their collective misery.

The exception was General John J. Pershing's recently formed First United States Army. What made the Americans different was their physique and, above all, their enthusiasm. American columns, consisting entirely of healthy volunteers of prime military age, swung purposefully up to the front in a manner that had not been seen since the heady, idealistic days of August 1914.

The pre-war strength of the US Army had been tiny and since the American declaration of war it had expanded at such a rate that its growth had outstripped its equipment procurement programme. Nevertheless, so anxious had the British and French been that American formations should take the field that they had willingly made good the shortfall, supplying tanks, artillery, machine-guns, steel helmets and many other items.

On 26 September the US First Army, with the French Fourth Army on its left, opened what became known as the Meuse-Argonne offensive. The task of the Americans was to clear the Argonne Forest, a heavily wooded area broken by steep-sided ridges and sharply incised ravines. At this period the German Army, though disillusioned by the failure of the spring offensives that it had been promised would bring victory, and demoralised by successive defeats, had recovered some of its fighting spirit and was determined to keep the enemy out of its homeland. In the Argonne it was holding positions ideally suited for defence, employing machine-gun posts with interlocking arcs of fire, together with barbed wire entanglements and chicken wire fences cunningly strung to create killing grounds in the dense undergrowth, which itself reduced an attacker's visibility to a few yards. After a few days of this sort of difficult forest fighting, in which contact with neighbouring units was almost impossible, Pershing gave orders that advances were to be continued 'without regard of losses and without regard to the exposed condition of the flanks'. As a direct result of these instructions a situation arose from which grew one of the war's most remarkable stories, the legend of the Lost Battalion, although the troops involved knew exactly where they were and were not, in the strict sense, a battalion at all.

On the extreme left of the advancing American line was Major General Robert Alexander's 77th Division, recruited from New Yorkers of many different national origins. Early on the morning of 2 October Alexander gave orders for a general advance along the divisional front, setting the objective as the east-west La Viergette – Moulin de Charlevaux road. Following an artillery barrage the division moved forward on a two-brigade frontage with 153rd Brigade right and 154th Brigade left. The former was quickly checked by heavy fire from high ground to its front, but 154th Brigade made steady progress, pushing back the enemy slowly.

Leading the brigade advance was 1/308th Infantry, commanded by Major Charles Whittlesey, a tall, serious, bespectacled Wall Street lawyer known to his men as Bird Legs. A deep, precipitously sided ravine filled with brush ran diagonally across the battalion's line of advance, splitting the battalion with A, B and C Companies to the right of the obstacle and D Company to the left. Following up was 2/308th, commanded by Captain George G. McMurtry, another lawyer but one who had previously served with Theodore Roosevelt's Rough Riders at San Juan Hill during the Spanish-American War. Conforming to Whittlesey, McMurtry had his E, G and H Companies to the right of the ravine and F Company to the left. Attached to both battalions were detachments from C and D Companies 306th Machine Gun Battalion.

The 308th Infantry had already been in action during the six preceding days and both Whittlesey and McMurtry were operating well below half their established strength. While they were fighting their way forward they incurred a further 90 casualties, but captured 30 prisoners and three machine-guns.

'Upon reaching the objective', wrote Alexander, 'a position for the night was taken up. This position was about five hundred metres east of the Moulin de Charlevaux, on a steep bank which runs down from the road to the bottom of the ravine. The machine-gun sections were placed on the flanks of the line and the left flank was refused somewhat with a view to securing what was considered the most dangerous quarter. The men, of course, dug fox-holes and prepared to hold their positions as directed.'

The two battalion commanders had some 550 men with them, holding an oval area 350 yards long and 70 yards deep. From this a series of runner posts was set up to carry messages back to the main American line. Both battalion commanders were anxious about D and F Companies, which were out of contact and still on the wrong side of the ravine. As yet, neither felt that they were in any immediate danger and both believed that the American advance would catch up with them on the morrow.

In fact, theirs had been the only successful advance along the entire corps front and, to their left, the French had also failed to win any ground. Furthermore, after dark the Germans began infiltrating back into the trench line the Americans had overrun, dispersing the runner posts and reoccupying it in strength. Meanwhile, Alexander, aware of the gap that had opened between his left and the French, ordered two battalions, 3/307th and 3/308th, to swing half-left and establish a line between them and Whittlesey. The move, carried out after dark in the confusing forest landscape with intermittent contact with the enemy, only resulted in muddle. Dawn on 3 October found both battalions scattered and in the wrong place, but at about 0700 Captain Nelson M. Holderman's 82-strong K Company of the 307th worked its way into Whittlesey's perimeter.

Whittlesey had already sent out E Company, commanded by Lieutenant Karl Wilhelm, to contact D and F Companies and bring them in. Heavy firing quickly indicated that Wilhelm had run into trouble. Shortly afterwards Lieutenant Lenke arrived back with only nineteen men, to report that they had been ambushed and that the runner posts had gone; Wilhelm, with eighteen more survivors, managed to get across the ravine and reach safety.

It was now evident to Whittlesey, McMurtry and Holderman that they were cut off. The majority of their men had gone into action with only two days' field rations, much of which had already been consumed. The ammunition state, too, left something to be desired. With Whittlesey's permission, McMurtry circulated the following note to company commanders: 'Our mission is to hold this position at all costs. No falling back. Have this understood by every man in your command'.

Next, Whittlesey summoned Private Omer Richards, who reported with his wicker basket containing eight homing pigeons, some of the 600 supplied by British breeders to the US Army. Whittlesey scribbled notes to Alexander giving his approximate position and requesting ammunition, food and support. Two birds were then released after the messages had been inserted into metal tubes on their legs, and reached the divisional loft safely.

Alexander had already tried to get his brigades moving again at dawn, but a heavy autumn mist hung among the trees and made any form of control, let alone direction keeping, impossible. As one company commander recalled, 'I found myself with two runners adrift in a blind world of whiteness and noise, groping over something like the surface of the moon. One literally could not see two yards and everywhere the ground rose into bare pinnacles and ridges or descended into chasms half-filled with rusty tangles of wire'. The attack stalled, was repeated during the afternoon and stalled again, this time with heavy casualties.

In the meantime the Germans had thrown a girdle around Whittlesey's position, approximately 200 yards out from the perimeter. The defenders began to come under sniper, machine-gun, mortar and artillery fire but succeeded in beating off an attack. By then one third of their number had been killed or wounded and the scant medical supplies had been used up. Whittlesey sent off a third pigeon, requesting that food and ammunition should be dropped by aircraft. After dusk he made his way round the companies, reassuring the wounded and encouraging the rest. After this the general opinion of the troops was that Bird Legs wasn't so bad after all; in fact, he was all right.

During the afternoon Alexander was summoned to the corps headquarters of Lieutenant General Hunter Liggett, where the next phase of the battle was planned. It was here, evidently, that the press learned that a sizeable body of American troops was trapped behind enemy lines and within a day or so reports concerning a Lost Battalion began to circulate in the more popular American newspapers. The phrase is believed to have originated in a cable from a news editor requesting further information. In passing, it is worth mentioning that one of the reporters present was Damon Runyon, later famous for his portraits of New York life. To the public it seemed that if Whittlesey was forced to surrender the enemy could claim a victory, and that was not politically acceptable. Pressure was brought to bear on Pershing himself, who in turn personally urged Alexander to make 'a vigorous attempt' to break through.

On 4 October the US First Army made good progress everywhere save on its left flank. Within the pocket, half of Whittlesey's men had now been killed or wounded. McMurtry, hit in the knee by shell splinters, was still able to hobble around, as was Holderman, who had been wounded three times. The sight of the medical orderlies stripping bandages from those who had died and using them at once on the latest casualties prompted Whittlesey to despatch several more pigeons with the message: 'Situation is cutting into our strength rapidly. Men are suffering from hunger and exposure and the wounded are in a very bad condition. Cannot support be sent at once?' Hour succeeded hour without any sign of relief, punctuated by regular volleys of stick grenades exploding among the American trenches, flung by the enemy on the slopes above.

Worried by the failure of his morning attack, Alexander ordered his divisional artillery to shell the enemy surrounding the pocket. During the afternoon an aircraft flew directly over the trapped Americans and released a flare. Within minutes the number of shells bursting inside the perimeter had increased dramatically, and the source of the majority was clearly American or French.

While casualties continued to mount Whittlesey scribbled in frantic haste: 'Our own artillery is dropping barrages directly on us! For Heaven's sake stop it!' Richards extracted another pigeon from his basket, only to have it break free. There remained only one bird, a black cock named Cher Ami. Richards clipped the message capsule to its leg and let go, but after completing his orientation circles Cher Ami landed on a branch and began preening. Sticks and stones failed to dislodge him. Finally, after the enraged Richards had climbed the tree and shaken his branch, he took off and headed towards his loft. The Germans, well aware of the significance of pigeons, opened fire on him. One bullet removed part of a leg, made a hole through his breastbone and put out an eye. He staggered and began to lose height. Then he recovered and flew on, disappearing far beyond the enemy to the south. Shortly after, the rain of American shells ceased abruptly. This 'friendly fire' incident killed or wounded 80 more of Whittlesey's men; had the message not got through and the bombardment continued it seems probable that the pocket would have been wiped out. As it was, Cher Ami became a national hero. His wounds having been treated and now in honourable retirement, he was taken back to the United States, where he died a year later; suitably preserved and mounted, he can still be seen at the Smithsonian Institution.

An attack was launched on the pocket as soon as the American artillery ceased firing. It was beaten off and when it was dark enough volunteers, ignoring the risk of snipers, made the perilous journey to the turgid stream at the bottom of the ravine to collect water. At about 2100 flares went up all round the perimeter, more grenades landed among the trenches and a voice called for the Americans to surrender. The demand, angrily rejected, was followed by another assault, which was also broken up.

On 5 October an attempt was made to supply the pocket by air. The problem was that the combination of mist, smoke and tree cover made it very difficult for the pilots to identify it from above. One aircraft was lost and such small packages as were dropped fell tantalisingly beyond the perimeter. Enemy activity during the day was confined to hurling grenades, now tied together in bundles for greater effect, down the upper slopes, and sniping. The sound of heavy fighting to the west indicated that the French were gaining ground and hopes of relief began to rise, only to be dashed when the Germans recovered their losses with a prompt counter-attack. A simultaneous attempt by one of 77th Division's regiments to break through was repulsed and Alexander, rapidly losing patience, dismissed the commanding officer of the unit concerned.

The following day also passed without a major attack on the pocket and it began to look as though the enemy had decided to starve the Americans into surrender. Hunger, in fact, had become so intense that many men had resorted to chewing fallen leaves and tree bark. Little or no water could be spared for the groaning wounded who now lay everywhere. That night, however, Whittlesey, lacking any other means of communicating with Alexander, sent back an officer and two men with a situation report. By a combination of stealth and good shooting they got through, bringing with them details of a gap in the German defences, and this priceless information was used in the planning of the next day's attack.

7 October almost saw the pocket overrun. As dawn broke the pangs of hunger became too much for nine men of H Company, who ventured out to recover one of the air-dropped ration packs. The Germans had been waiting for just such an attempt and ambushed them, killing five and capturing the rest. The survivors found themselves in the presence of an English-speaking lieutenant who had spent six years in the United States as the representative of a German tungsten company. He drafted a note for Whittlesey in which he explained that the bearer, Private Lowell R. Hollingshead, had refused to answer his interrogator's questions and was acting under duress, continuing:

'It would be quite useless to resist any more, in view of present conditions. The suffering of your wounded men can be heard over here in the German lines and we are appealing to your humane sentiments to stop. A white flag shown by one of your men will tell us that you agree with these conditions'.

Whittlesey discussed the note with McMurtry and Holderman. McMurtry had a bullet lodged in his shoulder and his knee had festered to the size of a football, so that he could only move with difficulty supported by a stout branch. Holderman had sustained four wounds but could still get about, using two rifles as crutches. The three agreed that no reply was necessary and Whittlesey gave instructions for the white air recognition panels to be taken in lest they be interpreted by the enemy as a surrender signal. When word began to spread around the perimeter that a surrender demand had been received it resulted in a barrage of obscenities being hurled at the German lines.

Having received their answer, the Germans launched a major attack, led by flamethrowers, during the afternoon. A few men, terrified and at the end of their resources, broke and fled before these terrible weapons, only to be halted by Whittlesey and thrown back into the line. Two of the Hotchkiss machine-guns were temporarily lost but a third cut down the flamethrower operators and the heart went out of the attack. Holderman, propped upright on his temporary crutches beside the machine-gunner, was banging away with his Colt .45in automatic pistol, downing his fifth opponent just as he received his fifth wound.

As the attackers faded away the sounds of renewed fighting came from the trees between the pocket and the American front line, but this time it came closer and closer. At length it became clear that the Germans were pulling back to the north, not just because their line had been penetrated by Alexander's renewed attack, but also because advances elsewhere on the American sector had left them outflanked and in danger of being cut off themselves. At about 1900, just as the last of the light was going, a patrol of the 307th Infantry, led by Lieutenant Richard Tillman, made its way into the pocket without encountering any opposition. More and more men from the regiment arrived, willingly distributing their own rations to the starving survivors while the medical orderlies did what they could for the wounded who lay in slit trenches and shellholes everywhere. For the first time since they had arrived, Whittlesey's men enjoyed an undisturbed night's rest.

Alexander walked up to the position early the following morning. and found Whittlesey, gaunt and haggard, still attending to the welfare of his wounded. The meeting between the two was brief, formal, but not lacking in warmth – an exchange of salutes, a handshake and a quiet 'How do you do?'. Alexander was clearly awed as he surveyed the charnel house that had formed the Lost Battalion's position, and Whittlesey was too exhausted to want conversation. After a while, he led out his remaining 194 unwounded men, leaving behind 107 killed and 190 stretcher cases requiring evacuation. Of 63 men there was no trace; they had either been blown to pieces, were prisoners in enemy hands, or were wandering somewhere in the woods, their minds driven beyond the limits of endurance.

If the Lost Battalion had been overrun or forced to surrender there would undoubtedly have been an inquest and the probability is that during the subsequent recriminations Whittlesey himself would have been made the scapegoat, just as the unfortunate Major Reno was after the Custer disaster on the Little Big Horn.[1] As it was, the Army had been provided with a classic example of leadership and dogged determination, and its standing soared. Having consulted with Liggett, Alexander informed Whittesley that he had been promoted to lieutenant colonel, McMurtry to major and that both of them had been awarded the Medal of Honor, as had Holderman.

Whittlesey cared very little about his decoration and on his return home he studiously shunned publicity. A man of conscience, he had fought only because in his eyes not to fight would have been the greater sin. He had hated many of the things he had had to do and sought to make amends by becoming President of the Red Cross Roll Call. Perhaps, for someone of his sensitivity, this was not the right thing to do, for there would be times when, in the course of a week, he would be required to visit severely wounded men in hospital, attend the funerals of two or three veterans and provide comfort for the bereaved. The cumulative effect of this honourable and necessary work was to induce a state of profound depression. In the autumn of 1921 he set his affairs in precise order, boarded a liner bound for Cuba, and jumped overboard to his death.

Notes
1. See *Last Stand*, Chapter 4, The Little Big Horn.

9

A Fondness for the Bayonet: 2nd Hampshires At Tebourba, Tunisia, 30 November – 3 December 1942

The landing of Lieutenant General Kenneth Anderson's Anglo-American First Army in Algeria on 8 November 1942 presented the Axis Powers with a serious problem that demanded an immediate answer. The nub of this was that the remnants of Field Marshal Erwin Rommel's shattered divisions were streaming westwards after their defeat at El Alamein and could not be reinforced rapidly enough to halt the pursuit of the victorious British Eighth Army. If, therefore, the Axis wished to retain a presence in North Africa – and it was strategically essential that they should do so – they would have to create a redoubt into which Rommel could retire, recover his strength and continue the war. Tunisia presented such a redoubt, partly because it offered a conveniently short sea and air passage from Sicily, partly because Anderson's troops had not yet advanced that far east, and partly because the Mareth Line to the south and the mountains to the west provided a series of excellent positions that all but girdled the country.

Once the decision had been taken it was implemented with impressive speed. By sea and air, reinforcements poured into Tunisia with the tacit approval of the Vichy French colonial government. The leading elements of what was to become a sustained build-up included parachute troops, part of the 10th Panzer Division, one company of Heavy Tank Battalion 501 equipped with Tigers, which had not seen action in Africa before, and a number of Marsch (reinforcement) battalions consisting of soldiers of doubtful quality, the inclusion of which in itself confirmed the urgency with which the situation was viewed. The Luftwaffe quickly established itself on good airfields close behind the predicted front and in so doing achieved a marked tactical advantage over the Allied air forces, which were flying from distant airstrips in Algeria that were often rendered inoperable by winter rains.

The Allies were, of course, aware of the Axis intentions and sought to foil them by a rapid advance on Tunis itself, using Major General Vyvyan Evelegh's 78th Division, reinforced with units from the US 1st Armored Division, and parachute drops to secure important locations along the route.

The advance began on 24 November and was made along three separate axes. At first all went well; Medjez-el-Bab was captured, then Tebourba, and in a dashing action on Djedeida airfield the Stuart light tanks of 1/1st US Armored Regiment and the armoured cars of 2nd Derbyshire Yeomanry destroyed twenty Stuka dive-bombers for the loss of only one tank.

The Allies had reached a point approximately twenty miles short of Tunis and, for the moment, that was as close as they would get. At this juncture the German commander, General Walther Nehring, ordered a counter-attack under the overall command of Major General Wolfgang Fischer of 10th Panzer Division.

In the meantime, the advance of Brigadier E.E.E. Cass's 11th Infantry Brigade, consisting of the 2nd Lancashire Fusiliers, 1st East Surrey Regiment and 5th Northamptonshire Regiment, had been halted with heavy casualties between Tebourba and Djedeida and the decision was made that it should be reinforced with the 2nd Hampshire Regiment, belonging to the recently-landed 1st Guards Brigade.

Commanded by Lieutenant Colonel James Lee, the 2nd Hampshires were a regular battalion which contained a high proportion of tough, experienced soldiers; indeed, upon mobilisation in 1939 the battalion had been brought up to strength with 300 reservists, almost all of whom had seen active service on the North-West Frontier of India or in Palestine and possessed two or three campaign medals apiece. The battalion had then fought in France and had returned from Dunkirk with only one man missing; in the process it had brought out all its rifles, light machine-guns, anti-tank rifles and 2in mortars, an astonishing achievement upon which it was congratulated by Anthony Eden, the then Minister of War. Lee himself had been commissioned into the Hampshires in 1919, serving with the 1st Battalion in Egypt and India. He joined the 2nd Battalion in 1939 and commanded its Y Company in France. He played several sports to a high standard and as well as being an able leader he inspired the genuine liking and respect of his men.

The afternoon of 29 November found the Hampshires bivouacked in a copse near Medjez-el-Bab, where they had relieved the Lancashire Fusiliers. At about 1800 the battalion's liaison officer at brigade headquarters, Lieutenant Symes, arrived with orders to move forthwith and relieve the Northamptons in their positions approximately four miles east of Tebourba. By 1900 the battalion was aboard its troop-carrying lorries and travelling through the Tebourba Gap in almost total darkness. On route one vehicle, containing a platoon of W Company, overturned, seriously injuring many of the occupants. The platoon did not rejoin until after the battle, and as W

147

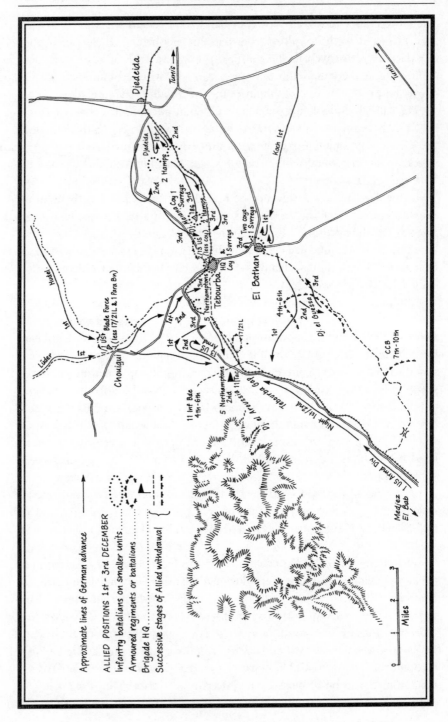

Company had already detached another platoon to guard prisoners of war, its effective strength had already been reduced by half.

The column arrived in the centre of Tebourba at 2130. The men clattered out of their trucks and were met by guides who led them on the final stage of the march up to the front. By midnight they had relieved the Northamptons and begun digging in. The position itself consisted of an elongated strip of woodland, incorporating the Medjez-el-Bab to Tunis railway, with the Medjerba river running along its southern edge. It was overlooked by high ground across the river and more high ground to the east and north. It was, therefore, totally unsuitable as a defensive position and was, in fact, nothing more than the area in which the Northamptons' advance on Djedeida, one and a half miles further on, had been halted by the stiffening enemy defence.

That afternoon Lee had received a depressing visit from the commander of V Corps, Lieutenant General Charles Allfrey. At this stage V Corps consisted of little more than 78th Division and was a somewhat pointless interjection by the administratively minded Anderson between Evelegh and himself. Allfrey thus had nothing to contribute beyond a blunt comment that the overall situation was most unpromising and that 78th Division was in for a sticky time. With this gloomy prediction still fresh in his mind, Lee had made a preliminary reconnaissance of the position he had to take over and was shocked to discover its shortcomings. He asked Brigadier Cass for permission either to continue the attack on Djedeida, or to withdraw approximately two miles to a much stronger position between Hill 186, already held by an East Surrey company, and the river. Cass, however, was adamant; the Hampshires would remain where they were.

Lee therefore deployed his battalion as follows: X Company at the forward, i.e. eastern, edge of the wood, with 10 Platoon in front, 11 Platoon covering its right-rear and 12 Platoon in a small farm between the railway and the river; Y Company on a hill named Djebel el Hamada to the left of X Company with 15 Platoon right, 13 Platoon left and 14 Platoon rear; Battalion HQ, including three detachments from the Anti-Aircraft Platoon and half the Pioneers, was located in the wood behind X Company; the rump of W Company dug in behind Battalion HQ; and Z Company, in reserve, provided all-round protection at the rear of the wood. X, Y and Z Companies were each allocated one section of 3in mortars and the battalion's own 2pdr anti-tank guns, plus an attached troop of 6pdr anti-tank guns, were sited in depth along the wood. HQ Company, together with the tracked Carrier Platoon, the rest of the Pioneers, one Anti-Aircraft detachment, the transport vehicles and the regimental aid post, were located in a second wood a mile and a half behind Z Company; the battalion's B echelon was located near the railway about two miles west of Tebourba. Altogether, the Hampshires' strength amounted to 689 all ranks.

Also attached were two troops of 25pdr guns, one of which was to provide fire support under the direction of its Forward Observation Officer, who set up his observation post with Y Company on Djebel el Hamada. The second troop was integrated into the anti-tank defence, and here a word of explanation is necessary. By this phase of the war the 2pdr was already considered obsolete and, save at close range, it was unable to penetrate the thicker armour that was being fitted to the enemy's tanks. The 6pdr could kill the latest versions of the PzKw III and PzKw IV at longer range but was in short supply. On the other hand, experience in the Western Desert had shown that the 25pdr, though designed for the field artillery role, was an excellent tank killer when firing armour-piercing shot over open sights. Against this, none of the British guns had the slightest chance of penetrating the Tiger's massive frontal armour, although the 25pdr could punch a round through the vehicle's thinner side and rear plates at about 1000 yards, depending on the angle of strike. The problem was that Tiger commanders

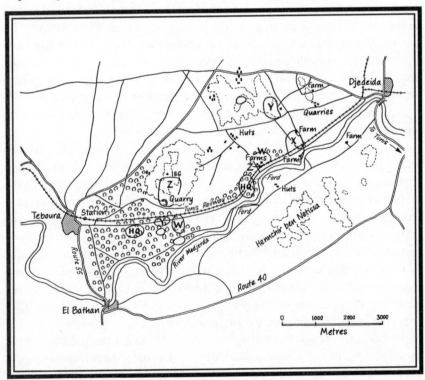

rarely presented these comparatively vulnerable areas and, that being the case, the infantryman's only real defence lay in recently developed shaped-charge weapons such as the PIAT or the Bazooka, which were not yet on general issue, or in calling down a medium artillery strike, which was not always available; otherwise, as General Allfrey had already indicated, the outlook was bleak.

On the morning of 30 November Brigadier Cass visited the battalion and repeated his orders that it was to hold its ground, Sporadic shelling and mortaring indicated that the enemy was obviously aware of the Hampshires' presence. There was also intense Luftwaffe air activity; from Djebel el Hamada Y Company could see Djedeida airfield in the distance, with Stuka squadrons landing and taking off in the manner of a cab rank. Having noted that his entire position could be observed from an area of high ground to the left-rear of Y Company, Lee decided to establish a daylight standing patrol thereon, this task being accomplished by Captain B.P. Page and one section of his Carrier Platoon. At about 1530 a half-track filled with German infantry was spotted near the railway and destroyed with a direct hit by X Company's mortars. After dark X and Z Companies both sent out fighting patrols but these returned without any direct contact with the enemy, although they provoked machine-gun fire on fixed lines when the outskirts of Djedeida were probed.

If the events of the day had seemed routine enough to the Hampshires, this was far from being the case. One of the German Army's greatest strengths during World War II was its ability to form battlegroups from any troops to hand and fling these against the flanks and rear of any penetration of its lines, often with devastating results. Fischer, having scraped together every tank in Tunisia, had formed four such battlegroups with which he intended to achieve nothing less than the total destruction of Cass's brigade by means of a double-envelopment directed at Tebourba. To the north, Battlegroup Hudel, with 40 tanks, was to eliminate the Allied armour providing flank protection at Chouigui; it would then join forces with Battlegroup Lüder, which possessed a further 20 tanks, and advance straight down the road to Tebourba. To the south, Battlegroup Koch, led by Lieutenant Colonel Walter Koch, who had led the spectacularly successful glider assault on Fort Eben Emael in 1940, was to capture El Bathan and close the Tebourba Gap approximately two miles west of Tebourba. The combined effect of these two pincers would be to entrap 11th Brigade in a pocket. However, while these operations were in progress Fischer's intention was divert the attention of Evelegh and Cass to the east, where the Hampshires were to be pinned down by Battlegroup Djedeida. This included several of

151

the Marsch battalions, the ranks of which contained not only malcontents and ne'er-do-wells unloaded by other units but also military criminals who could win remission if they fought well.

Fischer's counter-attack began on 1 December. At Chouigui the Stuart light tanks of 1/1st US Armored Regiment and the Derbyshire Yeomanry's armoured cars were no match for their opponents and quickly withdrew to Tebourba. The flank protection force's organic armoured regiment, the 17th/21st Lancers, immediately moved north from the town but soon found itself engaged in an unequal battle against the combined Hudel and Lüder Battlegroups. The Lancers were equipped with an incompatible mixture of Valentine and Crusader tanks; the former, designed for infantry support, were heavily armoured but slow, and the latter, intended for use within armoured brigades, carried average armour and were extremely fast. This might not have mattered too much in the sort of defensive battle they were fighting, had they been adequately armed. As it was, the regiment's tanks were armed with 2pdrs and a small proportion of 6pdrs, both of which were outranged by the 75mm L/48 gun mounted on the latest models of the PzKw IV. Naturally enough, the Germans fought the battle at ranges of their own choosing and sustained little damage. The Lancers, who were being simultaneously harried by artillery fire and dive bombers, lost tanks steadily but were aware that Combat Command B (CCB) of the 1st US Armored Division was approaching through the Tebourba Gap and when dusk put an end to the fighting they were still holding open a narrow corridor north of Tebourba.

CCB, consisting of 1/ and 2/13th Armored Regiment, equipped respectively with Stuart light and Lee medium tanks, two armoured infantry battalions and an armoured artillery battery, went into action on 2 December. The Americans lost heavily but their Lees enabled them to engage on more equal terms and this, plus the combined weight of the Allied artillery, brought the advance of Battlegroups Hudel and Lüder to a halt.

On the southern flank Battlegroup Koch, unwisely stripped of some of its parachute units by Fischer to reinforce Battlegroup Djedeida, had not done so well. It had been decisively repulsed by two East Surrey companies at El Bathan but then swung wide to the west and actually penetrated the Tebourba Gap during the evening of 1 December. The arrival of CCB, however, had led to its withdrawing onto Djebel el Guessa, about two miles from the river, on 2 December, then abandoning the feature the following day. Nevertheless, the fact remained that most of Cass's brigade was now held within a sack, the narrow neck of which was being held open with difficulty and was well within range of the enemy's artillery.

Although they were aware of heavy fighting taking place to their rear, little or nothing of this was known to the Hampshires, situated at the very bottom of the sack, as their own hands had been kept very full indeed. On the morning of 1 December considerable enemy activity was reported by Lee's forward companies. An attack was anticipated and to meet this Y Company adjusted its position slightly, moving 15 Platoon to the right so that it could cover a small farm and two gravel pits between it and X Company. During the afternoon frontal attacks, covered by mortar and machine-gun fire, were launched against X and Y Companies. That against Y Company was stopped in its tracks and those of the enemy who managed to penetrate the wood on X Company's sector were driven out by a hail of fire from the company's Brens, supplemented by 25pdr concentrations.

That evening the Germans attempted to infiltrate the farm between the two companies. Lee, determined that they should not secure such a lodgement, ordered Z Company to clear the position. Unfortunately, the counter-attack, delivered by 16 Platoon under Lieutenant O.G. Griffith, an attached Welsh Guards officer, had to be made down an exposed forward slope and incurred serious casualties, including Griffith, although some of the men succeeded in reaching the farm, which was then set ablaze.

Considering that the platoon's position was dangerously exposed, Lee ordered it to pull back at dusk. When it returned seven or eight of its members were found to be missing and more were known to be lying badly wounded. As soon as it was dark Lieutenant E.G. Wright, the Second-in-Command of Z Company, although wounded himself, went out with several teams of stretcher bearers, rescuing Griffith and eight more of the wounded, as well as rounding up seven of those previously reported missing, an action for which he was awarded the Military Cross.

A German version of events is provided by the diary of Lieutenant Hans Holler, an anti-tank gunner whose role in leading an infantry assault underlines the mixed nature of the troops at Fischer's disposal.

'On 1 December we attack, supported by one Luftwaffe 20mm flak gun and some paratroopers from Battlegroup Koch. A farm, 300 metres to our right, is on fire. The Tommies, tucked away behind the hill [i.e. Y Company on Djebel el Hamada] prevented us advancing further. The situation is extremely unpleasant. We are meant to be a battlegroup, but we have no contact with anyone on the right or left – in fact, no neighbours at all. In the evening we dig in where we are with shells bursting around us regularly. A wounded Tommy is lying 50 metres in front of us in the branches and leaves, but it is only possible to bring him in after dark. He has been shot through the lung.'

The Hampshires' casualties for the day had not been excessive. X Company had lost seven killed and eighteen wounded; Y Company twelve wounded; Z Company one killed and sixteen wounded or missing. On the other hand, it must be remembered that thus far Battlegroup Djedeida had only mounted diversionary holding attacks while the jaws of Fischer's trap closed around 11th Brigade. On the morrow Fischer's intention was to smash his way through the battalion and overrun the pocket, and to this end he reinforced Battlegroup Djedeida with tanks, including several of 1/501st's Tigers.

Patrols reported no activity during the night but shortly after first light the enemy came on again, this time in strength and accompanied by an estimated seven tanks. Once more, their targets were X and Y Companies, whose positions were raked by flanking machine-gun and sniper fire from the high ground across the Medjerda. The anti-tank gun screen went into action at once. Two tanks and a tractor unit towing an infantry gun were quickly set ablaze on the slopes in front of Y Company and nearby a third tank lay silent and immobile. A fourth tank, however, apparently invulnerable, halted only twenty yards from the company's right-hand platoon, commanded by Lieutenant Seth-Smith, and began to pump high explosive shells into each of the slit trenches in turn; nothing more was heard or seen of this platoon.[1]

A fifth tank, having crossed the southern spur of Djebel el Hamada, trundled along the edge of the wood shelling and machine-gunning Battalion HQ. It then retired but evidently transmitted the location as the headquarters was promptly mortared.[2] This attack killed Lieutenant Pritchard, the Signals Officer, and five of his men, totally disrupting the battalion's internal communications net for a while, as well as wrecking a carrier. To prevent a recurrence, Lee moved his command post behind W Company, to which he attached the pioneers and anti-aircraft gunners.

Meanwhile, X Company was being subjected to repeated heavy attacks. Whenever the enemy penetrated the wood, they were driven out by a series of bayonet charges led by the company commander, Captain C.L. Thomas, and Lieutenant J.R. Hart. Rarely on a modern battlefield has a regiment resorted to the bayonet with such frequency and zeal as did the Hampshires throughout the fighting at Tebourba and here, perhaps, can be seen the workings of the regimental system at its best. The Hampshires, also known as 'The Tigers' because of their cap badge, were a Minden regiment and as such would acknowledge no peers save five other Minden regiments.[3] It is doubtful whether anyone in Lee's battalion was giving Minden a conscious thought at that moment, but the lessons of that astonishing victory, including the will to win and the value of sustained aggression, had been drummed into every recruit and clearly provided intense motivation at the subconscious level. On one of the occasions when his position was penetrated by enemy infantry and tanks,[4] Thomas recognised that the latter were almost blind in woodland. He gathered together the only five men in the area and, firing a Bren light machine-gun from the hip, led them in a savage counter-attack between the tanks, scattering the infantry behind. Yet, gallantly as it was fighting, X Company could not withstand this sort of pressure indefinitely. Its strength was gradually whittled away and, one by one, its four anti-tank guns, which had destroyed two tanks, fell silent with their crews sprawled around them. Shortly after 1200 the enemy attacked again in large numbers, accompanied by two more tanks. Thomas, recognising that this time they could not be held for long, ordered his Second-in-Command, Captain A.J. Pearce-Serocold, another attached Welsh Guards officer, to warn Lee that the position was about to be overrun. Apart from Pearce-Serocold, only one sergeant and five men came back from X Company. For his very gallant and aggressive conduct of the defence Thomas was subsequently awarded the Distinguished Service Order.

Lee's reaction was to move the reinforced W Company forward into the position previously occupied by Battalion HQ. By now his internal communications had been restored, save to Y Company, although traffic had to be relayed through Z Company's set; against this, his radio rear link to Brigade was lost about the same time.

Just as W Company were moving forward, one of the 25pdrs opened fire at a PzKw IV crawling across the shoulder of Djebel el Hamada and set it ablaze at a range of 300 yards. Hardly had the company settled in than its commander, Captain A.N.E. Waldron, later awarded the Military Cross, reported that large numbers of the enemy, having overwhelmed X Company, had renewed their advance through the wood and were closing in on his position. Lee immediately ordered him to mount a counter-attack in platoon strength. The task was given to Lieutenant A.W. Freemantle's platoon, which executed a ferocious bayonet charge that killed or wounded over 40 of the enemy and put the rest to flight. This remarkable success was achieved at the cost of six wounded, including Freemantle and his sergeant. The platoon, understandably elated, returned through the trees cheering, laughing and shouting, driving six very frightened prisoners before them.

After this the pressure eased, although the enemy's dive bombers, hitherto inhibited by the proximity of the two sides, made regular appearances. Lee had not heard from Y Company for some time and, observing enemy infantry and machine-gun teams on the high ground to the left rear of Djebel el Hamada, was forced to assume that it had shared the fate of X

Company. At about 1600, however, a message arrived from the company commander, Captain J.W. Brehaut, delivered by his clerk and transport NCO. These two men had made an extremely brave dash across open ground swept by machine-gun fire on which they had already seen one runner shot down. Brehaut's message stated that the company had sustained very serious casualties but was still holding, although it had exhausted its ammunition and water. At Lee's instructions, a small party of men loaded one of the tracked carriers with fresh supplies and succeeded in fighting their way across the bullet-swept ground to the beleaguered company. Their commander, Captain H.E. Wingfield, was also awarded the Military Cross.

Lieutenant Symes arrived from Brigade as dusk was falling, anxious for a situation report. Lee told him to inform Brigadier Cass that the Hampshires were still holding, although that in view of the heavy casualties that had been incurred it was unlikely they would be able to withstand a similar series of attacks next day.

Across the lines the Germans were also taking stock. 'I had orders to attack at 0700, following an artillery barrage', wrote Lieutenant Holler in his diary. 'Tank support had also been promised. The barrage consisted of just ten rounds which fell dangerously short, fortunately without loss to ourselves. Without adequate artillery support we were unable to take the hill. I gave orders to move to the left, cross the railway and attack from that direction. Crossing the railway we suffered casualties, but gained some ground. On our left was a lovely house which had Tommies inside, but they were now surrounded. Behind the hill where we started was a Tiger tank, the first I have ever seen.'

At a higher level Fischer, who had been in the thick of the fighting, was almost incoherent with rage. He had no quarrel with Koch's paratroopers, but his furious contempt for the Marsch battalion's collection of no-hopers and military outcasts springs from the pages of his report: 'They displayed not the slightest interest, nor aggressive spirit, nor readiness for action. At times it was necessary for me to take personal command of companies, platoons and even squads'. In the final analysis, of course, it had been the Hampshires who thwarted his intentions of overrunning the pocket he had so expertly created.

There was no enemy activity after dark. Symes arrived back at Battalion HQ at about 2330, bringing with him an order to pull back about two miles – in fact, to the position Lee had originally suggested holding. The companies disengaged cleanly some two hours later and withdrew in good order. The manner in which this movement, perhaps the most difficult in war, was conducted, made a lasting impression on survivors of the battle.

'They had been slogging it out for three days and there were numerous casualties in both men and weapons', recalled Wingfield, writing some 50 years after the event. 'The chances to eat had been rare, water was scarce and sleep had been virtually impossible. Yet the withdrawal was later described as "immaculate". In complete silence they disengaged from the enemy, companies thinned out and made their way to their new positions. Digging started about two hours before dawn. Discipline remained unchanged and at the dawn "stand-to" everyone's cheerfulness and good spirits were quite remarkable'.

Lee positioned the battalion with W Company on the right, Z Company on the left, holding the southern slopes of Point 186 but not the summit, and Y Company, now sadly depleted, to the rear and covering the gap between them, astride the railway line. Battalion HQ was located a little to the south of Y Company with Headquarters Company several hundred yards behind. With the exception of the open slopes of Point 186 the position was, if anything, more closely wooded than that which the Hampshires had just left. In immediate support were two troops of 25pdrs, one of which was employed in the anti-tank role, and one troop of 6pdr anti-tank guns sited in a lay-back position behind the battalion. The summit of Point 186 was held by the East Surreys' A Company; two more East Surreys' companies, B and C, were in Tebourba, and the fourth, D, was on the north bank of the Medjerda, opposite El Bathan.

Fischer had followed up the Hampshires' withdrawal very quickly. At first light on 3 December the British positions were subjected to a sustained artillery and mortar bombardment. This lasted until 1000 when the Germans launched a general and very determined assault with infantry and armour along the entire line. Fischer was well aware that the key to the position, and indeed Tebourba itself, was Point 186. After a furious battle the East Surreys were driven off the summit. The effect was to turn the Hampshires' flank and expose the left-hand section of Z Company to intense machine-gun and mortar fire. The company commander, Major H.W. Le Patourel, informed Lee and despatched several squads to recover the summit. These managed to reach the top of the hill but sustained heavy casualties and were driven back by the volume of fire directed at them.[5] Because of the extremely dangerous nature of the situation Le Patourel then assembled a small group of volunteers, including Lieutenant B.N.P. Lister and three men, and personally led them in an apparently suicidal attempt to dislodge the enemy. For this action Le Patourel, a Channel Islander like many members of the regiment, was awarded the Victoria Cross. To quote from his citation:

157

'The party was heavily engaged by the machine-gun fire and Major Le Patourel rallied his men several times and engaged the enemy, silencing several machine-gun posts. Finally, when the remainder of his party were killed or wounded, he went forward alone with a pistol and some grenades to attack the enemy machine-guns at close quarters, and from this action he did not return.'

It was thought at the time that Le Patourel had been killed and the award was made posthumously. Only later was it discovered that he had been seriously wounded and was picked up by the Germans after the battle. He spent several months recovering from his wounds in hospital in Italy and was repatriated by the Italians in 1943.

A subsequent attack by two East Surrey companies also failed to recapture the summit. Elsewhere, the enemy's attempts to penetrate the battalion's front were fiercely repulsed throughout the morning, often by means of locally inspired bayonet charges. By 1500, however, large numbers of infantry, supported by tanks, had worked their way round W Company's right flank into the Hampshires' rear. Captain Waldron immediately responded with a bayonet charge that broke up the attack and Captain Brehaut dealt similarly with a party of Germans that had worked its way between W and Z Companies. By now Z Company, exposed not only to the murderous fire from the summit of Point 186 but also to that of three hull-down tanks to the east, had been reduced to the strength of a single weak platoon. Both 25pdr troops had been fighting their guns over open sights all day and had accounted for five tanks, although by 1700 the field troop had only one gun left in action.

It had begun to look very much as though little time was left to the Hampshires. The enemy had again begun working their way past W Company and were moving round Point 186 to isolate the battalion from the rear. Lee called in his companies and deployed them in a hollow square around his command post. He was stubbornly reluctant to accept defeat and his idea was to mount a concentrated attack on Point 186 after dark and hold it until he received further orders. However, a quick count revealed that he had only ten officers and 200 men at his disposal and that very little ammunition and water remained. The only alternative left, therefore, was to break out and rejoin the rest of the brigade.

He gave orders for as many men as possible to arm themselves with automatic weapons; simultaneously, grenades and ammunition were collected from the dead and those too seriously wounded to move. As soon as it was sufficiently dark, the battalion deployed in extended line with its right on the railway. Bayonets were fixed and the line began moving forward through the trees. As soon as it was in contact with the enemy Lee gave the order to charge. For a few confused minutes there were impressions of flaring automatic weapons, the flash of bursting grenades reflected from the flat sides of two tanks, the thud of bodies falling, screams as bayonets struck home, shouted commands and the sound of running feet. There were casualties on both sides, but suddenly the Hampshires were through. Breathless, they rallied in the outskirts of Tebourba. Here they formed up and marched through the strangely silent, deserted streets past roofless, gutted buildings, sprawled bodies, and wrecked or abandoned transport vehicles. With a sinking feeling they realised that the rest of the brigade had gone and that they were still entirely on their own.

Brigadier Cass, recognising that Tebourba could not be held, had been forced to make a difficult and unpleasant decision. His personnel casualties and equipment losses – the latter including eight 25pdrs, fourteen anti-tank guns and ten light anti-aircraft guns – had been very heavy and now his task was to preserve as much as possible of his brigade's fighting strength. His orders were to conduct a fighting withdrawal on Medjez-el-Bab and the Northamptons had already moved back to the first covering position in the Tebourba Gap while CCB 1st Armored Division conformed south of the river. The East Surreys had pulled out of Tebourba at last light, covered by the remaining tanks of 17th/21st Lancers. With no radio link to the Hampshires, and no means of getting a message through to them, Cass was faced with the bitter necessity of having to abandon them, although their B (Administration) Echelon had got clear.

On emerging from the western edge of Tebourba the remnants of the battalion's fighting companies found that the main road to Medjez-el-Bab had already been cut by the enemy, who had it covered by machine-guns firing along fixed lines from the hills and had emplaced several tanks to fire along it.

Short of ammunition as they were, the Hampshires could not fight their way through. Lee decided that the battalion should split into small groups which, having been issued with water and rations from bogged down East Surrey transport vehicles, would make their own way through the enemy's lines.

On 4 December the regimental Chaplain and Medical Officer, who had worked tirelessly throughout the battle to get the wounded away and themselves come out with B Echelon, assisted the Quartermaster, Lieutenant C.A. Northmore, to set up a collecting point in a wood near Medjez-el-Bab. Here came the survivors in a steady trickle that finally ended two days later. Lee was not among them. Only six officers, of whom Captain Brehaut was the senior, and 194 men remained of the 2nd Hampshires.

Here, too, came the correspondent of *The Times*, who wrote:

'Yesterday, I found resting in a wood the heroes of this astonishing feat of arms. They were grimed but their fighting spirit was as high as ever and they have begged to be allowed to return to the hills to search for the Colonel.....They are filled with contempt for the enemy, whom they have repeatedly put to flight with the bayonet....They are savagely angry with the enemy, too, after seeing mortar shells dropping among their helpless wounded....Out of their matter of fact talk, lurid glimpses of the fighting emerge. There was Corporal Wiggins* who was last seen in a ring of Germans swinging round and spraying them with a tommy-gun. There was Captain Page and a party who found a 25pdr with the crew killed and, though infantrymen, managed to make it work and knocked out a German tank with the first shot. And there were many stories of German invitations to surrender, all of them refused.'

A more personal tribute was paid to the battalion in his report by Captain J.A.C. Shaw, Royal Artillery, who served as Forward Observation Officer during the final day's fighting:

'In spite of enormous casualties on the previous day, and to a lesser extent during this engagement, and in spite of the enemy's great superiority, the Hampshires never ceased to fight with the greatest bravery and determination. The fact that even during the final phases of the enemy's assault the commanding officer was personally controlling all fire of the unit, and that their final break-out from the position was carried out in perfect order, are in themselves sufficient tribute to the unit's magnificent discipline and esprit de corps. It is impossible to assess the effect of their resistance on the enemy, but it is certain that they inflicted tremendous casualties upon them.'

Although none of the Hampshires were aware of the extent of their achievements at the time, these were considerable. Tactically. they had foiled Fischer's plan and enabled most of 11th Brigade to escape. Strategically, they had so delayed and mauled the enemy that he was unable to follow up his victory promptly. By the time he got himself moving again the defences of Medjez-el-Bab had been put in order and the town was held after more bitter fighting. If this vital road junction had been lost the probability is that the Allied line could only have been re-established much further to the west. As it was. Medjez-el-Bab and the Medjerda Valley provided the springboard for the final drive on Tunis the following spring.

Lee, now a prisoner, was awarded the Distinguished Service Order. Including those awards already mentioned, the battalion earned the follow-

* Awarded the Military Medal.

ing during the Battle of Tebourba: one Victoria Cross, two Distinguished Service Orders, five Military Crosses, four Military Medals and numerous Mentions in Despatches.

It was mid-December before the first reports of the action appeared in the British press, catching the public imagination. Immediately, messages of congratulation began to reach General Sir Richard Haking, the Hampshires' Colonel, at his office in Winchester, where the regiment had its Headquarters. They came from two former Chiefs of the Imperial General Staff and other senior officers, local civic dignitaries, the Dean and Chapter of Winchester Cathedral, the Colonel of the Rifle Brigade, which also had its Headquarters in Winchester, the Colonel of the East Surrey Regiment, the veterans of the Hampshire British Legion, and numerous former members of the regiment. The common threads running through them all were immense sense of pride and inspiration generated by the 2nd Battalion's achievements at Tebourba, which were the equal of anything in the regiment's history, and great sadness at the loss of so many brave men. Perhaps the most memorable tribute to the men of Tebourba was made by King George VI who, at a passing-out parade of officer cadets told them in his quiet way just what was expected of them: 'I recommend you to read the story of the 2nd Battalion of The Hampshire Regiment in Tunisia in 1942. That was a triumph of individual leadership and corporate discipline.'

Lee escaped from his prison camp in September 1943, was recaptured but managed to escape again the same night and reached Switzerland. On his retirement in 1949 he settled in Wrington, Somerset, and for the remaining twenty years of his life played a leading part in every aspect of village and community life, as well as serving as an umpire at the Wimbledon lawn tennis championships for no less than fifteen seasons.

Notes

1 & 2. From their behaviour it seems probable that these two tanks were Tigers. Initially, the German heavy tank battalions were intended to perform the breakthrough role, although this changed to that of corps 'fire brigades' during the last two years of the war, when Germany was placed on the strategic defensive.

3. At Minden on 1 August 1759, in response to a misunderstood order, six British and three Hanoverian regiments advanced alone and unsupported against the entire French army. They were charged three times by the French cavalry, which they destroyed with their disciplined musketry. They were then counter-attacked in flank by the French infantry but changed front and drove their opponents off the field after a protracted fire-fight. The British regiments, known collectively as the 'Unsurpassable Six,' later became the Suffolk Regiment, the Lancashire Fusiliers, the Royal Welch Fusiliers, the King's Own Scottish Borderers, the Hampshire Regiment and

the King's Own Yorkshire Light Infantry. An account of the battle can be found in the author's *At All Costs*.

4. There are strong grounds for believing that at least one, and probably two, of these tanks were Tigers. Lieutenant Colonel Wingfield writes: 'At this stage of the game we were quite unaware of any new German tank in North Africa – the PzKw IV was quite enough to be getting on with, as it was! On the other hand the tank that milled around X Company slit trenches and was stalked by Captain Thomas, the company commander, was in my view a Tiger. It was Cecil Thomas who later queried its type with me and voiced an opinion that Tigers were being used against us.'

5. The German MG34 (sustained fire) and MG42 light machine-guns had a respective rate of fire of 850 and 1200 rounds per minute (rpm); that of the British Bren light machine-gun was 500 rpm. The German MP38 and MP40 submachine-guns, often referred to as Schmeissers, could produce 500 rpm and were reliable. The Thompson submachine-gun issued to the Hampshires had a comparable rate of fire. In general, however, the average German infantry platoon could produce a higher volume of fire than its British counterpart.

10
The Defence of Kohima,
6–18 April 1944

B y the beginning of 1944 even the most optimistic members of Japan's ruling military clique had been forced to accept that the fortunes of the Axis powers were in decline. Italy had been knocked out of the war the previous year. The German Army, forced into retreat in Russia yet simultaneously compelled to fight fierce defensive battles in Italy and prepare for an Allied invasion of France, was dangerously overstretched. In the Central and South Pacific, Japan herself was in retreat before an American war machine that grew stronger by the day, while in China, where much of her strength was tied down, the sheer size of the country inhibited victory. Only in Burma were the Japanese armies still holding their own.

The commander of the Burma Area Army was Lieutenant General Masakuzo Kawabe, who had been told that the last thing the Japanese people wished to hear was bad news from his theatre of war. Kawabe was aware that the reconquest of Burma was a long term Allied objective. The easiest way to achieve this would be by means of an amphibious landing in the area of Rangoon followed by an advance northwards, the effect of which would be to cut off his armies from their sources of supply. However, he also knew that because of demands for landing craft in the Pacific, in the Mediterranean and for the invasion of France, the Allies were unlikely to mount amphibious operations in the Burmese theatre until the following year, at the earliest. The only alternative remaining to them, therefore, was to invade from the north. In this context, the Chindwin river offered him an obvious defensive barrier, but since he lacked the resources to cover this adequately along its entire length he decided instead that he would secure a line along the crest of the Naga Hills, beyond the Chindwin and across the Imphal Plain. Once this had been occupied, he believed that the British would never be able to break out of India and resume large-scale operations in Burma, as routes through the towering hills were few and could be easily guarded. The only stumbling block was the presence of the British IV Corps, commanded by Lieutenant General G.A.P. Scoones, on the Imphal Plain, but this he did not consider to be an insuperable obstacle.

Kawabe detailed Lieutenant General Renya Mutaguchi's Fifteenth Army for the operation, which he called U-go. The plan required one division, Major General Sato's 31st, to isolate IV Corps at Imphal by cutting the road behind it at Kohima, 50 miles to the north; simultaneously, the 15th and 33rd Divisions, commanded respectively by Major Generals Yamauchi and Yanagida, would encircle and destroy IV Corps. All three divisions would then construct impregnable defences at strategic points along the crest of the Naga Hills, denying the British further access to Burma from Manipur and Assam. To draw off British troops, a diversionary offensive, codenamed Ha-go, was to be mounted in the Arakan coastal region shortly before the Fifteenth Army began its advance.

Unfortunately for Kawabe, Ha-go proved to be an expensive failure. For the first time, British and Indian troops inflicted a costly defeat on the Japanese, with the result that General Sir William Slim, commanding the British Fourteenth Army, was able to reinforce the Manipur sector with troops who had fought in the Arakan, the precise reverse of the situation Kawabe had intended to create. Furthermore, since the arrival of Spitfires in Burma, the Royal Air Force had obtained complete air superiority, enabling Slim to order IV Corps to stand its ground at Imphal, where it would be reinforced and supplied by a continuous air lift. This, again, upset Kawabe's calculations. In the past, whenever British and Indian troops had found themselves isolated, they had tried to fight their way out and suffered heavy losses, including most of their equipment and stores, in the process. The Achilles heel of the Japanese Army was its primitive supply system, but in Malaya and during the First Burma Campaign it had always managed to feed itself on captured rations. It followed, therefore, that if Mutaguchi's divisions could not eat their fill from IV Corps' depots they would not eat at all and, sooner or later, the entire U-go strategy would collapse.

Sato's 31st Division, consisting of the 58th, 124th and 138th Infantry Regiments, each the size of a British brigade, and 31st Mountain Artillery Regiment, crossed the Chindwin on 15 March and advanced rapidly in four parallel columns along tracks that had been secretly reconnoitred the previous month. Behind them came a 15,000-strong herd of oxen and goats that was intended to feed the division until Mutaguchi wiped out IV Corps and arrived from the south with fresh supplies. Apart from the cattle and the men's meagre marching rations, the only other source of food lay in the infrequent Naga villages and in this respect the Nagas, being loyal to the British, were less than helpful. The Nagas also provided warning of the Japanese approach, as did the teams of V Force, which in Burma performed a similar role to the SAS in other theatres of war. As a result of this Sato was compelled to fight his way through an outer screen of outposts held in strength. He incurred heavy losses dislodging the 50th Indian Parachute Brigade at Sangshak, and again at Jessami, Kharasom and Phek, in the hills to the east of Kohima, where detachments from the 1st Assam Regiment fought to the last, their Brens glowing red with heat as they shot the heart out of one attack after another. They also cost him priceless time which could never be recovered.

Against this, British failure to identify Sato's objective resulted in dangerous confusion that could have resulted in a major setback. For a while, Slim believed that Sato had his sights set on Dimapur, to the west of Kohima. Dimapur was situated on the Calcutta – Ledo railway line and had become an enormous base with accumulated stores piled high beside the tracks for several miles in both directions. The loss of these would undoubtedly keep Mutaguchi's entire army well supplied for many months to come, but that was not the only consideration. The railway was a vital supply artery of Lieutenant General Joseph Stilwell's Chinese-American army in northern Burma and if it was cut the fighting ability of the latter would be seriously reduced. In this context the possession of Kohima had little relevance to either side. Yet, as reports of Sato's movements continued to come in, it became clear that he was focusing his entire attention on the hill town. At the eleventh hour his purpose became apparent – Kohima offered a series of superb defensive positions that could hold out indefinitely against a relief force attempting to reach the besieged IV Corps at Imphal. Therefore, it must be denied to the enemy at all costs.

Kohima was situated at the point where the winding Dimapur-Imphal road, approaching from the west, turned due south. The town, itself 5000 feet above sea level, was dominated by mountains up to twice that height. It was the civil administrative centre for the area and in happier times was a cool hill station in which planters and their families could obtain some relief from the sweltering heat of the plains below. The war, however, had turned Kohima into an intermediate-sized base camp, incorporating a general hospital, reinforcement depot, supply facilities and workshops. As the road neared the town, it wound round the shoulder of a projecting spur on which a military hospital had been laid out: it turned sharply right in the town centre, with the entrance to the Deputy Commissioner's bungalow in the inner angle, then ran south for approximately one mile with a sharp drop on the left and a low wooded ridge on the right. The DC's bungalow, in fact, marked the northern end of a ridge and was built on a terraced hillside. Above the bungalow was a tennis court, and above that was the focal point of town's expatriate social life, the Club. From this point the small hills con-

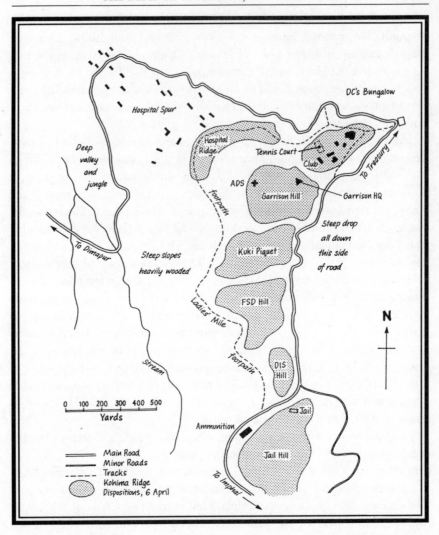

DC's Bungalow

Hospital Spur

Hospital Ridge

Tennis Court

Club

Deep valley and jungle

ADS

Garrison Hill

Garrison HQ

To Treasury

To Dimapur

Steep slopes heavily wooded

Kuki Piquet

Steep drop all down this side of road

Ladies' Mile

FSD Hill

footpath

footpath

N

DIS Hill

Stream

Jail

Ammunition

0 100 200 300 400 500
Yards

Jail Hill

To Imphal

Main Road
Minor Roads
Tracks
Kohima Ridge
Dispositions, 6 April

stituting the ridge were occupied by the supply base; first Garrison Hill, then Kuki Piquet, then FSD (Field Supply Depot) Hill, then DIS (Detail Issue Store) Hill. To varying degrees, these features were occupied with bashas, that is, windowless bamboo huts with a space between the top of the walls and the roof, that served as stores, bakeries and workshops. Across the Imphal road from DIS Hill was a feature named Jail Hill. On high ground to the north of Kohima was a wooden fort that had withstood a fortnight's siege by Naga headhunters in 1879 but was now used as government offices and known as the Treasury. Beyond this was the Naga township, straggling across the hillside.

On 22 March the newly appointed garrison commander, Colonel Hugh Richards, arrived with orders to put the town's defences in order. The troops at his disposal included the rear party of the 1st Assam Regiment, joined later by 260 survivors from the fighting at Jessami, Kharasom and Phek, the 3rd Assam Rifles, a paramilitary force intended for internal security duties, the Sher Regiment, a State force commanded by its own officers with three British training officers, two companies of the 5th Burma Regiment, two platoons of 5/27th Mahrattas, composite companies formed from British convalescents from the hospital and Indian troops from the local reinforcement depot, a company of Gurkhas and some men from V Force. Also present were a large number of non-combatant and administrative personnel who were not only of no military use, but had also been thrown into a panic by the approach of the Japanese. The fighting troops were deployed onto the more important features and commenced digging in. There was, unfortunately, an acute shortage of barbed wire, for which rows of sharpened stakes did not provide an adequate substitute.

On 30 March, much to Richards' relief, the 4th Battalion Royal West Kent Regiment arrived. Commanded by Lieutenant Colonel John Laverty, known to his men as Texas Dan, the battalion was a thoroughly experienced Territorial unit which had fought in France prior to Dunkirk, in the Western Desert at Alam Halfa and First Alamein, and more recently in the Arakan, where it had incurred some 200 casualties. In common with all British and Indian units that had fought in the Arakan, its men respected the suicidal courage of the Japanese but had long since lost their awe of them. Indeed, the cold-blooded massacre of the patients and staff at a dressing station during the critical Battle of the Admin Box[1] had provoked such fury that the Japanese were now universally regarded as a species of dangerous animal that must be exterminated on sight; and, since the Japanese showed little mercy and sought none, the arrangement suited everyone.

Together with 1/1st Punjabis and 4/7th Rajputs, the Royal West Kents belonged to Brigadier Frederick Warren's 161 Brigade, which had been flown directly to Dimapur from the Arakan at short notice. When he arrived, Warren was told that his brigade was to be detached from its parent formation, the 5th Indian Division, and placed under the command of the local area commander, Major General R.P.L. Ranking, whose function was largely administrative. Obviously, Warren did not like this, any more than Laverty liked being placed under Richards' command at Kohima.

Meanwhile, XXXIII Corps, consisting of Major General John Grover's 2nd British Division, containing a high proportion of regular battalions, and four independent brigades, had been activated under the command of Lieutenant General Montagu Stopford and was moving up to the front. Stopford believed that his first priority was the defence of Dimapur and ordered Ranking to take the necessary steps. Despite strenuous objections raised by Warren, Richards and Charles Pawsey, the Deputy Commissioner, who had been resident in the area for twenty years, Ranking insisted that 161 Brigade should be withdrawn to positions near Dimapur. Slim did not approve of the decision but allowed it to stand. The Royal West Kents perforce had to abandon their half-finished trenches and bunkers and leave Kohima the day after they arrived.

By 4 April the leading elements of 2nd British Division had reached Dimapur and Stopford felt strong enough to send 161 Brigade back to Kohima. The Royal West Kents, with one battery of 3.7in howitzers belonging to 24th Mountain Regiment Indian Artillery, a company of Sappers and a field ambulance, set off at first light next day, with the rest of the brigade due to follow shortly. The men were in a black mood, forcefully expressing a wish that the generals would 'make up their bloody minds'. As the trucks ground their way up the long, curving road from Dimapur they encountered crowds of frightened soldiers and civilian labourers running in the opposite direction. They were non-combatants whom Richards regarded as useless mouths. He had sent them out after issuing arms and ammunition which, if the worst happened, would simply have fallen into Japanese hands. The fugitives claimed that the Japanese had already reached Kohima and that there had been heavy fighting. Laverty chose to disbelieve them, confiscated their arms and drove on up the long, winding road to Kohima. There, taking only their weapons and basic battle order equipment with them, the West Kents left their lorries and moved up onto the ridge to complete the trenches they had begun the previous week. Hardly had they done so than Japanese guns began to shell the halted convoy, wrecking many of the vehicles or setting them ablaze. Most of the men lost their warmer clothing and blankets, although after dark it became possible to salvage a few items such as cooking utensils. The garrison's sole 25pdr gun fired one round in reply and was immediately knocked out, confirming that the Japanese artillery observers had a complete overview of the position. In view of this, it seemed likely that the four 3.7in mountain guns would share a similar fate and they were dismantled.

Laverty deployed his A Company (Major Tom Kenyon) as a central reserve on Garrison Hill, B Company (Major John Winstanley) on the eastern side of Kuki Piquet, C Company (Major Robert Shaw) on DIS Hill, and D Company, commanded by Captain Donald Easten, on FSD Hill. The West Kents' command post was dug close to that of Colonel Richards, on the upper slopes of Garrison Hill near the Club. Nearby, Major R. de C. Yeo, commanding the mountain battery, set up his observation post with a telephone line to Richards. Superficially, the proximity of these headquarters suggested that a good relationship existed between them, but their location was simply a matter of expediency. As already mentioned, Laverty objected strongly to being placed under Richards' command, and the West Kents as a whole regarded the latter's garrison troops with a sweeping contempt that was not altogether justified. There were, it was true, units whose presence was a liability rather than an asset, but there others, like the Assam regiments, who would never voluntarily yield a foot of ground, and experience alone would reveal the difference between the two. In the event, though Richards did his best to perform the role of garrison commander, Laverty ignored him, communicating directly with Brigadier Warren, who also treated Richards as though he did not exist. It was an unfortunate situation that might have led to disaster, had the circumstances of the ensuing siege not been unique.

On 6 April the Japanese infantry closed in around Kohima. At about 0400 they infiltrated the Naga village and, five hours later, quietly captured many of the unsuspecting defenders when they paraded for breakfast. During the day they also stormed Jail Hill, reducing the defended area of Kohima to a triangle measuring 700 by 900 by 1100 yards. In such a small space it was inevitable that their 75mm field guns, emplaced on ridges to the south, their 37mm anti-tank guns, firing high explosive over open sights, and their numerous mortars, would cause a great deal of damage. Of equal concern to Richards and Laverty was the fact that not only had some of the composite companies fled at the first hint of danger, the nerve of some British base administrative officers had failed as well. Arthur Campbell's novel *The Siege*, based closely on fact, mentions one such character, known as The Man in the Hole because he did nothing but cower within his ever-deepening slit trench. Laverty was worried about the effect he would have on morale but concluded that the best policy was to leave him where he was, out of sight. Throughout the siege many of the base personnel, often too terrified to work, let alone fight, spent their days scurrying from one imagined safe area to another, their only contribution being to divert the attention of the enemy's snipers from those manning the trenches. Richards, it had to be admitted, had been absolutely right to send out as many of the non-combatants as he could.

In the meantime Warren, bringing the rest of 161 Brigade up from Dimapur, had taken a decision that was to have a crucial influence on the outcome of the battle. Although he sent up a Rajput company to reinforce

Laverty, he was aware that the reduced Kohima perimeter could not accommodate two more infantry battalions, and he decided to establish a defensive box at Jotsoma, just two miles west of the town. There, from the reverse slopes of a ridge, the three remaining 3.7in howitzer batteries of Colonel Humphrey Hill's 24th Mountain Artillery Regiment could fire in support of the besieged garrison. In Kohima, Yeo and his team of Forward Observation Officers quickly registered the defensive fire tasks that would be needed. Such was the accuracy maintained by these Indian gunners that, although in places the opposing lines were only 30 yards apart, not one of their shells landed within the British perimeter. Equally accurate was Laverty's own 3in mortar platoon, commanded by Sergeant King.

During the night of 6th April the Japanese 58th Regiment mounted a series of attacks on DIS Hill. The first began with sniping, intended to draw a response that would reveal the position of the British trenches, and with voices shouting 'Let me through, for God's sake – the Japs are after me!'. The West Kents, having experienced such jitter tactics in the Arakan, were not impressed and remained silent. Then came a sudden patter of gym shoes as the first company crossed the road from Jail Hill. King's mortars and the guns at Jotsoma went into action at once, blasting holes in the packed ranks. Light machine-guns firing on fixed lines, aimed rifles and flung grenades cut down more but some broke through until C Company, emerging from its trenches, killed them with bayonet thrust or butt-stroke in savage hand-to-hand fighting. The survivors fled into the darkness.

During the night the 58th Regiment mounted three more attacks on DIS Hill. Every prospect of surprise having vanished, these were made with bugles blowing and shrill yells of 'Banzai!'. Silhouetted against the road below, most of the attackers were cut down as they clambered upward through the trees. A number who managed to infiltrate the position went to ground inside bashas and captured trenches. For those with the time to digest the lessons, they revealed serious weaknesses in Japanese tactical methods. First, there was the mindless repetition of attacks over the same ground on which previous attacks had failed. Secondly, throughout the siege, attacks continued to be delivered in company strength or less, disclosing a serious underestimation of the defenders' will and capacity to hold; if Sato's regimental commanders had mounted attacks in battalion strength the West Kents would undoubtedly have been hard pressed to contain them. Thirdly, most of the Japanese who reached their objectives seemed incapable of exploiting the situation, preferring instead to conceal themselves and await events, thereby reflecting the failings of an over-rigid discipline that stifled initiative.

Such academic considerations, however, lay in future for the men of C Company. For the moment all they knew was they were dog tired, had incurred 40 casualties of their own, including two company commanders wounded in succession, were now commanded by Captain Thomas Coath, sent forward by Laverty from B Company, and that there were still Japanese aplenty in and around their positions. Furthermore, as dawn broke on 7 April the enemy's mortars and artillery became increasingly active, the latter sending over air-bursts against which there was little defence until head cover for the slit trenches had been completed.

Laverty ordered D Company to clear the enemy from some bashas in which they had taken refuge. Easten gave the task to Lieutenant Peter Doresa's platoon, reinforced with personnel from company headquarters and some Gurkha volunteers. With assistance from C Company, Doresa's men set fire to most of the bashas. In due course, choking Japanese and Jifs[2] staggered out, only to be cut down by rifles, tommy-guns and grenades as they tried to escape. One large basha, a bakery, remained unsubdued. The Japanese within, protected by ovens and piled sacks, had a machine-gun with which they were raking C Company's southern trenches. As the building, which incorporated one brick wall and a tin roof, refused to burn, Easten sought the advice of Lieutenant John Wright of the Bengal Sappers and Miners. Wright taped slabs of gun-cotton to an old door, which the two officers carried up the hill and placed against the brick wall, running for cover as the detonator was activated. The building was completely wrecked by the explosion, those Japanese who emerged being shot down instantly by C Company. Inside was an officer, on the point of dying from his wounds, and a corporal who, having incurred the unutterable disgrace of being captured alive, thereby damning himself for all eternity, willingly disclosed the identity of his regiment and its dispositions; at the first opportunity, this lost soul took his own life.

The position was not finally cleared until next day, 8 April. A Japanese light machine-gun team which had taken cover in a captured trench near a burning ammunition hut suddenly became active. They were clearly in a position to cause a great deal of trouble if another attack was mounted and had to be eliminated as quickly as possible. Lance Corporal John Harman, a D Company sniper, told Easten that he had spotted a route forward that would enable him to deal with the gun, provided his section gave him covering fire with its Bren.

John Harman was a complex, introverted character. Well educated and from a wealthy background, his home was on Lundy Island in the Bristol Channel, where he was more at ease with nature than with his fellow men.

Once, on holiday in Spain, he had been told by an old man of similar out-look that he would live to the age of 70, and he still believed him. He had declined the chance to become a candidate for a commission because he pre-ferred the freedoms of a private soldier; in fact, his recent acceptance of a sin-gle stripe represented a triumph for Easten's powers of persuasion. He had begun his military career as a trooper in the Life Guards but transferred vol-untarily to the infantry when that regiment was mechanised, joining the 4th Royal West Kents in the Arakan. He had made a few friends in the battalion, though none claimed to fully understand him. Few were inclined to chal-lenge him; one does not willingly pick fights with a man who, though his height might be two inches less than six feet, not only has the shoulders of an ox and a huge chest, but also a strange, distant light in his eyes. Perhaps the only sure thing about John Harman was that at Kohima he became one of those rare individuals clearly possessed by the joy of battle.

At soon as his section's Bren began to stutter Harman crawled forward from his slit trench then, before the Japanese could react to him as a mov-ing target, sprinted 35 yards to fling himself down below the level of the enemy fire slit. Bullets passed over him in a continuous stream, but the Japanese were unable to depress their weapon sufficiently. Calmly he took out a grenade with a four-second fuse. The watchers heard the ping as the safety clip flew off, followed by Harman's steady count to three, then a muf-fled crump as the grenade entered the aperture. Having verified that both his opponents were dead, Harman returned to his section with their weapon.

The companies of the 58th Regiment, the most experienced under Sato's command, had been cut to ribbons during their attack on DIS Hill. The slopes were littered with their dead, including the best of their officers and NCOs; about 100 more had been wiped out during the mopping up oper-ations. Major Shimanoe, one of the regiment's battalion commanders, described the action as 'a crushing defeat'. Nevertheless, the 138th Regi-ment had not only completed the encirclement of Kohima, but also that of Brigadier Warren's defensive box at Jotsoma. On 8 April it mounted attacks against Hospital Ridge and the DC's bungalow. At the former, held by the Assam Rifles, the Japanese made some small gains, from which they were dri-ven by a counter-attack the following day. At the latter, the perimeter was struck by a heavy artillery concentration, then assailed by an attack in com-pany strength that broke cover from dead ground across the road. The defenders, consisting of British and Gurkha soldiers from the Reinforcement Depot, joined by Yeo's Indian gunners fighting as infantry, resisted fiercely but were slowly driven out of the bungalow's grounds and back onto the tennis court above. Richards saw the danger at once and stabilised the line with two platoons, one from the Assam Regiment and one from 1/7th Gurkha Rifles. Simultaneously, Laverty instructed Sergeant King's 3in mortars to switch their fire from Jail Hill to the DC's bungalow, and ordered Kenyon's A Company, hitherto in reserve, to take over the sector.

One of the most horrific aspects of this horrific siege was the plight of the wounded. The Advanced Dressing Station (ADS) always had far more patients than it could accommodate. The garrison's senior medical officer, Lieutenant Colonel John Young, and his doctors worked day and night in makeshift operating theatres dug out of the hillside, but the stream of casualties was endless. Although trenches had been dug to accommodate the wounded these were quickly filled. The less urgent cases among new arrivals, therefore, had to wait on their stretchers in the open where, since the Japanese made no attempt whatever to spare the ADS, they sustained further wounds. Young, who had himself reached Kohima on foot through enemy held territory, asked Richards' permission to relieve the congestion by taking out 100 of the walking wounded the same way. Richards approved and the necessary arrangements were made. Guided by a Naga and escorted by a platoon of Rajputs, the long column left the perimeter after dark at a point near Hospital Spur and during the next seven hours covered seven pain-filled miles over the heavily wooded spurs to emerge near Milestone 42 on the Dimapur road, where lorries were waiting to transport the wounded to safety. During the night Richards also sent out more of the non-combatants along the same route. Naturally, the return journey of Young and the escort was much quicker and they reached the perimeter just before first light. Shortly after, the Japanese closed off this gap in their lines and soon the ADS was overflowing again. On another occasion Young, anxious to obtain bedding for his patients, led a party down the spur to the wrecked transport lorries, dealt personally with a sentry, and returned with blankets and other much-needed stores.

On 9 April the Japanese renewed their suicidal attacks on DIS Hill. C and D Companies, reinforced with a Rajput platoon, fought them off but sheer weight of numbers ensured that the enemy secured lodgements. At a critical moment Lance Corporal Harman, bayonet fixed, was seen hurtling downhill through the shattered trees towards a Japanese trench that contained five men armed with automatic weapons. Leaping a rise, he was suddenly on them, shooting his way into the trench. The occupants stood no chance at all against the big man, who was fighting like a Norse berserk and clearly beyond the reach of fear and pain. The watchers could see the movements of his rifle butt as he spitted or smashed his opponents into oblivion. There were two screams followed by a single shot, then he clambered out of the trench, holding aloft a captured machine-gun for the benefit of the cheering the West Kents. Perhaps a sense of release had drained his energy for, to his comrades' horror, he began to walk slowly back, ignoring their shouted warnings to run. A burst of fire caught him in the base of the spine and he fell. Easten brought him in but it was obvious that the wound was mortal, and also that Harman knew it. 'Don't worry about that, sir', he said as Easten tried to staunch the flow of blood. A few minutes later he spoke again, for the last time: 'I've got to go. It was worth it – I got the lot'. For this action, which prevented the premature fall of the hill, and that the previous day, Lance Corporal John Harman received the posthumous award of the Victoria Cross.

Although the Japanese had sustained horrendous casualties, attrition had reduced the size of C and D Companies' platoons to that of sections. Such losses meant that Laverty could no longer afford to hold the entire perimeter and during the evening of 10 April he abandoned DIS Hill, pulling back the now combined C/D Company to FSD Hill, where it joined B Company.

By now, the pattern of the siege, one of the most savage and bestial in history, had been firmly established. The overall situation has been concisely summarised by John Colvin in his excellent study of the battle *Not Ordinary Men*. At Kohima 8-9,000 Japanese had been fought to a standstill by a garrison that never exceeded 600 unwounded fighting men. Another 3,000 Japanese had closed in around 161 Brigade's box at Jotsoma or were preparing to contest the advance of 2nd Division from Dimapur. By day the Kohima garrison endured the accurate fire of mortars, anti-tank guns and snipers who strapped themselves into trees; by night artillery concentrations heralded screaming charges which, because the opposing trenches were often only yards apart, would end in hand-to-hand fighting unless they could be stopped by the combined efforts of the Jotsoma guns, Sergeant King's mortars, Brens firing on fixed lines and hurled grenades. Because so much of the fighting took place at close quarters the dead of both sides remained intermingled with the living. Few forgot the stench of this vilest of battlefields, a compound of decomposition, human waste that could not be disposed of, unwashed bodies and expended explosives. More often than not there was barely sufficient water for drinking; at other times the heavy tropical rain, welcome at first, soaked the men and chilled them to the marrow. Sleep was counted in minutes, waking just the precursor of a continuous conscious nightmare.

It seems incredible that the body and mind could endure such a level of sustained horror for so long. Yet, day after day, the hungry, red-eyed and desperately weary West Kents, without whom the defence would undoubtedly have collapsed, remained a barbed thorn in Sato's side. Reasons for this are not difficult to find. As might be expected in so experienced a battalion, a mutual trust and confidence existed between officers and men, and there were still enough of the original hands left for it to have retained the flavour of its Kentish origins; recently, it had been brought up to strength with a draft from the South Wales Borderers, heirs the inherited traditions of Isandhlwana and Rorke's Drift,[3] who were respected as soldiers and quickly absorbed. Within the battalion family, therefore, the men fought for their comrades as much as themselves. They fought with a deep sense of personal loathing for their enemy, unusual in British troops, induced by their knowledge of Japanese atrocities. They fought, too, to keep the enemy away from their wounded, knowing what would happen to them if the position was overrun. And, of course, they fought because Texas Dan Laverty had told them that this was the place where they were going to halt the Japanese invasion of India, and that was that. As the ordeal continued from one day to the next with no apparent end in sight, considerations of survival focused no further ahead than standing off the next attack. Many of the walking wounded, rather than risk the hazards of the ADS, preferred to remain in their trenches and fought on as best they could.

There were also moral factors which inspired continued effort, such as the willing self-sacrifice of John Harman; the presence of Company Sergeant Major Haines who, though blinded, was guided among the trenches by his minder, encouraging the riflemen with the familiar sound of his voice; the endurance of Sergeant King, the mortar specialist, who, holding together a smashed jaw with his hand, continued to direct the fire of his weapons; and the periodic arrival under fire of Colour Sergeant Eves, the battalion's senior cook, and his dwindling band of helpers, dragging dixies of hot food and tea around the companies to supplement the endless hard tack biscuits and cold rations. There was the battalion chaplain, Captain the Reverend Roy Randolph, spiritually tortured by the unbelievable agony inflicted by man on man, yet constantly touring his flock to bring comfort to the wounded and dying; and Laverty himself, the father of the battalion family, a tough disciplinarian who never seemed to rest, spurring on his officers and men with a few gruff words of encouragement and a smile from tired eyes. It was, of course, a two-way traffic. Whenever Richards arrived in the West Kents' trenches the begrimed, bloody riflemen, who appreciated his visit, would hail him with a cheery: 'Don't worry, sir – you're winning!' It meant a lot to a man whose problems were beyond calculation. The West Kents also liked Charles Pawsey, the Deputy Commissioner, who had chosen to endure the siege rather than abandon his Nagas; one could only admire a man who had watched his home blown to pieces yet, with his open-necked white shirt, grey slacks and companionable dog, still presented a picture of imperturbability and took his turn.

Laverty had requested that his dwindling supplies be replenished with air drops. These began on 13 April, initially with a disappointing outcome. The first drop, of urgently needed 3in mortar rounds, was mistakenly made on the Treasury and used against the garrison that night. The second contained 3.7in howitzer ammunition intended for the guns at Jotsoma and was therefore useless. The third consisted mainly of water jerricans, many of which were punctured by Japanese fire during their descent, but also included medical supplies, for which Young and his surgical team were grateful. Further daily drops produced much better results, although the parachutes snagged among the splintered trees and snipers inevitably took a toll of those recovering the loads.

At Laverty's urging, Richards issued an Order of the Day to all troops on 14 April, congratulating them on their magnificent stand, assuring them that a relief force was on the way and urging them to stand fast until the battle could be brought to a successful conclusion. It was heartening, although spirits raised by the prospect of relief began to sink again when none came, despite the sounds of distant fighting to the west.

Meanwhile, the fight for Kohima raged on without respite. Richards and Laverty struggled to employ their dwindling assets to the best advantage, amalgamating some of the hardest hit sub-units and rotating others on the worst sectors. Yeo and his observers continued to direct the Jotsoma guns with deadly effect and, when they were not breaking up infantry attacks, were sometimes rewarded with the sight of a known Japanese gun position being blown apart. No area was as bitterly contested as the tennis court, where the two sides remained closest to each other. Nightly, the Japanese, refusing to learn from their mistakes, formed up for their attack on the terrace below, chattering as they did so. As each attack was heralded by whistles, bugles and shouts, Yeo's guns and King's mortars, accurate to the foot, would open fire promptly. Those of the attackers who survived the rain of high explosive would swarm over the edge of the court straight into the crossfire of Brens on fixed lines and a barrage of bursting grenades. A few grenades would be thrown in return, a few brave men would run on to be killed on the edge of the garrison's trenches, then the attack would be over, only to be repeated as soon as the Japanese had brought together sufficient troops. Very quickly, the tennis court became covered with bloated bodies, blackening under the sun, providing a feast for the million flies that crawled and multiplied.

During the night of 16/17 April the Japanese finally absorbed some of the lessons of their repeated failures, attacking FSD Hill in great strength, supported by a heavy bombardment that included a high proportion of phosphorous shells. Regardless of their losses, the screaming assault waves swamped the heavily outnumbered defenders, forcing them back to Kuki Piquet. A series of counter-attacks led by an Indian officer, Major Naween Rawlley, thrice recovered some of the lost ground but finally it had to be accepted that FSD Hill had fallen.

The following night Kuki Piquet shared its fate. Once again the defenders were swamped by sheer weight of numbers and although they put up a ferocious fight among the blazing bashas, only a handful succeeded in making their escape. Here died the blinded CSM Haines, encouraging his men to the last. On Garrison Hill Sergeant King, blood oozing from his shattered jaw, declined all assistance until he saw his mortar rounds bursting among the enemy, now capering like demons against the flames on Kuki Piquet, finally halting their advance.

When Richards emerged from his command post on the morning of 18 April the end seemed in sight. The trenches were filled with dead British and Indian soldiers; there were now 600 wounded lying in the ADS; only Garrison Hill remained to him, enclosed by a perimeter no more than 350 yards across; and the Japanese were now only 100 yards from the command posts and the ADS. Unless a miracle took place the Japanese had only to mount another concentrated attack and Kohima Ridge would be theirs. By now, hopeful anticipation of relief had been replaced by cynicism. It was true that fighting was clearly visible between Kohima and Jotsoma, that patrols from 4/7th Rajputs had worked their way through to the garrison and even that arrangements for the prompt evacuation of the wounded had been discussed, but the mood in the trenches that dawn was one of quiet acceptance that the end could not be long delayed.

Brigadier Warren's 161 Brigade had experienced no difficulty in holding its defensive box at Jotsoma, but on its own was too weak to break through to Kohima. The relief, therefore, could not be effected until Major General Grover's 2nd Division arrived from Dimapur. Sato, aware that Grover's leading brigade had left Dimapur on 11 April, used part of his 138th Regiment to establish a roadblock in its path at Zubza. This, coupled with the densely wooded mountain terrain on either side of the road, had proved to be a formidable obstacle. Grover decided that tanks would be needed to batter a way through, but those allocated to him, two squadrons of Lees belonging to 149 Regiment Royal Armoured Corps, had not yet reached Dimapur. However, at Dimapur were five more Lees, the spare vehicles of a squadron that was already fighting at Imphal. The troop leader, Lieutenant R.H.K. Wait, had only skeleton crews with him but quickly recruited some willing volunteers, mainly from 99 Field Regiment Royal Artillery, and drove up to Zubza on 13 April. That night the Japanese, fully aware of the implications, twice tried to break into his harbour area, carrying magnetic anti-tank mines. The first attack was beaten off, the second annihilated. Next day, while the divisional artillery battered the dominant feature covering the roadblock, Wait's tanks smashed in the enemy's bunkers and the 1st Queen's Own Cameron Highlanders went in with the bayonet, leaving none of the defenders alive. Warren's box at Jotsoma was relieved shortly after. The delay that followed came close to proving fatal. According to the plan, the Kohima garrison was to have been relieved on 16 April, but Grover, anxious to secure his flanks, postponed the operation twice, finally setting it for 18 April. In the meantime, two troops of 149 Regiment RAC had arrived and were preparing to spearhead the final breakthrough.

At about 0800 something happened that lifted the first-light mood of black fatalism from the exhausted men lining the Kohima weapon pits. A sudden screaming of 25pdr and heavier 5.5in shells was followed by explosions erupting on all the enemy's positions. Clearly, the 2nd Division's artillery was now within range and it was being used by Yeo and his observers to punish the Japanese as they had never been punished since the battle began. Next, flights of Hurribombers roared in to bomb and strafe. Then, in the distance, those with binoculars saw eight Lees crawling up the road from Dimapur, followed by tracked carriers, infantry, lorries and ambulances. At Milestone 45 the tanks were held up for an hour by a roadblock but succeeded in fighting their way through; the Lee, though obsolete in other theatres of war, was still a good tank to use on jungle roads and tracks, since its 75mm gun, housed in a limited-traverse sponson, could fire armour piercing or high explosive rounds ahead, while its 37mm gun, mounted in a top turret with all-round traverse, fired a canister round that was deadly against troops in the open and could also be used to strip vegetation from around a concealed position. The column halted beneath Hospital Spur, down which the last of the non-combatants stampeded to safety while Young directed the removal of over 300 wounded to the waiting transport. Vindictively, a Japanese gun opened fire, killing many before it was spotted and destroyed by the tanks. At noon 1/1st Punjabis from 161 Brigade, unbelievably spick and span in their relatively clean uniforms, moved into the perimeter to take the strain off the worn-out garrison.

Early on 20 April the 1st Royal Berkshire Regiment relieved the West Kents. It was usual when such a relief took place for members of the two regiments to exchange good natured banter regarding each other's real or imagined shortcomings, but on this occasion there was very little. Somehow, the obvious references to the West Kents being 'The Dirty Half-Hundred'[4] did not seem appropriate in the circumstances; haggard, hollow-eyed, bearded, filthy and bandaged, their uniforms ragged and stained, they had clearly been subjected to an ordeal beyond normal understanding. Some of the Berkshires, anyway, were retching involuntarily at the sights and stench of this most revolting of battlefields.

Laverty was the last of his battalion to leave, and Richards waited until the remnants of his original garrison had filed off the hill. The West Kents were taken to a camp near Dimapur where they had a hot bath, shaved, donned clean uniforms, fed on bully beef rissoles and treacle pudding, then slept without fear. Such small things must have seemed like unimaginable luxuries to men emerging from weeks of unimaginable squalor.

Of the 444 West Kents who had fought at Kohima, 61 were killed and 138 sustained serious wounds; most of the remainder had incurred wounds or injuries of some sort and in normal circumstances would have been classed as unfit for duty. The Assam Regiment's casualties during the siege amounted to 15 killed and 21 wounded out of the 260 men present. Losses among Richards' garrison troops included an estimated 250 killed and 350 wounded.

Just why the Japanese infantry failed to make one final effort after they had taken Kuki Piquet remains a mystery. This failure cost them the battle and ultimately the campaign. Even so, it took Grover's 2nd Division until the middle of May to loosen their hold on Kohima Ridge. Survivors later described the effect of ample and flexibly handled British artillery as crushing, but said it was the tanks that finally broke their spirit. On 12 May two troops of Lees, commanded by Captain P.S. Field, smashed up no less than twelve bunkers with point blank direct gunfire on FSD, DIS and Jail Hills, enabling the British infantry to take possession of the first two. Simultaneously, a Lee commanded by Sergeant Waterhouse was grinding its way to the summit of Garrison Hill along a track carved by a bulldozer. Next day, while Field dealt with further bunkers on Kuki Piquet, Waterhouse spearheaded an attack on the tennis court, deliberately dropping over the terrace to crush one bunker, then shooting up every position in sight, including the ruins of the DC's bungalow. By the end of this 40-minute action not one Japanese remained alive in the area; casualties among Waterhouse's supporting infantry amounted to one man slightly wounded.

By the end of May the remnants of Sato's division, starving, diseased and shooting their own wounded to prevent capture, were staggering back through the mountains towards the Chindwin, pursued by the 7th Indian Division. Sato believed that Mutaguchi, his Army Commander, had failed to support him and initiated a public feud so bitter that both were removed from their commands. Stopford's XXXIII Corps, with 149 Regiment in the lead, pressed on along the road to relieve IV Corps at Imphal. Kawabe's U-go offensive was over; it had cost him 53,000 in dead alone, and the result was a defeat from which the Burma Area Army never recovered.

The battle honour 'Kohima' was carried with justifiable pride on the colours of nineteen British and Indian regiments; the much rarer honour 'Defence of Kohima' was awarded only to the Queen's Own Royal West Kent Regiment and the 1st Assam Regiment.

Notes

1. See *Last Stand!* Chapter 11.
2. Jifs were former Indian prisoners of war, captured in Malaya or during the first Burma campaign, who had been persuaded by renegade politicians to join the so-called Indian National Army and fight for the Japanese. Jifs were believed to be implicated in the massacre of wounded during the Admin Box battle, and were responsible for the murder of several Royal Norfolk Regiment convalescents at Kohima, where they also used loudspeaker broadcasts in unsuccessful attempts to persuade the garrison's Indian soldiers to desert. The Japanese clearly had little regard for the fighting value of their Jif units. With Indian independence on the horizon, the British wisely left the judgement of such men to the Indians themselves.
3. See *Last Stand!* Chapter 5.
4. As with many regimental nicknames, different explanations exist as to its origins. One has it that during a battle in the Peninsular War continuous heavy firing blackened hands and faces with expended powder; another is that it stems from the black facings (collar and cuffs) worn by the regiment at this time, although these were not unique. The regiment was originally numbered as the 50th, hence the 'half-hundred'.
5. Gallantry awards won by the West Kents during the Siege of Kohima included one posthumous Victoria Cross (Lance Corporal Harman); one Distinguished Service Order (Lieutenant Colonel Laverty); three Military Crosses; three Distinguished Conduct Medals; and four Military Medals. Many more were earned.

11
Hinge of Victory: The Defence of Mortain, 7-12 August 1944

Regarded as the archetypal Prussian officer, Field Marshal Gerd von Rundstedt was a product of cadet academy and General Staff training, above politics, remote, austere and possessed of such gravitas that even Hitler accorded him a grudging respect. In the summer of 1944 he was serving as Commander-in-Chief West, although such was the level of interference from Hitler and the Oberkommando des Wehrmacht (OKW) that at one stage he complained that his real authority did not extend beyond changing the sentries at his own gate. He was unable to prevent the Allied landings in Normandy on 6 June and when a critical counter-attack failed three days later he reached the conclusion that, in the long term, the writing was on the wall for Nazi Germany. Even so, he believed that, given a free hand in the conduct of operations, he could have made the Allies pay a fearful price for their victory. He had hoped to fight a protracted withdrawal, inflicting heavy losses for every piece of ground given up, believing that he might buy sufficient time for the war to be ended by political means, thereby saving Germany from the consequences of total defeat. It was not to be, for Hitler prohibited any withdrawals whatever and because of this the German armies in Normandy were bled white by Allied air power, naval gunfire and a crushing weight of artillery. On 1 July, tired and beginning to feel the weight of his 68 years, Rundstedt picked up the telephone and asked to be connected with Field Marshal Wilhelm Keitel, the Chief of OKW.

Keitel was a man of very different stamp. By instinct, he would have preferred to be a gentleman farmer, but his family had propelled him into the Army. Both he and his wife were intensely loyal to Hitler and it was to this, plus the fact that he had evolved into a hard-working bureaucrat of limited intelligence, that he owed his appointment. Many within the Army believed that his ambitions had far outstripped his abilities and spoke of him contemptuously as Lakaitel – the lackey. On the rare occasions that he ventured to disagree with Hitler on professional grounds, the latter was able to bully him into total submission very quickly. Aware of his limitations, he attempted to conceal these by becoming a dedicated sycophant and the Führer's principal source of gossip.

When Rundstedt informed him of the hopeless strategic situation that had developed in the West, Keitel, despite his exalted rank and position, was unable to offer any constructive solution.

'What shall we do?' he asked.

'Make peace, you fools!' replied Rundstedt, enraged by the ineffective response. 'What else can you do?'

Needless to say, details of the conversation were relayed to Hitler in the shortest possible time. Next day a representative arrived at Rundstedt's headquarters to present him with the Oak Leaves to his Knights' Cross and inform him that he was to be replaced by Field Marshal Gunther von Kluge immediately.

Kluge was a capable, energetic officer but he had no fresh solutions to offer and was no more master in his own house than Rundstedt had been. On 17 July he also assumed direct responsibility for Army Group B when its commander, Field Marshal Erwin Rommel, was seriously wounded and evacuated to Germany. In the meantime the German armies continued to be written down as they were forced to react to the Allied strategy, which was to maintain continuous pressure on the British and Canadian sectors, thereby pinning down the bulk of the German armour, while at the southern end of the Allied line the American First Army prepared to break out of its beachhead.

So successful was this strategy that on the eve of the breakout, code-named Cobra, there were 645 German tanks in the line opposite the British and Canadians but only 190 opposite the Americans. On 25 July, in the wake of a bomb carpet that turned the German forward defences into a cratered moonscape, the Americans broke through and began advancing southwards towards Avranches. Kluge was slow to react, but on 28 July he ordered the 2nd and 116th Panzer Divisions to leave their positions opposite the British sector and move into the danger zone. Aware of the move, General Sir Bernard Montgomery promptly mounted a series of holding offensives designed to prevent the transfer of further German units. The first of these, Operation Bluecoat, achieved such deep and unexpected penetrations that Kluge was compelled to plug the gap with 21st Panzer Division and a Tiger battalion, followed by 9th and 10th SS Panzer Divisions, all of which were harried incessantly by fighter bombers as they moved into the line. This holding strategy was then taken up by the Canadians on the Allied left with a drive aimed at Falaise that further pinned down the German armour and was barely contained by the 12th SS Panzer Division 'Hitlerjugend' at the cost of its own destruction.

Back on the American sector Lieutenant General George S. Patton's US Third Army was activated on 1 August. Patton's four corps streamed through the gap at Avranches in succession, VIII Corps swinging right into Brittany, XV Corps driving hard for Le Mans, and XX Corps, followed by XII Corps, heading south to the Loire before swinging east. Three-quarters of Third Army was, in fact, wheeling towards the Seine, pivoting on First Army's VII Corps at Mortain.

Kluge was only too aware that with his right held fast by the British and Canadians and his left already turned, any northwards pressure by Patton would ultimately entrap all the German armies in Normandy. His advice to Hitler, therefore, was that the panzer and panzergrenadier divisions should be used as a screen behind which the rest of his command should withdraw across the Seine. Hitler, however, rejected the idea out of hand. He was still recovering from the injuries he had sustained in the 20 July Bomb Plot and in a climate where senior officers were being arrested and shot or strangled with piano wire it was obviously unwise to argue with him, especially as Kluge had himself been an unwilling conspirator.

Having been led by his toadies to believe that the Normandy Front was inherently stable, Hitler was primarily concerned with restoring his fortunes on the Eastern Front, where the German Army Group Centre had been all but annihilated by a major Soviet offensive. Nevertheless, having assumed the mantle of the Army's Commander-in-Chief some years earlier, the Führer could not escape making some sort of decision and, like many of the decisions he made at this phase of the war, this was to be influenced by two factors. The first of these was his personal conviction that Destiny required him to play the role of the Feldherr or Warrior King, and that when the situation looked bleakest his enemies would play into his hands, enabling him to win a decisive strategic victory, just as Frederick the Great had done two centuries earlier. The second was that all his planning was done from the map, without any knowledge of the terrain or the tactical conditions prevailing at the front. He was apparently unaware, for example, that the close, leafy, rolling country of the Normandy bocage was so unsuited to armoured operations that any major offensive would have to be based on the local road network; and he disregarded altogether the Allies' total air superiority and the terrible effects of their flexibly-handled artillery.

The orders he gave Kluge were crisp and clear. The field marshal would assemble a force of eight panzer divisions and with this he would counter-attack along the axis Mortain-Avranches, severing the narrow corridor through which Patton's troops received all their supplies. 'When we reach the sea', he continued, 'the American spearheads will be cut off....The deci-

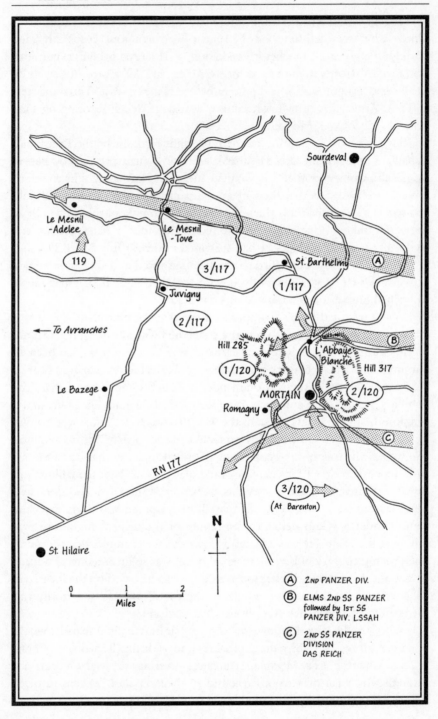

Sourdeval

Le Mesnil
-Adelee

Le Mesnil
-Tove

St. Barthelmy

119

(A)

3/117

1/117

Juvigny

2/117

To Avranches

(B)

Hill 285

L'Abbaye
Blanche

Hill 317

1/120

2/120

MORTAIN

Le Bazege

Romagny

(C)

RN 177

3/120

(At Barenton)

N

St. Hilaire

0   1   2
Miles

(A) 2ND PANZER DIV.

(B) ELMS 2ND SS PANZER
followed by 1ST SS
PANZER DIV. LSSAH

(C) 2ND SS PANZER
DIVISION
DAS REICH

sion in the Battle of France depends on the success of the attack. The Commander-in-Chief West has a unique opportunity, *which will never return*, to drive into an exposed enemy area and thereby change the situation entirely'.

Superficially, the plan was attractive, for if Patton's army could be deprived of fuel and ammunition at such a critical juncture not only would a serious check be imposed on the Allied strategy, but Kluge would also gain the time he needed to stabilise the front. Some German commanders, notably General Paul Hausser, the commander of the Seventh Army, were enthusiastic about the idea and foresaw no difficulty in closing the Avranches gap, although they had serious reservations about the second phase of Hitler's plan, which involved swinging north into the flank of the original American beachhead. The major difficulty lay in assembling sufficient troops for the counter-stroke, for so deeply was the German armour involved in the fighting on other sectors that Kluge was only able to scrape together four armoured divisions (2nd and 116th Panzer, 1st SS Panzer 'Leibstandarte SS Adolf Hitler' (LSSAH) and 2nd SS Panzer 'Das Reich', grouped together as XLVII Panzer Corps under General Baron Hans von Funck) with just 185 tanks and assault guns between them. One factor beyond German control was flying conditions which, if good, would allow Luftwaffe participation and, if bad, would ground the Allied air forces. Another was the nature of the opposition that might be encountered between Mortain and Avranches, but at this stage the Germans were inclined to undervalue the fighting abilities the American troops in Normandy and were not unduly worried. H Hour for the counter-offensive, codenamed Liège, was set for 2200 on 6 August.

In fact, the only formation lying in the path of the projected drive was the US 30th Infantry Division, commanded by Major General Leland Hobbs, a West Point classmate of General Dwight D. Eisenhower, the Allied Supreme Commander. According to Bradley, another West Point contemporary, he was an extrovert with 'a stubborn streak a mile wide' and a tight disciplinarian who was able to impose his personality on his troops. The 30th Division was a National Guard formation that originally drew its recruits from the Carolinas, Georgia and Tennessee. However, since its mobilisation in the autumn of 1940 it had been used as a quarry to provide cadres for fresh divisions as the Army expanded steadily and comparatively few of the old hands were left. The division had begun landing in Normandy shortly after D Day and had fought in the apparently endless Battle of the Hedgerows, sustaining heavy casualties in the capture of St Lô and the Cobra breakout. Many of its losses had been caused by short bombing and because of this the division's attitude to the USAAF was ambivalent, to say the least.

On 5 August Hobbs' regiments began taking over the positions occupied by the 1st Infantry Division, which had liberated Mortain two days previously. Immediately to the east of the picturesque little town 2/120th Infantry Regiment occupied Hill 317, from the summit of which views extended across a wide area in every direction. 1/120th were emplaced on the lower slopes of Hill 285 to the north-west of the town. Most of 3/120th, however, together with a company of Shermans from the division's 743rd Tank Battalion, was despatched south-east towards Barenton, which was reported as being clear of the enemy; in the event, the town was found to be strongly held and the task force was forced to dig in for the night. The three battalions of 117th Infantry Regiment were positioned in and to the west of the village of St Barthelmy, two miles north of Mortain. Hobbs' third regiment, 119th Infantry, was in reserve some seven miles west of St Barthelmy, less one battalion that had been temporarily detached to 2nd Armored Division. The divisional artillery was deployed along a line stretching southwards from a point three miles west of St Barthelmy; in the opinion of Brigadier General James Lewis, Hobbs' artillery commander, who had inherited the battery positions from 1st Division, this left the guns too exposed in the event of an enemy counter-attack, but on 5 and 6 August the thoughts of most officers were more concerned with maintaining the offensive than with precautionary defence. Hobbs' own headquarters were located in a château at La Bazoge, six miles west of Mortain.

Although F.W. Winterbotham claimed in his book *The Ultra Secret* that Bradley was given four days' warning of the German counter-offensive, this was contested by Ralph Bennett in *Ultra in the West*, published four years later. The dispute is further discussed by Alwyn Featherston in *Saving the Breakout* and the conclusion reached is that the first intimation from Ultra did not reach Bradley until late on 6 August. Thus far, he had not been inclined to attach too much importance to the evidence produced by his own intelligence sources regarding the enemy's preparations, but the involvement of Ultra clearly indicated that something major was in the offing. A teleprinter warning was despatched to Major General J. Lawton Collins at VII Corps, who relayed it to Hobbs:

'Enemy counter-attack expected vicinity Mortain from East and slant or North within the next 12 hours....RCT (Regimental Combat Team) 119 remain division reserve, moving one battalion vicinity of Le Tellevil to protect lines of communication there and to the North. 30th Division also reinforce battalion on Hill (317). Acknowledge receipt of this message without delay'.

It was too late, for although Operation Liège had begun over two-and-a-half hours behind schedule, there was no time to warn the troops at the front and the Germans achieved complete tactical surprise.

Despite this advantage, Kluge's counter-offensive got off to a poor start. On the right the 116th Panzer was unable to move at all because it had not been fully relieved in the sector of the line it was holding. To its left 2nd Panzer succeeded in capturing St Barthelmy after heavy fighting and then advanced slowly against stiffening opposition for a further seven miles before being fought to a standstill by Combat Command B 3rd Armored Division. Further south, Das Reich managed to capture the town of Mortain, but not the dominant hills to the east and west, and advanced a few miles beyond. LSSAH, also delayed by late relief and a difficult approach march, was to have exploited the initial breakthrough but did not really enter the battle until the following morning.

The most critical fighting took place in and to the north of Mortain itself. During the early hours of 7 August panzergrenadiers of Das Reich, followed by tanks, overran the 120th Infantry's south-eastern perimeter outposts and broke into the town. Taken completely by surprise, the Americans were at first unable to offer organised resistance, although here and there isolated tanks were picked off by dogged bazooka teams. Most of those in the town, however, were forced out to the north and west, or joined those on Hills 317 and 285, or were compelled to seek refuge in cellars where they remained throughout the battle.

Dawn broke accompanied by a heavy mist that completely grounded the Allied air forces. This enabled the Germans to maintain their westwards progress, albeit slowly, and to mount the first attacks on the two hills, which were broken up with the assistance of Hobbs' divisional artillery.

At about this time Funck's troops received their first serious check. It occurred at a road junction named L'Abbaye Blanche, which took its name from the large white abbey lying just to the east the little river Cance. Here, three bridges crossed the stream, two close to the abbey while the third, the Pont de la Vacherie (Dairy Bridge), lying approximately four miles to the north, carried a road leading to St Barthelmy that joined the road northwards from Mortain.

Holding this area of obvious tactical importance was a small force commanded by Lieutenant Tom Springfield of the 823rd Tank Destroyer Battalion. Springfield had with him four M5 3in towed anti-tank guns, two of which he had dug in under cover of a hedgerow covering Dairy Bridge, some 40 yards distant, while the remaining two were positioned to cover any threat that might develop from the north. The southern end of the position,

187

though still under Springfield's command by virtue of seniority, was Lieu-tenant Tom Andrews' 1st Platoon of F Company 120th Infantry, reinforced with two M1 57mm towed anti-tank guns from the regiment's anti-tank pla-toon. Andrews covered each of the two abbey bridges with one of his guns and backed these with minefields, bazooka teams and machine-gun posi-tions. Bisecting the entire position diagonally from north-east to south-west was a railway with a station situated approximately two miles south-west of Dairy Bridge.

At about 0500 a troop of Das Reich's reconnaissance battalion, consist-ing of a light armoured car, a motorcycle with sidecar, a Kübelwagen (the German equivalent of the Jeep), and an open staff car, crossed Dairy Bridge and turned onto a secondary track between the railway and the river, head-ing towards the Abbey bridges. As the column approached the first bridge one of Andrews' 57mm guns banged twice, setting the armoured car and staff car ablaze; simultaneously, machine-gun fire cut down the motorcycle combination crew and wrecked the Kübelwagen. None of the survivors escaped and the wreckage of their vehicles blocked the track for the remain-der of the battle.

Minutes later it became clear that the purpose of the reconnaissance troop had been to provide left-flank protection for one of Das Reich's panz-ergrenadier regiments moving north towards St Barthelmy. As the head of the column crossed Dairy Bridge, Springfield noted that the road beyond was so steep that the drivers were forced to change down. The leading vehi-cles began to bunch as they crawled up the hill and at that precise moment two of his M5s opened fire. Five shots wrecked five vehicles, including three half-tracks, a PzKw IV tank and an ammunition lorry that erupted in a gigan-tic, ear-shattering fireball. Conscious that his column had come under microscopically accurate fire, deprived of the information that in other cir-cumstances might have been provided by his reconnaissance troop, and see-ing the road ahead immovably blocked with a tangle of burning wreckage, the German regimental commander and his staff abandoned their own vehi-cles and took refuge in a barn near the bridge, where they remained pinned down for the next eight hours.

Someone, however, set about initiating a response. The Germans were uncertain of the precise whereabouts of Springfield's guns although they knew the general area in which they were located, and they began shelling it. In fact, the guns were positioned near the crest of a narrow ridge, so that the shells either burst on the forward slope some way in front of them or passed harmlessly overhead. Heavy mortars joined in, their opening salvo landing so close that Springfield ordered one of his guns to take out a nearby church steeple that he suspected was being used as an artillery observation post. After that, the mortar fire drifted ineffectively away into empty space.

At about 0600 two German 75mm howitzer half-tracks, accompanied by an infantry company, put in an attack on the American position from the north. This was clearly intended to outflank the two guns that had caused the damage at the bridge, but quickly ran into trouble when it was engaged by the two other guns and their local defence squad. It is some measure of Springfield's leadership that as his platoon fought its way through the Normandy campaign, he had insisted that his men collect any abandoned automatic weapons that they came across, so that it now possessed a formidable array of .50 and .30-calibre machine-guns and ample ammunition. Consequently, when the unsuspecting half-tracks were suddenly blown apart, the German infantry found itself completely outmatched in the ensuing firefight. After fifteen minutes the survivors abandoned the unequal contest and withdrew. Thus far, Springfield had succeeded in severing lateral communication between the two wings of the enemy offensive without incurring a single casualty.

At St Barthelmy, the 1/117th Infantry and their attached tank destroyer platoons were engaged in a bitter, one-sided battle against elements of 2nd Panzer and LSSAH. Under immense pressure, the Americans were forced to give ground slowly but were not finally forced out of the town until approximately 1230. At Mortain itself 1/120th Infantry still held Hill 285, despite the enemy having secured a lodgement on the upper slopes, and 2/120th, supplemented by fugitives from the town, was fully occupied in beating off attacks on Hill 317. These sometimes involved tanks, whose routes to the summit were limited and therefore predictable, but despite this they were pressed home to within grenade throwing range. At this stage of the battle only one artillery battalion was available to support the defenders, the rest being either engaged in other fire missions or being forced to limber up and move to new battery positions by the German probes reaching westward from Mortain. In some cases the enemy tanks broke into the gun positions, leaving the gunners no alternative other than to remove the breech blocks and beat a hasty retreat through the mist; the guns thus temporarily abandoned were all subsequently recovered.

Then, at about noon, the mist began to disperse and the situation on the confused battlefield underwent a dramatic change. Senior Allied officers, now fully briefed as to the implications of the German counter-offensive, reacted at once. Major General Elwood Quesada, commanding the USAAF's IX Tactical Air Command, conferred over the telephone with Air Vice Marshal Sir Harry Broadhurst of the British Second Tactical Air Force and the two agreed that they would deal jointly with the situation that had developed at Mortain. Broadhurst had ten rocket-firing Typhoon squadrons in Normandy which would be used to attack the German armour, while Quesada's fighter squadrons would fly top cover and prevent intervention by the Luftwaffe.

Broadhurst's squadrons had, in fact, been standing by since before dawn and were quickly airborne, the first of them reaching the battlefield at about 1230. The Typhoon, armed with four 20mm cannon and eight 60lb high explosive rockets, was regarded at the time as the supreme tank buster, although this view was not confirmed by subsequent analysis. The explosion of each rocket was equivalent to that of a medium artillery shell; a direct hit would certainly disable the majority of German tanks, and even a near miss could cause serious damage. Against this, direct hits were comparatively rare, being very difficult to obtain with an unstabilised missile fired from an air-craft flying at over 400mph. On the other hand, when employed against

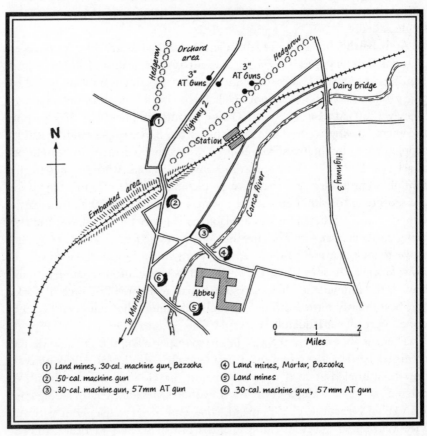

① Land mines, .30-cal. machine gun, Bazooka ④ Land mines, Mortar, Bazooka
② .50-cal. machine gun ⑤ Land mines
③ .30-cal. machine gun, 57mm AT gun ⑥ .30-cal. machine gun, 57mm AT gun

long nose-to-tail columns of enemy vehicles, now stalled on the narrow bocage roads, their effect was devastating. Roaring low in pairs across the battlefield, the Typhoons used their rockets and cannon to deadly effect, creating a tangle of wrecked tanks, armoured cars, half-tracks and supply vehicles that blocked the Germans' principal axes of advance. Many crews, terrified by the sustained onset against which there was no defence, simply abandoned their vehicles and sought shelter elsewhere. Altogether, Broadhurst's squadrons expended 2088 rockets, 80 bombs and many thousand rounds of 20mm cannon ammunition, claiming 81 tanks destroyed and 54 seriously damaged. This proved to be optimistic, for subsequent examination of the 78 armoured vehicles found on the battlefield revealed that more than half had been destroyed by artillery or anti-tank weapons; on the other hand, as some tanks are known to have been recovered by the Germans after the air attack, it seems that the true figure will never be established.

As already mentioned, losses from 'friendly fire' are not a modern phenomenon and the 30th Division had already sustained casualties on at least two occasions as a result of USAAF bombing. Now, it sustained several more at the hands of the RAF, including one man killed and several wounded at Springfield's L'Abbaye Blanche roadblock. Many of the Americans were bitterly philosophical about such incidents, expecting nothing better from airmen. Others, however, took a wider view, one member of the 117th Infantry stating that without the intervention of the Typhoons the story of Mortain would have been different; another commented that although the Germans had been halted they could not have been held without their assistance.

The real impact of the Typhoon attack was on men's minds. For most of the embattled Americans it uplifted their morale, while for the Germans it was nerve-shattering and deeply depressing. 'The activities of the fighter-bombers are almost unbearable', Funck signalled to his superiors. 'LSSAH reports that air attacks of such intensity have never before been experienced. Its attack has been stopped'. And again, later in the afternoon: 'The attack has made no progress since 1300 hours because of the large number of enemy fighter-bombers and the absence of our own air force....There is bitter fighting around Mortain. The situation of our tanks is becoming very alarming. The 116th has not advanced one step today'. His complaint regarding the Luftwaffe was understandable although nothing could be done about it since Quesada's fighters were engaging the German aircraft as soon as they were airborne.

By now, too, the Americans' own counter-measures were beginning to take effect. Bradley moved the 4th Division and CCB 3rd Armored Division into position to block the deepest penetration and swung CCA 2nd

Armored Division in a wide arc through St Hilaire and Le Teilleul to secure Barenton, from whence it could menace the right-rear of the narrow German advance. At VII Corps, too, Collins was busy reinforcing 30th Division so that ultimately Brigadier General Lewis, the latter's senior artilleryman, had no less than twelve and a half batteries at his immediate disposal, armed with twelve 8in, twelve 4.5in, 48 155mm and 78 105mm guns. Concentrations fired by some of these had already halted the German spearheads by the time the Typhoons arrived and with the clearing of the mist it became possible to direct the remainder against the trapped columns and other objectives, under the direction of artillery observers on the encircled Hill 317.

By evening it was clear that the German counter-offensive was going nowhere, least of all to Avranches. Fully aware of the realities of the situation, Kluge cancelled Operation Liège and was immediately subjected to a furious tirade from Hitler. The Commander-in-Chief West, the Führer raged, had been half-hearted; the attack had been launched before adequate resources had been assembled and it had been clumsily executed. Why had LSSAH been routed through St Barthelmy, where resistance had been heaviest, instead of through Mortain, where Das Reich had achieved a penetration? Some regard this last criticism as valid; yet it was not, for had LSSAH been directed to reinforce Das Reich's apparent success, it would simply have run into a different set of problems at L'Abbaye Blanche and the untaken Hills 285 and 317.

Nevertheless, Hitler remained quite convinced that his plan would succeed, given the required motivation and necessary resources. He ordered II SS Panzer Corps to be withdrawn from the British sector and committed to a renewed assault at Mortain. That such an attack might succeed against a fully prepared defence when its predecessor had failed despite taking the Americans by surprise was, to say the least, highly improbable, yet Kluge could only obey. He was to set, in turn, two dates for the renewal of Operation Liège, but both were overtaken by events elsewhere and in due course it became quite impossible to comply with Hitler's demands.

Many campaign studies regard the halting of the German armour with concentrated artillery fire and air attacks during the afternoon of 7 August as marking the end of Operation Liège. This may be true in the strategic sense, but as the German intention was to renew the counter-offensive it was essential that they should eliminate such thorns in their side as the roadblock at L'Abbaye Blanche and Hills 285 and 317, possession of which would confer obvious advantages and enable the entire Mortain area to be used as a springboard. Thus, while the senior Allied commanders could feel some satisfaction on the evening of 7 August, for the soldiers of Hobbs' now weary

and fragmented division the battle would continue with undiminished ferocity for several more days.

Patrols probed the defences at L'Abbaye Blanche at first light on 8
August. Shortly after, three PzKw IVs and four half-tracks launched an
attack from the north. Springfield's two anti-tank guns facing in that direction knocked out all save one tank, which may have been able to reverse out
of action in a damaged state. The panzergrenadiers, however, were already
closing in and a two-hour fire-fight ensued, ending when Springfield led five
of his men in a counter-attack that secured fifteen prisoners.

Simultaneously, the southern end of the roadblock came under heavy
machine-gun and artillery fire and an armoured reconnaissance troop
attempted to rush one of the Abbey bridges from the south-east. Here the
sting was taken out of the attack by Private First Class Robert Vollmer,
armed with a bazooka, who, in quick succession destroyed an armoured car,
a motorcycle combination, a second armoured car and a machine-gun post
that had provided covering fire for the attack. After this, apart from regular
shelling, the Germans left the roadblock alone, although they still attempted
to push vehicles up the hill beyond Dairy Bridge, losing three Panthers and
several other vehicles in the process.

The 1/120th on Hill 285 was also attacked at first light on 9th August
but succeeded in holding its own. Of greater importance to the Germans,
however, was the capture of Hill 317, possession of which would place
them in a much stronger position if Operation Liège was reactivated.
Indeed, so much importance did they attach to the feature that the elements of Das Reich that were already mounting attacks against it were reinforced by part of the newly arrived 17th SS Panzergrenadier Division 'Götz
von Berlichingen'.

Nominally, the hill was held by 2/120th with Lieutenant Joseph Reaser's
K Company at the northern end of the summit, Lieutenant Ralph Kerley's
E Company on the south-eastern corner and Lieutenant Ronal Woody's G
Company on the south-western slopes overlooking the town. In addition,
there were a number of fugitives from the regiment's C, F, H, Anti-tank and
Cannon Companies, a handful from the 823rd Tank Destroyer Battalion and
six forward observation officers from the 230th Field Artillery Battalion, giving an overall total of approximately 700 men. Unfortunately, the Second
Battalion's command post had been located in the town and it was overrun
during the early hours of the battle, forcing the commanding officer, Lieutenant Colonel Eads Hardaway, and his staff into temporary hiding; worse
still, when Hardaway and his group attempted to work their way up the hill
they were quickly captured. As a result of this each company commander

fought a separate, uncoordinated battle with the stragglers fitting in as best they could. It was not, in fact, until the morning of 8 August that some measure of overall control was established when Captain Delmont Byrn, the commander of the regiment's Heavy Weapons Company, led an E Company patrol that succeeded in making contact with G and K Companies, despite the constant enemy shelling. Thereafter, Captain Reynold Erichson, normally the commander of F Company, assumed command of the troops on the hill by virtue of seniority. G Company was pulled back onto the summit, creating a much tighter defensive perimeter.

Most of the German attacks were pressed to very close quarters. Hill 317's real teeth, however, were its artillery observers who were not only able to direct Lewis's guns in defensive fire tasks that broke up each assault, but also employ them in counter-battery work that steadily wrote down the value of the German artillery. When not so employed, the observers were able to bring down concentrations on any group of German vehicles that was unwise enough to disclose its presence.

During the afternoon of 9 August an SS officer carrying a white flag appeared in front of E Company's position. He was blindfolded and taken up to Kerley's command post, where Erichson happened to be present. He informed them of Hardaway's capture, described the situation on Hill 317 as hopeless, suggested that Erichson's duty to his men lay in surrender, and promised that unless he did so by 2000 the entire battalion would be annihilated. Erichson declined and Kerley, irritated by the German's pomposity, told the SS man where to go in the bluntest of Anglo-Saxon phrases.

What was intended as the final assault, delivered by infantry from 17th SS Panzergrenadier Division with a company of Das Reich's Panthers in support, commenced at 2015. It was broken up by the combined fire of seven artillery batteries but was pressed so close that at one point Kerley requested fire on his own position. Five minutes later the Germans were in retreat.

The repulse of the attack had a profound effect on the Americans' morale. Hitherto, they had done their job but been a prey to fear and anxiety; now, they were fiercely intent on holding the hill, whatever the cost. As Byrn later put it to Alwyn Featherston, 'It was like nobody expected to live anymore. Once that decision was made, you could go on, just doing what you were doing, living day to day, hour to hour'.

Determined as the defenders of Hill 317 were, they were now seriously short of ammunition, food, water and medical supplies. They were desperately tired and casualties were mounting daily. Worst of all, the artillery observers' radio batteries, upon which they depended for their very survival, were running down to the point that transmissions were barely audible.

Colonel Hammond Birks, commanding 120th Infantry, initiated several attempts to relieve or reinforce them but none succeeded in crossing the 800 yards that separated the hill from the new American line. He also managed to arrange an air-supply drop despite unbelievable procrastination of staff officers at VII Corps. When this took place during the afternoon of 10 August much of it fell outside the perimeter although some ammunition and a little food were recovered. After this the 230th Field Artillery succeeded in firing several smoke shells filled with medical supplies onto the hill; the drug and plasma containers did not survive the impact but the dressings were usable.

The end, when it came, was something of an anti-climax. Throughout 11 August enemy columns began moving eastwards, harried by the artillery observers on the hill. Sounds of movement continued during the night. By the following morning the Germans had gone. The relief of Hill 317 took place immediately and 357 dog-tired men walked slowly down its slopes into the ruins of the town with nothing but food and sleep on their minds; behind them lay more than 300 of their comrades, killed or wounded, the latter receiving adequate medical attention for the first time since the battle began.

The final destruction of the German armies in Normandy began just four days later. Profiting from the Hitler's obsession with the renewal of Operation Liège, Patton's Third Army had used the Mortain salient as a hinge and swung north to menace Kluge's left and rear. Simultaneously, combined British and Canadian advances from the north drove in his right. By 16 August three major German formations – Seventh Army, Fifth Panzer Army and Panzer Group Eberbach, the last containing the divisions employed at Mortain – were pinned inside a pocket some 25 miles long and fifteen wide. This continued to shrink under relentless Allied pressure until, on 21 August, the last exit was finally closed. About 60,000 men were caught in the trap. Kluge was promptly dismissed but rather than return to Germany, where his unwilling complicity in the 20 July Bomb Plot would inevitably be exposed, he took his own life.

If Major General Leland Hobbs' 30th Division had not stood and fought at Mortain the end of the campaign would not, perhaps, have been quite so dramatic. Montgomery's memoirs make it clear that the inspiration for the great Allied double envelopment that created the Falaise Pocket was provided by Hitler's obsession with breaking through at Mortain, which actually created a situation from which there was no escape.

In the six days of fighting the 30th Division sustained 1834 casualties, including 165 killed and 442 missing, which can be regarded as remarkably light in the circumstances. Presidential Unit Citations were earned by 1/117th Infantry for its stand at St Barthelmy and by 2/120th Infantry and K Company 3/120th for their defence of Hill 317; by two platoons of the 120th's Anti-tank Company for their part in the defence of the L'Abbaye Blanche roadblock; and by A and B Companies 823rd Tank Destroyer Battalion for actions at L'Abbaye Blanche and St Barthelmy. Springfield received the Silver Star; and the five company commanders on Hill 317 – Erichson, Byrn, Reaser, Kerley and Woody – were all awarded the Distinguished Service Cross.

12
Bloodbath on Sulphur Island:
Iwo Jima, February – March 1945

There are few places on earth less attractive than Iwo Jima, a small kite-shaped island in the Volcano-Bonin group, situated some 660 nautical miles south of Tokyo. Measuring less than five miles from north to south and half that distance from east to west at its widest point, it has no natural water supply and its sterile, stony soil provides sustenance only for a few stunted trees, gnarled bushes and coarse grass. Those who choose to live there store rainwater in small cisterns, fertilise their plots with seaweed to the extent that vegetables and sugar cane can be grown, and eke out their diet with fish. The island's only natural asset is sulphur, lying just below the surface.

Nature has divided Iwo Jima into three distinct areas. At its southern tip is the conical Mount Suribachi, an extinct volcano rising to 550 feet above sea level. Immediately to the north is a narrow area of land separating beaches to the east and west. On both sides this is bordered by a deep layer of soft, black, volcanic ash which the wind blows into a shifting pattern of steep sand terraces. Movement across these, the famous Sands of Iwo Jima, is difficult on foot and in places impossible even for tracked vehicles. The northern part of the island consists of a domed plateau about one mile in diameter, incorporating several low summits that would appear on tactical maps as Hills 382, 362A, 362B and 362C, representing their height in feet above sea level. The plateau itself is composed of a jumble of shattered volcanic rock formed into twisted ridges and gorges with occasional level areas. Here the hot sulphur below warms the ground and vents steam in many places. The coastline around the northern plateau rises steeply with few exits from the narrow beaches so that anyone wishing to land on the island has to do so further south. No natural harbour exists and the act of landing is itself complicated by heavy surf and a steeply shelving shoreline.

If Nature had been unkind to Iwo Jima, Geography was equally so. The fact that the island lay approximately midway between Tokyo and the Mariana Islands, whence American B-29 heavy bombers had begun raiding the Japanese homeland in the autumn of 1944, gave it an immense strategic importance. The reason for this was that the B-29s were sustaining serious losses from enemy fighters over Japan, and could not be escorted because their own fighters lacked the necessary range for the round trip. The American Joint War Planning Committee quickly appreciated that by establishing a fighter base on Iwo Jima this problem could be solved. Furthermore, an airfield on the island could also be used to receive B-29s damaged over Japan. Finally, since Iwo Jima was sovereign Japanese territory administered

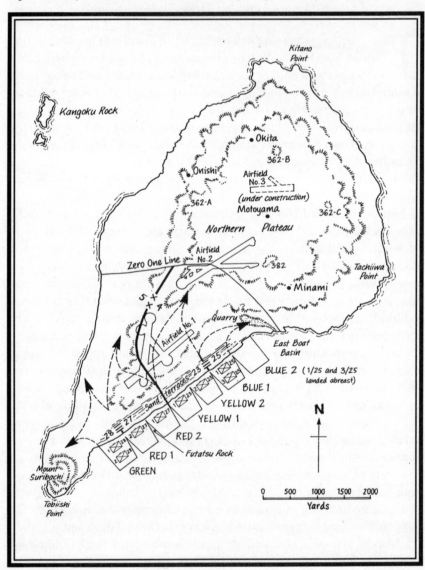

by the Tokyo Prefecture, its loss would be a tremendous psychological blow to the enemy. In October 1944, therefore, it was decided that the island would be captured at the earliest possible moment.

The Japanese, too, had recognised the strategic importance of Iwo Jima. In June 1944 Lieutenant General Tadamichi Kuribayashi was appointed garrison commander. The troops at his disposal included his own recently activated 109th Division, consisting of the 2nd Mixed Brigade, formed from a number of independent infantry battalions, the 145th Infantry Regiment, part of the 26th Tank Regiment, and a large number of attached artillery, mortar, anti-tank, anti-aircraft, machine-gun, rocket and engineer battalions. Also present were several naval units, including coastal artillery, anti-aircraft and construction personnel. Ultimately, there were about 21,000 troops on the island, some 7000 more than American intelligence sources suggested. Heavy weapons included 33 coast defence guns of 80mm calibre and over; 46 artillery weapons of 75mm and over; twelve 320mm mortars; 65 81mm and 150mm mortars; 69 37mm and 47mm anti-tank guns; 94 medium and 200 light anti-aircraft guns; a number of large calibre rocket projectors; and 27 Type 95 Light or Type 94 Medium tanks.

Although two airfields had already been completed and an additional airstrip was under construction, Kuribayashi recognised from the outset that in themselves these were indefensible. He decided to concentrate resistance in the most favourable terrain, that is on Mount Suribachi and the northern plateau. Large supplies of cement and other construction materials, originally earmarked for Japanese garrisons that had been overrun or bypassed by the American drive across the Pacific, were diverted to Iwo Jima, enabling Kuribayashi to initiate an intense programme of fortification. A strict disciplinarian, he drove his men hard. They laboured round the clock in shifts of three hours on and five off, the short working spell being necessary because of the exhausting effects of sulphur fumes.

By the time they had finished, Iwo Jima had been turned into a vast killing zone in which there was barely a foot of ground not covered by one or more weapons. Concrete bunkers and pillboxes were built to deliver flanking fire along the beaches and were protected against the effects of naval gunfire by sand ramparts on the seaward side. All over Mount Suribachi and the northern plateau natural caves were enlarged and interconnected by passages and stairways, creating a honeycomb of gun positions, artillery observation posts, command centres and shelters, many so deep that they offered complete protection against the heaviest shells. Anti-tank ditches were dug so as to channel probable lines of advance into minefields that incorporated naval mines, aerial bombs and anti-personnel mines. The whole system was then elaborately camouflaged, leaving dummy positions exposed to absorb the effects of shelling and air attack.

Kuribayashi accepted that Japanese naval and air power had declined to such low levels that he would have to fight with little or no support from the Home Islands. He also accepted that the Americans, when they came, would possess immense firepower and, drawing upon past experience, strictly forbade massed 'banzai' charges that would simply result in valueless loss of life. Instead, he insisted that the troops would fight from their positions, that there would be no withdrawals, and that those same positions would become their graves. Later, he modified this slightly by permitting local commanders to mount limited counter-attacks at their discretion, but restricted the possible effectiveness of these by digging in his tanks, thereby reducing their potential to that of static pillboxes. At the suggestion of his artillery commander, Colonel Kaido, he agreed that instead of engaging in counter-battery work, the Japanese guns would either concentrate on preregistered killing grounds or employ the full weight of their firepower against the enemy's armour. In the event that the American tanks could not be stopped by the artillery, special Human Combat Tank Destruction Squads were formed to deal with them; these, the anti-tank equivalent of the kamikaze squadrons, consisted of volunteers willing to risk their lives while placing a magnetic hollow-charge explosive device under a tank's belly plates or on other vulnerable areas. Finally, Kuribayashi emphasised that the troops must use their subterranean communication to infiltrate back into areas captured by the enemy, a tactic that was to cause the Americans a great deal of trouble.

D Day for the assault on Iwo Jima, codenamed Operation Detachment, was ultimately decided upon by the Americans as being 19 February 1945. An immense undertaking, it would be under the overall command of Admiral Raymond Spruance with Vice Admiral Richmond Kelly Turner as Joint Expeditionary Force Commander and Lieutenant General Holland M. Smith, US Marine Corps, in command of the Expeditionary Troops. Altogether, including the crews of the vast armada of warships, transport vessels and landing craft, half a million men were involved, although only Major General Harry Schmidt's V Amphibious Corps would make the assault landing and complete the destruction of the Japanese garrison. Schmidt's command contained the 3rd Marine Division (Major General Graves B. Erskine), the 4th Marine Division (Major General Clifton B. Cates), the 5th Marine Division (Major General Keller E. Rockney) and corps troops including two medium artillery battalions and several naval construction battalions (Seabees), whose task was to put the island's airfields into working order as quickly as possible. After three intensive years of amphibious warfare in the

Pacific, the Marine Corps had acquired immense expertise in overcoming the varied aspects of resistance it might encounter and each division contained its own organic artillery and tank units, the latter equipped with Sherman medium tanks of which a proportion were flamethrowers and tank-dozers. The assault landing divisions would each be carried ashore by two amphibious tractor (amtrac) battalions equipped with armoured landing vehicles, tracked (LVTs) that could deposit riflemen and heavy weapons above the water line and simultaneously provide local fire support.[1] Beach exits would be cleared by armoured bulldozers and temporary roads laid over the soft sand with sections of Marston airstrip matting laid from trailers. Supplies would be brought in by amphibious lorries called DUKWs and smaller tracked amphibians known as Weasels, the latter capable of towing a disposable floating trailer; these vehicles were manned by five amphibian truck companies, three of which consisted of US Army personnel. Having studied conditions on Iwo Jima closely, the planners even provided water condensing equipment so that the troops ashore did not have to rely on supplies from the ships. Every known contingency had been allowed for and, even though the Japanese could be expected to fight to the death as usual, training had been thorough and it was anticipated by the staff of V Amphibious Corps that the capture of the island would be completed in fourteen days; Smith, regarding this as pessimistic, believed that ten would be sufficient.

Air attacks on Iwo Jima had begun in June 1944, culminating on 8 December with the beginning of the longest and heaviest aerial bombardment of the Pacific War when for 72 days B-24 and B-25 bombers had rained tons of high explosive on the island. Periodically, too, the Navy had also closed in to bombard known or suspected defences. Some optimists believed that the garrison's defensive capacity had been neutralised, but the more hard-bitten Marines were sceptical – they had witnessed too many bombardments under which human survival seemed impossible, then been forced to fight their way ashore in the teeth of a very active enemy's defensive fire. The climax of the preparatory bombardment of Iwo Jima began on 16 February (D-3) and continued until the landings when, interspersed with further air strikes, the battleships *Tennessee, Arkansas, Nevada, Texas, Idaho* and *New York*, and the cruisers *Salt Lake City, Chester, Tuscaloosa, Pensacola* and *Vicksburg* each pounded a designated sector of the island.

Throughout it all, the Japanese sat tight in their deep shelters, sustaining comparatively few casualties and returning to their work as soon as the immediate danger had passed. However, on D-2 the commander of their coastal artillery made a serious error of judgement. At 1045 the American naval demolition teams began swimming towards the island's south-eastern beaches, which had been selected as being the most suitable for the landing, their task being to verify beach and surf conditions and dispose of any obstacles they found. They were covered by 40mm gun and rocket fire from twelve LCI(G)s lying 1000 yards offshore. The Japanese mistakenly took this activity for the opening stages of the main landing and unmasked their coast defence batteries prematurely. They damaged every one of the LCI(G)s, nine of them seriously, killing 38 seamen and wounding 132. Earlier that morning the *Tennessee* and the *Pensacola* had also been hit, the latter sustaining extensive damage and 155 casualties when she was straddled. Now, their sustained firing enabled the *Nevada* to pinpoint the enemy guns, notably those located in a quarry wall at the northern end of the landing beaches, so that she was able to silence them with salvos of 14in shells. Other warships put down a smokescreen along the beaches, enabling the underwater demolition teams and the battered LCI(G)s to withdraw.[2]

H Hour had been set as 0900 on 19 February. During the preceding 90 minutes the naval bombardment, now supplemented by the 16in guns of the newly arrived battleships *Washington* and *North Carolina* and thousands of 5in rockets fired by LCI(R)s, reached a crescendo. During carefully orchestrated pauses in the firing, waves of carrier aircraft roared in to pound selected areas with bombs, rockets, napalm and machine-guns. Iwo Jima, blanketed in explosions and smoke, seemed to be ablaze, an impression reinforced by the tons of displaced sand hanging like a pall over the island. To the Marines, circling in their amtracs, Iwo Jima gave the appearance of being dead.

The assault plan required the 4th and 5th Marine Divisions to be landed simultaneously along the 3500-yard-long south-eastern beach. On the extreme left one of 5th Division's regiments, 28th Marines, were to advance across the narrow neck of the island then wheel south to secure Mount Suribachi. On the right of the divisional sector, 27th Marines were also to cross the island but would then turn north to secure the western end of what had been designated the Zero-One Line, that is, a line drawn on the map connecting several conspicuous features that were the initial objectives. On 4th Division's sector the 23rd Marines (left) were to clear Airfield No 1, part of Airfield No 2 and tie in with 27th Marines on the Zero-One Line. Simultaneously, 25th Marines (right) would assist in clearing Airfield No 1, expand the beachhead to the north and clear the southern edge of the plateau as far as their Zero-One Line objectives.

Promptly at 0830 the first wave of amtracs formed line abreast and headed for the beach; five minutes later the second wave did likewise. They touched down shortly after 0900 but found the sand terraces too soft and too steep to surmount. Riflemen charged down the lowered ramps only to find themselves wading ankle-deep in black sand.

At first it seemed as though the protracted bombardment had done its work. For several minutes there was no response to the landing, then the enemy's machine-gun, artillery and mortar fire increased in intensity until by 0930 the advancing lines were pinned down and scraping cover for themselves in the sand. Along the increasingly congested shoreline stalled amtracs and jeeps were hit and began to burn. From the sea, Mount Suribachi seemed to be sparkling like a Christmas tree as dozens of fire slits were unmasked.

It was at this point that the Japanese most regretted the loss of their coastal artillery. No less than eight Marine battalions had obtained a footing and now their heavy weapons, including tanks and armoured bulldozers, were being brought in by landing craft. For a while, the most important men ashore were the bulldozer drivers, who hauled tanks into action up the sand terraces. Elements of B and C Companies 1/28th Marines reached the island's western shore at 1035, but behind them they left numerous unsubdued and often invisible fire positions that kept their comrades pinned down. The clearing of these continued throughout the day but by nightfall, though Mount Suribachi had been isolated, both divisions dug in well short of their Zero-One Line objectives, having incurred 2420 casualties, including 501 killed. Naval gunfire support and airstrikes seemed to make little impression on the enemy, and tank losses, caused by buried naval mines and aerial bombs as well as the unexpected volume of anti-tank and artillery fire, rose to unwelcome proportions. Nevertheless, the tanks' direct gunfire more often than not proved to be the decisive factor in eliminating individual positions.

Most Marines had anticipated a major counter-attack during the hours of darkness and were surprised when this did not materialise. For the next two days, while 28th Marines closed in around Mount Suribachi, the two divisions succeeded in swinging the line northwards. On 21 February the Japanese launched a kamikaze attack with 50 aircraft on the American shipping, damaging the fleet carrier *Saratoga* so badly that she had to return to Pearl Harbor for repairs, sinking one escort carrier, *Bismarck Sea*, and damaging another, *Lunga Point*, as well as a transport and an LST. This proved to be the only outside assistance received by Kuribayashi and it had no effect on the fighting ashore.

It took 28th Marines three days to fight their way up the slopes of Mount Suribachi. Where tanks could assist with direct gunfire from below the going was reasonably straightforward. For most of the climb up steep, rugged slopes, however, it was a matter of dealing with each fire position and cave entrance individually, using manpack flamethrowers, grenades and satchel charges under intense fire; many Japanese were simply sealed inside their positions when the entrance was blown in. At about 1030 on 23 February a 40-man patrol led by Lieutenant Harold G. Schrier of E Company reached the summit. Discovering a length of pipe, they secured a small American flag to it and fixed it in the ground, simultaneously cutting down a Japanese swordsman who emerged from his bunker to object. Shortly after this an unknown marine boarded LST 779, beached near the foot of the mountain, and obtained a larger flag with which he climbed to the summit. The raising of this was photographed by Joe Rosenthal of Associated Press and became the best known image of the Pacific War. Now, translated into three dimensions, it forms the Marine Corps Memorial in Washington.

The waist of the island was also now in American hands, the Seabees had commenced work on Airfield No 1 and the Marines' divisional artillery was ashore. Nevertheless, progress on the northern plateau was agonisingly slow and costly, being measured in a few hundred yards each day. The Intelligence Officer of 5th Marine Division explains why in his report:

'Volcanic eruption has littered the whole northern end of the island with outcrops of sandstone and loose rock. A series of irregularly eroded, criss-crossed gorges with precipitous sides resulted in a series of compartments of various shapes. These were usually small but some extended for several hundred yards. The compartments were lined with a labyrinth of natural and artificial caves which covered the approaches from all directions. Fields of fire were usually limited to 25 yards, and a unique or at least unusual characteristic of the Japanese defensive positions in this area was that the reverse slopes were as strongly fortified as were the forward slopes.

'In attacking these positions, no Japanese were to be seen, all being in caves or crevices in the rocks and so disposed as to give an all-round interlocking ghost-like defence to each compartment. Attacking troops were subjected to fire from flanks and rear more than from their front. It was always difficult and often impossible to locate exactly where defensive fires originated. The field of fire of the individual Japanese defender was often limited to an arc of 10° or less; conversely, he was protected from fire except that coming back on this arc. The Japanese smokeless, flashless powder for small arms was of particular usefulness here. When the position was overrun or threatened, the enemy retreated further into his caves where he was usually safe from gunfire, only to pop out again as soon as the occasion warranted unless the cave was immediately blown.'

The experience on the 4th Division's sector was very similar:

'The enemy remains below ground in his maze of communicating tunnels throughout our preliminary artillery fire. When the fire ceases he pushes OPs out of entrances not demolished. Then, choosing a suitable exit he moves as many men and weapons to the surface as he can, depending on the cover and concealment of that area, often as close as 75 yards from our front. As our troops advance towards this point he delivers all the fire at his disposal, rifle, machine-gun and mortar. When he has inflicted sufficient casualties to pin down our advance he then withdraws through his underground tunnels most of his forces, possibly leaving a few machine-gunners and mortars. Meanwhile our battalion CO has coordinated his direct support weapons and delivered a concentration of rockets, mortars and artillery. Our tanks then push in, supported by infantry. When the hot spot is overrun we find a handful of dead Japs and few if any enemy weapons. While this is happening, the enemy has repeated the process and another sector of our advance is engaged in a vicious fire fight, and the cycle continues.'

In this sort of battle, with the Americans above ground and the Japanese below, it was inevitable that the former's casualties would be heavy, especially among junior leaders. Together, losses, fatigue and the inexperience of replacements combined to reduce unit efficiency, but still the fight went on. There emerged, too, the close bonding between those who had survived the gruelling training of a national elite; of the 24 Medals of Honor awarded during the operation, no fewer than seven of the recipients had smothered enemy grenades with their own bodies to protect their comrades.

On 25 February, with the slowly advancing Americans approaching the widest part of the island, the fresh 3rd Marine Division moved into the centre of the line, completing the capture of Airfield No 2 two days later. By 3 March the division had secured Airfield No 3 and the 5th Division had taken Hills 362A and 362B. During the next two days Iwo Jima began to fulfil the purpose for which the operation had been mounted, the first damaged B-29 landing on Airfield No 1, followed by the USAAF's 15th Fighter Group.

Despite this, progress across the northern plateau remained painfully slow and it was not until 26 March that the last organised pocket of resistance was overrun. The Japanese public had watched the progress of the battle with much the same feelings that the Americans had watched the last days of Corregidor in 1942 and the British their embattled 1st Airborne Division at Arnhem. The Song of Iwo Jima, composed by Kuribayashi himself, was broadcast on Japanese radio. On 15 March Kuribayashi informed his superiors that he intended making a final banzai charge at midnight on the 17th, and bade his friends farewell. Whether he received the news that he had been promoted to full general is uncertain, as are the details of his end. No major

Japanese counter-attack is recorded on 17 March, but at first light on the 26th over 200 Japanese infiltrated down the coast and attacked bivouac areas near the western beaches, evidently with the idea of breaking through to Airfield No 1. During a confused battle lasting three hours the 5th Pioneer Battalion succeeded in accounting for 196 of the enemy. Of these no less than 40 carried swords, indicating an exceptionally high proportion of officers, but there was no hard evidence that Kuribayashi was among them. The 5th Pioneers sustained nine killed and 31 wounded, while casualties among Air Force personnel amounted to 44 killed and 88 wounded.

It had taken 36 days of bitter fighting to capture the island. Of the action, Admiral Chester Nimitz wrote, 'Among the Americans who served on Iwo Jima uncommon valor was a common virtue'. Marine Corps casualties amounted to a staggering 24,750 including 5885 known dead; to this had to be added 2798 Naval casualties, including 433 killed and 448 missing, presumed dead.

Only 216 Japanese had been captured by 26 March, and while it was correctly assumed that the majority of their comrades had been killed, there were still considerable numbers at large in their underground warrens. During April and May the Army's 124th Infantry Regiment, which had taken over the island as garrison troops when the Marines left, maintained aggressive patrols, killing 1602 of the enemy and capturing a further 867. Speaking shortly after the battle for Iwo Jima, General Holland Smith, who had no more love for the Japanese than any Allied commander, commented that it had been the toughest fight the Marine Corps had run across in its 168 years of history.

There was one aspect of the battle that troubled every Allied commander and politician. If the Japanese, fighting to the death in defence of an insignificant speck of their territory, could inflict such heavy casualties, what would be the probable human cost when it came to invading Japan itself? Consideration of this factor became an important element in the decision to end the war by nuclear means.

Notes

1. Amtracs, originally employed as cargo carriers, were developed into assault vehicles that could negotiate the coral reefs surrounding many Pacific islands and cross the lagoon beyond to disembark their riflemen above the waterline on the shore beyond. After experience revealed the need for heavy weapons support until tanks could be got ashore a proportion were fitted with Stuart light tank turrets, mounting a 37mm gun, or M8 75mm self-propelled howitzer turrets.

2. The Landing Craft Infantry (Gunboat) was armed with three 40mm anti-aircraft guns and ten 4.5in rocket launchers. For this action the flotilla received a Presidential Unit Citation, one Medal of Honor and ten Navy Crosses.

13
Pork Chop Hill: Korea, 16–18 April 1953

T he Korean War was almost three years old. The United Nations and the Chinese communist armies had dug in along natural defence lines stretching across the peninsula and were engaged in a contest of attrition. Armistice negotiations that had begun in June 1951 had twice been broken off but in March 1953, following the death of Josef Stalin, they were resumed.

During the ensuing talks, the communists, aware that the American public was becoming tired of the war, began testing the United Nations' resolve with a series of local actions at various points along the front, the intransigence or otherwise of their negotiators reflecting the outcome of these. The most important took place on the sector of Major General Bruce C. Clarke's US I Corps, typical being the loss to the communists in March of a prominent hill feature named Old Baldy.

Some 1500 yards to the west of Old Baldy lay Pork Chop Hill, so called from the overall shape of its contours. Pork Chop was an isolated feature situated on the enemy side of a valley that served as No Man's Land between the two opposing defence lines. The distinguished American military historian S.L.A. Marshall described it as 'a contemptible hill, ill-formed for all-round defence and too loosely tied in to the supporting neighbourhood'. It was, in fact, just 600 feet high and was overlooked by the Chinese-held heights of Old Baldy to the east and Hassakol to the north. Logic dictated that it should have been abandoned when Old Baldy was lost, but the Americans were disinclined to yield any more territory than they were compelled to. The intention was that Pork Chop would serve as an outpost that would absorb the first impact of any communist offensive directed at the American Main Line of Resistance (MLR) to its rear. The crest was encircled with a partially-roofed trench that was punctuated at 30-yard intervals by loopholed bunkers constructed from sandbags and timber. One problem was the shallow depth of soil covering the hill's bedrock. This meant that the sides of the trench had to be built up into breastworks, across which the defenders would have to lean if they wished to engage targets on the steep slopes below, thereby becoming dangerously exposed. Another problem was that a re-entrant on the reverse slope extended upwards to end in a hollow near the summit, effectively dividing the position into two tactical areas. The command post bunker was located in the centre of the defences and in the re-entrant was a cookhouse known as the Chow Bunker. Downslope of the trench the hill was girdled by two or more barbed wire entanglements save for patrol gaps and a larger open area to the east.

Pork Chop lay within the sector of Major General Arthur Trudeau's 7th Division and was the specific responsibility of the 31st Infantry Regiment, commanded by Colonel William B. Kern. On 16 April Kern's garrison on Pork Chop consisted of two platoons from E Company under the command of Lieutenant Thomas V. Harrold, with a total of 96 men including attached artillery observers and engineers.

Intelligence sources suggested that the Chinese would mount a major attack that night. During the day, the faint sound of singing had drifted across the valley from Hassakol, in the bulk of which the Chinese were

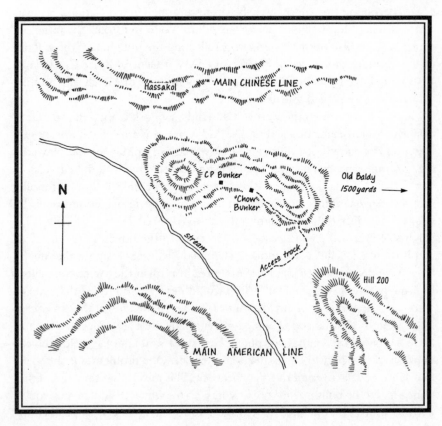

known to have followed their usual practice of constructing tunnels that would serve as forming up points for their assault troops. The sound was creepy, reminding some men of Indian death chants in the Old West. That, said the old hands, was more or less what they were; the Chinese were getting ready to die. Harrold had already been warned of the possibility of an attack, which the divisional staff believed would be delivered east of Pork Chop. Beyond passing on this information to his platoon commanders he remained confident about his own security; so confident, in fact, that after dark he not only stuck to his routine of manning ten two-man listening posts in the valley between Pork Chop and Hassakol, but also sent out a ten-strong patrol with the object of snatching a prisoner, as had been ordered some days previously. This reduced the effective garrison of the hill to 66 men.

At about 2230 two Chinese companies debouched from their tunnels and began advancing rapidly towards Pork Chop. They scattered the patrol, a few members of which managed to escape to the MLR by skirting the northern edge of the hill, and quickly overran the line of listening posts, from which only seven men succeeded in regaining the trench line.

Although they could see isolated weapon flashes and hear shots in the valley below, those on the hill had no idea what was happening, partly because no reports had come in from the listening posts, and partly because the warning of impending attack had not been passed down to more than a handful of men. The Chinese artillery, waiting in silence until its infantry were on the point of launching their assault, opened fire at 2300. Harrold, standing in the doorway of his command post bunker, could already hear the sound of bursting grenades and Chinese PPS submachine-guns in one of his platoon areas, and when the first shells began to fall he fired the coded the rocket signal indicating that the position was under major attack. At 2305 the hill was illuminated and two minutes later the first American shells, fired by a single battery, began to slam into the forward slopes.

It was not enough to stop the Chinese. They swarmed into the trench line, turning left and right to overwhelm or outflank one bunker after another, flinging stick grenades through doorways and fire slits. The distinctive sound of their PPSs, known to the Americans as burp guns, spread across the upper slopes of the hill. Harrold's telephone links to the listening posts had long since gone and those to his platoons quickly went dead in succession, cut by shellfire or because none remained alive to answer. By radio he requested, and received, additional artillery support, but by 0100 the fight was effectively lost. Only the CP bunker and one or two isolated posts continued to offer resistance.

Inside the CP were Harrold, Lieutenant Jack Attridge, one of the platoon commanders, Lieutenant Anderson, the artillery observer, and four NCOs. The Chinese were now swarming round the bunker and had gained its roof. Standing in the doorway, First Sergeant Howard Midgeley was using his submachine-gun to good effect, cutting down thirteen of the enemy in succession then stacking their bodies to provide additional protection. At a fire slit the company clerk, Corporal Riepenhoff, picked off six more with his rifle, formally requesting Harrold's permission to fire whenever a target appeared in his sights. In the meantime, Harrold reported the situation to his battalion commander, Major Swazey, who referred the matter upwards to Colonel Kern. At this stage it seems that neither the battalion nor the regimental commander understood that most of Pork Chop was now in enemy hands, for a little before 0200 Kern ordered one platoon each from F and L Companies to 'reinforce' Harrold.

The platoon from F Company got lost and never entered the fight. That of L Company, commanded by Second Lieutenant Earle L. Denton, advanced in column along the track connecting the MLR with Pork Chop, still under the impression that the hill was in American hands. It had almost reached the Chow Bunker when two light machine-guns, one of which was firing from the roof of the embattled CP, cut through its ranks. It fell back down the hill only to sustain further casualties when the Chinese artillery began shelling the reverse slopes. In the valley, Denton rallied his remaining twelve men near two tanks parked beside the track. For all his youth, he spoke to them like a Dutch uncle: 'What do you want to run off for? There's only good men in this platoon. We've got nothing but the best'. Shamefaced but now firmly under control, the survivors clambered aboard the tanks, which ran them back to the MLR; on the way, two more men were wounded by shell splinters. On arriving, Denton reported to his company commander, Lieutenant Forrest J. Crittenden, who then discussed the situation with Lieutenant Colonel John N. Davis at battalion. Davis decided upon a first-light counter-attack, using K and L Companies.

Back on the hill, the fight continued to rage around the CP. While Midgeley paused in his efforts to have a wound dressed, a grenade was pushed through a crack in the sandbags. Harrold, Anderson and Midgeley were all wounded by fragments and the radio was wrecked. By some miracle Harrold's telephone link to his remaining platoon, back in the MLR, had survived, and by this means he was able to maintain illumination of the hill and a steady bombardment of the captured areas. Those in the bunker then sealed the door and fire-slit with sandbags and anything else to hand. At about 0400 Harrold received a totally unnecessary warning, relayed from division, that the Chinese would probably try and blow up the bunker. With astonishing restraint he replied: 'Tell them we will try to hold. Tell them also that any force sent to relieve us will need flame throwers and heavy rocket launchers'. After a further hour within the claustrophobic darkness, it was apparent that the American artillery had shifted its fire to the forward slopes. That could only mean one thing – a counter-attack force was fighting its way up the hill. Pulling aside the sandbags, Attridge, now the only unwounded man in the CP, went out to guide it in. He was hit in the head before he had gone far and was forced to return. Once again, the door was sealed. Now, as the sounds of fighting intensified, the occupants could only await their fate.

The counter-attack had begun at 0430 with L Company on the right and K Company on the left. K Company's commander, Lieutenant Joseph G. Clemons, Jr, was briefed personally by Colonel Davis, whose impression was that the entire hill had been lost. Davis stressed the important need to close with the Chinese before it was fully light, suggested that Clemons should advance with two platoons forward and one in reserve, and told him that two platoons of L Company would simultaneously be attacking up Pork Chop's eastern spur. This last piece of information caused Clemons some reservations since it meant that the two companies were moving on converging axes, with the attendant risk of firing into each other.

K Company moved off at a cracking pace. In one respect this was unfortunate, for so steep was the gradient that by the time they reached the first belt of wire most of the men, heavily burdened with extra ammunition, were completely winded. On the other hand, their speed saved them from the worst effects of the Chinese artillery's defensive barrage, most of which passed overhead to explode in the valley between Pork Chop and the MLR. What followed became a junior leader's battle. Working their through gaps in the wire cut by the shelling of both sides, small groups closed in on the trench line and its bunkers, to be greeted by showers of stick grenades and rattling burp guns. They responded with their own grenades and automatic weapons. Casualties on both sides were heavy and even. A flamethrower enveloped one of the bunkers with jets of liquid fire, setting the door ablaze. In the growing light, however, the Chinese within had already identified the threat and escaped to higher ground, from which they hurled grenades, wounding the flamethrower operator several times. They then reoccupied the bunker, having beaten out the fire, but shortly after fell victim to several rounds from a 3.5in rocket launcher that blasted their way through the sandbags. At other bunkers, sustained fire from Browning Automatic Rifles (BARs) drove the defenders from their fire slits while grenade throwers crawled forward to administer the coup de grâce. In a dozen bitter little fights such as these K Company fought it way across the trench line to the CP, releasing Harrold and his companions. Further progress beyond was halted by heavy fire from the right which, as Clemons had feared, had its origins in L Company. Thus far, he calculated that the assault had cost him half his own men. Harrold, believing that all that remained of E Company was the platoon in the MLR, joined the steady trickle of walking wounded making their way down the re-entrant past the Chow Bunker.

Lieutenant Crittenden had decided to leave Denton's rallied platoon behind when L Company was ordered up onto Pork Chop's eastern spur. He had set off with just two platoons, a total of 62 men, but had become involved in heavy and costly fighting for an outlying bunker on the spur. Wounded himself, he handed over to Lieutenant Homer Bechtel, who was himself struck down shortly after. At about this time the company was decimated and scattered by a heavy artillery strike of unknown origin. Eventually, Lieutenant Arthur A. Marshall led all that remained, a mere dozen men, across the reverse slopes of the hill to join Clemons; just as they arrived, two were hit by machine-gun fire. At this moment, shortly before 0800, the American strength on Pork Chop amounted to 35 men of Clemons' K Company, ten from L Company and twelve shaken and mostly wounded survivors of E Company, who had held out in their bunkers until relieved.

At about 0815 Clemons was astonished to find himself talking to his brother-in-law, Lieutenant Walter B. Russell, commanding G Company 17th Infantry. This had been sent forward, Russell said, to help Clemons 'mop up'. Clemons gladly slotted the new arrivals into his overextended line and, having lost all his own radios, used Russell's to signal his immediate requirements of drinking water, medical supplies, ammunition, flamethrowers, ammunition, communications equipment and stretchers. Davis despatched Korean porters with these but, because of the shellfire falling on the upper slopes, the men declined to climb further than the Chow Bunker.

Pork Chop now became a meat-grinder. The Chinese, too, were reinforcing their troops on the hill and both sides battered each other continuously with their artillery. Trenches and bunkers were wrecked as men flattened themselves in craters against the worst effects of blast and flying shards of red-hot steel. Whenever the shelling slackened, close-quarter shooting started and grenades were exchanged across the pitted landscape. Hour by hour, the number of unwounded men dwindled.

At about midday, one of Davis' staff officers entered the CP bunker and handed Clemons an order. E Company's survivors were to be sent back at once; Russell's G Company was to withdraw promptly at 1500. With a restraint that betrayed nothing but cold fury, Clemons replied: 'Take this message back. Tell them I believe that the crisis here is not appreciated either by Battalion or Regiment. I have left but very few men. All are exhausted. Russell has only 55 men left. When they go out, it is not reasonable to expect that we can hold the hill.'

The reply was acknowledged but the order was not rescinded. Just how little those behind the lines appreciated what was happening on Pork Chop was revealed at 1445 when a press officer, accompanied by two photographers, entered the CP in the hope of gathering material for a report on a successful action. 'Forget the pictures', said Clemons. 'I want you to carry a message to Battalion.' The message read, 'We must have help or we can't hold the hill.'

At 1500 there was a lull in the shelling. Russell shrugged, shook hands with Clemons and, leaving his radio, led the remnants of G Company off the hill. During the lull, some of the replenishment stores were brought up from the Chow Bunker. Clemons deployed the 25 men remaining to him in two groups. The larger, under Lieutenant Tsugi O'Hashi and Sergeant First Class Walter Kuzmick, he positioned around the peak at the western end of the hill, while the rest remained with him in the CP. For the next four hours O'Hashi's group, which included a number of South Korean soldiers attached under the 'Buddy' system, was forced to endure shelling, grenading and small arms fire without the chance to hit back. They passed the time by alternately cleaning their weapons and digging to improve their position. At this stage few believed that they would leave the hill alive.

Davis, however, had not been idle. He had spoken to Colonel Kern and the latter, though as yet unaware of the extent of his regiment's casualties, was sufficiently alarmed to contact Major General Trudeau at Division. Trudeau was puzzled as to why the enemy was making such an issue of Pork Chop, since its possession would be of no more use to them than it had been to the Americans. He was not inclined to expend more troops in an apparently pointless battle, but after reporting the matter to I Corps, who in turn passed it on the Headquarters Eighth Army, he had himself flown forward to Davis' CP by helicopter to assess the situation for himself.

In the meantime, Davis was also doing what he could to support Clemons directly. If all had gone according to plan, L Company would now be up on Pork Chop fighting alongside K Company. Therefore, he reasoned, if the company was sent in again this would not in itself be regarded as committing additional troops. To his surprise, therefore, Second Lieutenant Denton found himself appointed L Company commander, with instructions to take it forward and hold Pork Chop. Young Mr Denton was not simply good at getting the best out of his soldiers – he was also a sound tactician. He had only 56 men available, the remnants of his own platoon and stragglers of the two platoons that had attacked with Crittenden, but he divided them into three squads and sent them, one man at a time with one minute intervals between, across the valley separating the MLR from the Chow Bunker. It took an hour, but the Chinese artillery obviously felt that such puny targets did not warrant its attention and L Company arrived without losing a single man.

Trudeau was still in Davis' CP when Clemons came through on the radio at 1645. He sounded calm and resigned but his words had a profound effect on the divisional commander: 'We have here about twenty men who are still unhit. They are completely spent. There is no fight left in this company. If we can't be relieved, we should be withdrawn.' Clearly, Pork Chop could pass into Chinese hands at any time and, should the higher command wish to recover it, the cost could be as high as a battalion a day. The situation demanded an immediate decision.

Major General Clarke, commanding I Corps, had already indicated that he was flying forward to Kern's CP, and there Trudeau joined him. The conclusion they reached was that since Pork Chop was of no military significance to either side, the Chinese were using it to test American resolve. Any weakness shown at Pork Chop would automatically be reflected in further communist intransigence at the Panmunjon armistice talks. Therefore, the hill must be held. Trudeau, wishing to avoid useless loss of life, obtained Clarke's assurance that the hill would not be abandoned in the foreseeable future. He then placed 2/17th Infantry under Kern's command and moved 1/17th Infantry into the immediate area with the promise that this battalion would also be made available if Kern felt that he could not win without it.

Shortly after Clemons had spoken to Davis, Denton walked into the CP bunker. His appearance was totally unexpected but very timely, as Clemons calculated that he was now down to sixteen men. Denton deployed his company in a position of all-round defence among the craters pitting the crown of the hill, sustaining six casualties from shellfire in the process. His men, however, remained well in hand, steadied by his repeated assurance that after two false starts L Company was doing its job, and doing it well. As the afternoon turned to evening comparative quiet descended on Pork Chop, but few doubted that it was anything more than the calm before the storm. Any movement was still punished; Lieutenant O'Hashi, leaving his position on the western crest to confer with Clemons, had his shoulder smashed by a grenade just as he reached the CP bunker door.

After the mauling received by Russell's G Company earlier in the day, 2/17th Infantry effectively consisted of only two companies, E and F. At 1800 Colonel Kern detailed Captain King of F Company to relieve Clemons

and Denton on Pork Chop. The company was slow to move off and its leading platoon did not arrive on the hill until 2130. Denton, spotting Chinese
reinforcements crossing the valley from Hassakol, called in an artillery strike
to disperse them. The Chinese responded with the heaviest bombardment
yet to strike the hill. F Company, caught in the open, sustained nineteen
casualties within a few minutes and scattered into such cover as could be
found. It took the better part of three hours to prise them loose and complete the relief.

Clemons and Denton wanted the illumination of the hill suspended while
they withdrew; understandably, King did not. At length a compromise was
reached, with only the forward slopes being illuminated. As they watched
their men disappearing downhill into the darkness, taking as many wounded
with them as possible, Clemons and Denton were forced to take refuge in
the CP bunker when the Chinese launched an attack. Grenades burst around
the door and, once again, an enemy light machine-gun crew established itself
on the roof. Corporal Chambliss, one of Denton's men, charged out into the
trench with his BAR, one burst of which sent both Chinese tumbling. The
remaining unwounded occupants then made a sally, clearing the immediate
area. Clemons managed to break away successfully and rejoin his company.
Denton had been about to follow when King plaintively asked him to stay
on until he was familiar with the position.

Ninety minutes later the Chinese attacked again. Grenades, lobbed
under-arm by a man on the roof, began to come through the door to burst
among the wounded. A burp gunner, blazing away as he ran through the
entrance, hit Denton in the hand and leg but was shot dead by Private First
Class John Baron. A second burp gunner poked his weapon through an
embrasure but was killed by Chambliss and two others before he could open
fire. Baron charged out into the trench to fire at the grenade thrower on the
roof, who fell with his legs dangling over the doorway. At this point three
heavy calibre shells exploded close to the bunker, caving in one wall and
blasting a wide opening in the roof. This proved to be too much for some
of the wounded men, who began screaming.

'Shut up!' yelled Denton. 'I don't want any cry babies in here!'

He was in radio contact with two self-propelled quadruple anti-aircraft
mountings which he knew were parked at the foot of the reverse slope. The
effect of these against infantry in the open was devastating and he asked
them to scythe the area around the bunker. The problem was that to the AA
gunners all the bunkers looked alike and they asked for an identification signal. Denton tied a grenade to a flare and Baron tossed it onto what remained
of the roof, killing another burp gunner who tried to stop him.

The flare had the opposite of the desired effect. The Chinese identified it correctly as a distress signal and they closed in for the kill in large numbers, grenading, firing burp guns and screaming. The end was clearly in sight when one man began to recite the Lord's Prayer. Then, quite suddenly, there was comparative silence. Peering out, the defenders saw the Chinese running in the direction of the forward slopes. From the east came the sound of Garrand M1 rifles and BARs, then there appeared a long line of American infantrymen, driving the enemy across the upper slopes of the hill.

If it was a miracle, the instrument of its working was Lieutenant Gorman Smith, commanding E Company 2/17th Infantry. At about 2330 Colonel Kern, aware of F Company's troubles and feeling that once again the initiative was passing to the enemy, decided to commit the company to Pork Chop. Smith decided to tackle the job his own way. Instead of climbing the reverse slopes, as previous counter-attacks had done, he decided to lead his platoons round the eastern shoulder of the hill and attack from what was in effect enemy territory; only results could possibly justify the enormous risks involved. Yet, all went exactly according to plan. The company's approach march was not detected, the climb met no resistance and the attack achieved complete surprise. At 0250 Smith was able to signal Kern: 'Pork Chop is under full control.'

The Chinese, however, were not prepared to let the matter rest there. At 0320 and again at 0430 they mounted counter-attacks which were beaten off. The fighting, complicated by the fact that scores of the enemy had gone to ground in shattered bunkers and trenches when Smith's company had driven their comrades off the hill, was as costly as anything that had gone before. Trudeau had already released 1/17th Infantry to Kern and the latter sent up the battalion's A Company to tighten the American grip on the feature. Although the Chinese continued to batter Pork Chop all through the next day, this move proved to be decisive. The indefatigable Denton managed to snatch a little sleep and finally left the hill during the afternoon, having spent several hours clearing booby traps from around the ruins of the CP bunker.

During the two day battle the 7th Division's artillery, and that of the neighbouring 2nd Division, fired a total of 77,349 rounds of ammunition. American casualties had been very heavy in proportion to the number of troops employed, while those of the enemy, though unknown, were undoubtedly heavier.

The Chinese ploy had failed. Both sides would commit even greater resources to the struggle for Pork Chop until the hill was finally evacuated just before the armistice was signed in July.

Bibliography

Adler, Major Julius Ochs, *History of the Seventy Seventh Division*, Winthrop, Hollenbeck & Crawford, New York, 1919

Baker, Anthony, *Battle Honours of the British and Commonwealth Armies*, Ian Allan, 1986

Barthorp, Michael, *The North-West Frontier – British India and Afghanistan 1839-1947*, Blandford Press, 1982

Bartley, Lt Colonel Whitman S., *Iwo Jima: Amphibious Epic*, The Battery Press, Nashville, 1988

Bodin, Lynn E., *The Boxer Rebellion*, Osprey, 1979

Brown, Dee, *The Fetterman Massacre*, Barrie & Jenkins, 1972

Callwell, Colonel C.E., *Small Wars*, Purnell 1976

Campbell, Arthur, *The Siege – A Story From Kohima*, George Allen & Unwin, 1956

Cannan, John, *The Antietam Campaign*, Combined Books, Conshohocken, Pa, 1994

Colvin, John, *Not Ordinary Men – The Battle of Kohima Re-assessed*, Leo Cooper, 1994

Costello, John, *The Pacific War*, Collins, 1981

Downey, Fairfax, *Indian-Fighting Army*, Bantam, 1957

Duncan, John and Walton, John, *Heroes for Victoria*, Spellmount, 1991

Ellis, Major L.F. et al, *Victory in the West*, Vol 1, The Battle of Normandy, HMSO, 1962

Featherston, Alwyn, *Saving the Breakout – The 30th Division's Heroic Stand at Mortain August 7-12 1944*, Presidio Press, Novato, Ca, 1993

Forbes, Archibald, *The Afghan Wars 1839-42 & 1878-80*, Darf, 1987

Forbes, Archibald et al, *Battles of the Nineteenth Century*, Cassell, 1896

Grinnell-Milne, Duncan, *Mafeking*, The Bodley Head, 1957

Howarth, David, *Waterloo – A Near Run Thing*, Collins 1968

Jeal, Tim, *Baden-Powell*, Pimlico, 1989

Katcher, Philip, *The American Civil War Source Book*, Arms & Armour Press, 1992

Kennedy, Frances H., Ed, *The Civil War Battlefield Guide*, Houghton Mifflin, Boston, 1990

Keown-Boyd, Henry, *The Fists of Righteous Harmony – A History of the Boxer Uprising in China in the Year 1900*, Leo Cooper, 1991

Latham, Captain H.B., *E/B RHA at Maiwand*, article in the Royal Artillery Journal 1928/29

Longstreet, Stephen, *War Cries on Horseback*, W.H.Allen, 1970

Macksey, Kenneth, *Crucible of Power – The Fight for Tunisia 1942-1943*, Hutchinson, 1969

Marshall, S.L.A., *Crimsoned Prairie – The Indian Wars on the Great Plains*, Macdonald, 1972

Marshall, S.L.A., *Pork Chop Hill*, The Battery Press, Nashville, 1986

Mason, David, *Breakout: Drive to the Seine*, Macdonald, 1969

Maxwell, Leigh, *My God, Maiwand! – Operations of the South Afghanistan Field Force 1878-80*, Leo Cooper, 1979

Naylor, John, *Waterloo*, Batsford, 1960

Paget, Julian and Saunders, Derek, *Hougoumont – The Key to Victory at Waterloo*, Leo Cooper, 1992

Pakenham, Thomas, *The Boer War*, Weidenfeld & Nicolson, 1979

Pericoli, Ugo, *1815 – The Armies at Waterloo*, Sphere, 1973

Perrett, Bryan, *Tank Tracks to Rangoon – The Story of British Armour in Burma*, Robert Hale, 1978 and 1992

Petre, F.L., *The Royal Berkshire Regiment*, Vol 1

Playfair, Major General I.S.O. et al, *The Mediterranean and Middle East, Vol 4*, HMSO, 1966

Rees, David, Ed, *The Korean War – History and Tactics*, Orbis, 1984

Robson, Brian, *The Road to Kabul – The Second Afghan War 1878-1881*, Arms & Armour Press, 1986

Rodenbaugh, Theo F. and Haskin, William L., *The Army of the United States – Historical Portraits of Staff and Line*, Maynard, Merrill & Co, New York, 1896

Rooney, David, *Burma Victory – Imphal, Kohima and the Chindit Issue, March 1944 to May 1945*, Arms & Armour Press, 1992

Scott Daniel, David, *Regimental History of the Royal Hampshire Regiment*, Vol 3, 1918-1954, Gale & Polden, 1955

Sears, Stephen W., *Landscape Turned Red – The Battle of Antietam*, Ticknor & Fields, New York, 1983

Stallings, Robert, *The Doughboys – The Story of the AEF*, 1917-1918, Harper & Row, New York, 1963

Tilberg, Frederick, *Antietam*, National Park Service, Washington, 1960

Toland, John, *No Man's Land – 1918, The Last Year of the Great War*, Doubleday, New York, 1980

Utley, Robert M., *Bluecoats and Redskins – The United States Army and the Indian 1866-1891*, Purnell, 1975

Wilmot, Chester, *The Struggle for Europe*, Collins, 1952

Index

Abbaye Blanche, 187, 191, 192, 196
Abbott, Captain, 31, 40
Abdur Rahman, 74, 77, 78, 95
Adams, Major General Sir Frederick, 24
Admin Box, Battle of the, 167
Akbar Khan, 29, 33, 34, 35, 36, 37, 38, 39, 40, 41
Alexander, Major General Robert, 139, 140, 141, 142, 143, 144, 145
Allfrey, Lieutenant General Charles, 149, 151,
American Horse, Chief, 71
Anderson, Lieutenant Colonel H. S., 87, 90,
Anderson, Lieutenant General Kenneth, 146, 149
Andrews, Lieutenant Tom, 188
Antietam, Battle of, 6, 47–58
Antietam Creek, 47–48, 49, 55,
Arakan, 164, 167
Argonne Forest, 138,

ARMY, BRITISH
Armies: First, 146; Eighth, 146; Fourteenth, 164
Corps: IV, 163, 164, 165, 180; V, 149; XXXIII, 167, 180
Divisions: 1st, 12, 21; 2nd, 167, 168, 174, 177, 178; 78th, 146, 149, 5th Indian, 167; 7th Indian, 180
Brigades: 1st Guards, 12, 24, 147; 2nd Guards, 12, 17, 21; 3rd, 24; 11th, 147, 151, 154, 159, 160; 161st, 167, 168, 169, 174, 177, 178; 50th Indian Parachute, 165
Regiments, Cavalry and Armoured: 9th Lancers, 77, 109; 17th/21st Lancers, 152, 159; 2nd Derbyshire Yeomanry, 147, 152; 149 Regiment RAC, 177, 178, 180; 5th Bengal Cavalry, 32, 34, 40; Guides Cavalry, 77; 3rd Light Cavalry, 79; 5th Punjab Cavalry, 77; 3rd Sind Horse, 79, 82, 86,
Regiments, Infantry: 2nd Grenadier Guards, 12 et seq; 3rd Grenadier Guards, 12 et seq; 2nd Coldstream Guards, 12 et seq; 2nd Scots Guards, 12 et seq; 1st East Surrey, 147, 149, 152, 157, 158, 159; Essex (44th), 34; 40; 2nd Hampshire, 147–162; 2nd Lancashire Fusiliers, 147; 5th Northamptonshire, 147, 149, 159; Oxford-

shire & Buckinghamshire Light Infantry (52nd), 23; 1st Queen's Own Cameron Highlanders, 178; 4th Queen's Own Royal West Kent, 6, 167–180; Royal Berkshire (66th), 6, 78, 79, 82, 84, 85, 86, 88, 90-96, 98, 178–179; Somerset Light Infantry (13th), 6, 28, 31, 39, 40, 41, 42;
Corps of Guides, 74-77; 1st Assam, 165, 167, 173, 179, 180; 3rd Assam Rifles, 167, 172; 35th Bengal Native Infantry, 31, 39, 40, 42; 1st Bombay Native Infantry (Grenadiers), 79, 82, 83, 85, 86–90, 92, 94; 30th Bombay Native Infantry (Jacob's Rifles), 79, 82, 85–90, 92, 94; 1/7th Gurkha Rifles, 173; 5/27th Mahrattas, 167; 1/1st Punjabis, 167, 178; 4/7th Rajputs, 167, 177; 7th Rajputs, 134–135
Bechuanaland Rifles, 101; British South Africa Police, 99, 104, 107, 115; Cape Police, 101, 106; Mafeking Cadet Corps, 110, 119; Mafeking Cape Boys, 101, 106, 109; Mafeking Railway Volunteers, 101; Mafeking Town Guard, 101; Protectorate Regiment, 99, 101, 104, 106, 109, 110, 112, 115; Rhodesia Regiment, 99, 108
Artillery: 99 Field Regiment RA, 178; 24 Mountain Artillery Regiment IA, 168, 170; E/B Battery RHA, 79, 82, 87, 88, 89, 92, 94, 95; 6th Light Field Battery RA, 31; Smoothbore Battery, 79, 82, 83, 84, 85, 87, 88, 89, 94; Mercer's Troop RHA, 12; No 2 Rocket Troop, 11–12
Bombay Sappers & Miners, 79, 82, 89, 90, 92
Royal Waggon Train, 20, 21

ARMY, CHINESE IMPERIAL
Organisation of, 121–122

ARMY, CONFEDERATE STATES OF AMERICA
Army of Northern Virginia, 7, 44, 46, 49, 53, 57
Divisons: Anderson's, 53; A. P. Hill's, 56; D. H. Hill's, 50, 52, 53; Hood's, 50; D. R. Jones', 55; McLaw's, 51, 52
Brigades: Law's, 50; Toombs', 55; Wofford's, 50

219